# The Village Atlas

The Growth of Birmingham and the
West Midlands
1831 - 1907

# The Village Atlas

The Growth of Birmingham and the
West Midlands
1831 - 1907

*The Alderman Press*

Published by The Village Press Limited
7d Keats Parade, Church Street, Edmonton, N9 9DP.

October 1989.

The Village Press 1989

**British Library Cataloguing in Publication Data**

The village atlas : the growth of Birmingham and the West Midlands, 1831-1907.

1. West Midlands, Metropolitan history, Maps, atlases
I. Bruff, Barry Robson, 1926-
912'. 4249

ISBN 0-946619-33-6

Typesetting by Stone Associates, Winchmore Hill.
Printed and bound in Gt. Britain
by The Bath Press, Bath, Avon.

# Acknowledgements.

The publishers would like to thank the staff of the Map Library and Photographic Department of the British Library for their help during the preparation of this Atlas.

The staff of the local History Department of Birmingham Central Library.

The staff of the Reference Library Enfield Middlesex.

# Introduction

One hundred years ago in the 1880's and 90's there was a wave of nostalgic interest in local history which has been exactly duplicated in this century. The thought of a new century looms, and as it approaches, so historians and writers take a look back and it seems they suddenly realise how much of their cities and their suburbs have disappeared beneath new acres of building. Villages which had once seemed a comfortable distance from a city, almost overnight, it seemed, found themselves gobbled up by the developer. The following extract was written over one hundred years ago. It could easily have been written today.

Every old house or old church or college may be said to be under sentence; for it "cumbereth valuable ground. It is almost pathetic to note the fine old houses in the suburbs standing in its fair gardens and lawns looking on the highroad; for it is already marked by the spoiler. Some forty or fifty years hence this rapacious greed will have wrought incalculable havoc. Business men and practical-minded persons seem to have a positive dislike to any old memorials of the kind. They would have them carted away: among the symmetrical modern structures they seem an eyesore. Soon or late, and more likely soon, there is certain to be a combined onslaught on the City churches, whose sites are coveted for palatial City warehouses, and such pressure it will be difficult to resist. When a substantial morsel of the old Roman wall is laid open to view in digging foundations, the utmost grace accorded is a day or two's delay to allow the antiquaries to come and see it.

This was written about London, but it was as true of every big city in Victorian times as it is now.

Writers and illustrators feverishly began to record local history and the changes that were taking place but the pace of change in Victorian times was astonishing; in one lifetime, hamlets that might once have contained a few cottages and three or four farms became suburbs with a population of twenty thousand. Several things combined to bring this about: a population explosion, new forms of transport, new industries and migration from the countryside to service them, were all contributing factors.

Birmingham was extremely well placed to become the hub of such extraordinary growth. Though in its early years it was no bigger or more important than some of its neighbouring parishes, Aston in particular, it was, from all accounts more centralised, with a vigorous market which attracted goods from all over the Midlands and this provided a more effective nucleus for growth.

The rapid expansion of the canal system which came to centre on Birmingham provided the first impetus for new industry. The canals provided a relatively quick means of transport for both raw materials and finished goods to all the major cities both north and south. The first increase of population took place along these waterways or the early railways. Balsall Heath, Aston, Lozells and Handsworth were the first areas where changes started to take place.

By the 1850's the railways were well established and there was fierce competition for traffic between them and the canals. The railways of course won the battle but there was a long period when the rivals combined resources such as wharfage and storage facilities.

Birmingham and the other manufacturing towns of the West Midlands were particularly well served for goods transport, much better in fact than the other great cities including London. Birmingham's other great advantage over other cities was its sheer variety of manufacturing. Not for nothing was it called the "city of a thousand trades". They ranged in size from the one-man business, carried on in a minute workshop at the back of the house, the owner perhaps helped by his wife and, I dare say, their small children, to the large manufacturer (for those times) employing as many as six hundred people, making everything from pearl buttons to cannon. Guns were Birmingham's oldest traditional industry and its hand-made sporting weapons were famous the world over.

One thing that stands out when one studies Birmingham's growth during the Industrial Revolution is the speed with which the manufacturers adapted to new ideas and inventions, steam power and electroplating being chief amongst these. It also had the entrepreneurs with the vision to bring in new ideas from abroad that revolutionised industry: screw-making machinery imported from Germany was a very important example of this.

The period during which all these changes took place was one of continuous growth. Some comparisons for Birmingham's population during this time may be relevant here. These are not always easy to make, as boundary changes took place from time to time but as these were mainly in the central areas during the early part of the century, the figures give a reasonably accurate picture.

The population and number of dwellings more than doubled between 1801 and 1841, from 60,822 and 12,044 to 138,215 and 27,272. In the sixty years from 1841 to 1901, which is roughly the period covered by the atlas, the population of Birmingham, as then constituted, rose from 177,922 to 431,327. With that of the parishes which were added in 1891, Harborne, Balsall Heath, Saltley and Ward End, the figure rose to 525,833.

As early as 1838 there was little or no land left for development in Birmingham itself and again, as in London, the building of the two main stations, New Street and Snow Hill, meant the destruction of hundreds of dwellings. Again, as in London, one by-product was a major slum clearance. (Likewise there is no mention of provision for rehousing the dispossessed.) Major roadwork schemes - Corporation Street in 1879 was one such - and new public building resulted in more slum clearance and by this time Birmingham was beginning to take shape as the city we know today. The first wards to be developed outside the city (although it was not to be granted the status of one until 1889) were in Aston, in the

Nechells and Duddeston district. By 1841 there was a population of 20,000, where previously there had been only a few farms and cottages.

A map of 1839 shows the city almost moated by canals, The Grand Junction connecting the Midlands to London, the Warwick, the Worcester, the Wolverhampton and the Fazeley canals radiated outward from the city like the spokes of a wheel and with their large wharf and storage areas, transformed Birmingham into an inland port. The building of the London-Birmingham Railway encouraged growth in the Deritend Ward to the extent that by 1841 the population had passed the 18,000 mark. The building of the Birmingham Small Arms (B.S.A.) factory sparked off another flurry of development.

Edgbaston alone among Birmingham's wards has retained its Victorian character. It was originally envisaged by its planners as a suburb for wealthy merchants and manufacturers and provided an oasis of greenery in the otherwise densely populated city.

The routes of the main roads, canals and railways continued to influence the pattern of growth. After Balsall Heath, Aston, Handsworth and Lozells, Erdington and Gravelly Hill were built over as the city reached towards Sutton Coldfield, although Erdington was never so densely built over as other wards. Eastwards Birmingham extended across Washwood Heath, Saltley and Sparkbrook.

Manufacturers too had been forced away from the city centre because of the high cost of land and the need to be beside either the canals or railways. The workers followed but their need was as much to get away from squalid living conditions in the city as to be near their workplace. In the central wards there was a continuous succession of building and rebuilding. Large houses were replaced by villas which within a few years were themselves demolished to make way for high density housing. As soon as Birmingham officially became a city, its corporation set about expansion in earnest. In 1891 Harborne, Balsall Heath, Saltley and Ward End were officially included within its limits, although most of these areas had already been extensively built over.

As previously stated, Aston parish, in terms of population, was equal to if not bigger than Birmingham itself and between 1851 and 1891, when the population of the city fell owing to redevelopment and resettlement, Aston Manor's rose from 6426 to 68,639. Erdington, once a fairly important village in the Aston Manor, was a classic example of the gradual, creeping development of a city swallowing a village.

Slowly at first, building took place along the road from Gravelly Hill to Erdington but once the station was built at Sutton Coldfield in 1862, work accelerated until the development was continuous and the village surrounded.

**Yardley** is another ancient parish which was transformed by the arrival of the railway in the 1850's. The population doubled every ten years through the latter half of the century, the figure of 2825 in 1841 rising to 59,165 in 1911.

**Harborne**, another village with its own ancient church and social fabric, was gradually enveloped also but somehow managed to retain its own identity, as the writer can testify, having lived there for some years. It had its own small industries, nailmaking at Camomile Green being one but growth here was slower than elsewhere, perhaps because Harborne was cushioned by the way that Edgbaston had been developed. Much of Harborne was woodland, evidenced by local names such as Lordswood, Ravenhurst and Beech Road. Lordswood occupied about 200 acres. There were also some large houses occupied by wealthy merchants of the city, Harborne Manor (later Bishop's Croft), Tennal House and Metchley Abbey amongst others.

Quinton became part of Birmingham in 1909 and virtually became part of Harborne in the development westward but the major part of this took place at a later date than that covered by this atlas.

**Handsworth**, another old parish, formerly part of Staffordshire, as was Harborne, covered nearly 8000 acres to the North-West of the city. Perry Barr is a place-name which has evolved from two former estates, Perry and Little Barr (Great Barr remains further to the north). When the railway station was opened in 1837 it was called Perry Barr and the name eventually came to be used for the whole district, north and south of the River Tame.

As in Harborne there was considerable woodland which was gradually eroded away for housing though the name Handsworth Wood remains. There was much small industry in the area near Birmingham due to the availability of water power but the building of Matthew Boulton's factory at Soho and the fact that both he and James Watt had homes in the area gave Handsworth its industrial base.

The southern part of the parish had much

the same social standing as Edgbaston but Handsworth and Smethwick stations, which opened in 1854, gave fresh impetus to building; the population grew steadily, and the open spaces were rapidly filled in. There was spectacular growth in the population between 1891 and 1901, with the figure rising from 32,756 ( it had been 6,138 in 1841 ) to 52,921 but after 1911 the figures scarcely increased at all.

**King's Norton**, formerly in Worcestershire, a parish of some 12,000 acres and thus rather larger than Handsworth, stretches some eight miles south and west of the city centre. The development, as previously mentioned, started along the railway and two canals, the Birmingham-Worcester and the Birmingham-Gloucester. Moseley was developed as a middle-class suburb. The station was opened in 1867 and had a fairly immediate effect on building but the area managed to retain its status. Kings' Norton had the advantage, unlike Handsworth, of a recognisable old village centre.

Development also took place along the Alcester Road and Pershore Road to Cotteridge and railway stations were opened at Lifford in 1840, King's Norton in 1849, and Bourneville in 1876 with the immediate effect of expansion of those suburbs. The population grew from 5550 in 1841,and 34,071 in 1881, to 89,044 in 1911. Except for Wythall and Rednal, King's Norton became part of Birmingham in 1911, as did Yardley. Here development was fairly rapid once the railway arrived. Stechford station opened in 1844 and Acocks Green in 1852. Yardley was another residential area favoured by local businessmen in its early stages of development but here there was greater pressure from population expansion in the 70's and 80's and the businessmen departed. Yardley grew rapidly from the 1850's on. From 2,825 in 1841, its population had grown to 31,395 by 1911.

**Northfield** was another ancient village huddled round its parish church. By 1840 new building north and west of the original village had already outgrown it.

**Selly Oak**, where road, railway and canals intersected, was obviously the first part to be developed. By 1882 it had become industrialised and building had taken place along the Pershore Road for almost its entire length. The Cadbury factory opened in 1879, shortly after the station was opened, and by 1900 the Bourneville Estate already covered 300 acres. The population trebled between 1891 and 1911, from nearly 10,000 to 31,000. Northfield

Station was opened in 1869 but the development of Bartley Green and Weoley Castle belong to a later era.

If a personal reminiscence might be allowed here - the writer remembers Bartley Green as the terminus for the Corporation buses and thus the starting point for Sunday summer walks to, Illey Romsley, Frankley and Clent. The overriding memory of that time is one of total peace and quiet in unspoiled countryside. Once the diesel engine of the bus had stopped its clatter, the only sound to be heard, apart from the birds, might be that of church bells from miles away. Looking at today's map, with the thick blue line of the motorway slicing through the middle of this beautiful countryside, one is inclined to wonder whether this is really progress.

**The Black Country** was the cradle of the Industrial Revolution. At its heart lay Dudley, with its iron and coal. Like Birmingham, the towns of the Black Country were peopled by independent-minded folk who preferred, if possible, to have their own workshop, however small, rather than work in a larger factory. Throughout towns and villages like Cradley Heath, Brierley Hill, Lye, Quarry Bank and Stourbridge, the nail-makers, chain-makers, glass-blowers and a hundred other trades turned raw materials into the tools of the new industries. At its height in the nineteenth century it must have been a fearsome sight with the smoke and flame of the blast-furnaces covering the sky twenty-four hours a day. The actor, Sir Cedric Hardwicke, who was born in Lye, gives a fascinating description of the Black Country in his autobiography, where he describes being driven by his father, a doctor, in a pony and trap when he visited his patients on his rounds. He describes the journey into some of the valleys as being like a descent into hell. It may very well have been hell to work there!

However, the towns thrived and the population grew.

**Wolverhampton**, with its huge variety of metal trades,can lay claim to be the capital of the Black Country. As the figures show, thousands of workers were attracted to its industries. From 14,736 in 1811, its population rose to 49,985 in 1851 and this figure had almost doubled to 94,187 by 1911. Hard to imagine it now as the centre of the wool trade, which it was for hundreds of years.

**Dudley**, The geology of the surrounding countryside made it inevitable that the old town of Dudley would become the powerhouse of the Black Country with its coal, ironstone, limestone and fireclay deposits so available to make it the steel town of the Midlands. Everything from nails to huge girders for bridge building came from here. Although its population was much the same as Wolverhampton's in 1811, at 13,925 it did not grow as fast, reaching 37,962 in 1851 and 48,733 in 1901.

Further west and south other industrial towns flourished.

**Kidderminster**, with a long-established weaving industry, became the centre for carpet making. Population there rose from 8,038 in 1851 to 13,493 in 1901.

**Redditch** was world-famous for its needle making and grew steadily, 2,429 in 1801; 4802 in 1851 and 13,493 in 1901.

**Coventry**, like Birmingham, was a city of many trades, though in the present century it has been mostly associated with cars and motorcycles. With such a variety of trades people flocked to it in the nineteenth century and its population grew from 17,923 in 1811 to 70,296 in 1901.

**Walsall**, on the edge of the Black Country, was the centre of the saddlery trade and the skills its people developed then have stood it in good stead with its host of metal and leather trades. The town showed the greatest growth in population of any town in the Midlands during the period covered by the atlas. It was a mere 9,176 in 1811, rising to 21,203 in 1851 but by 1901 it had reached an astonishing 70,296.

This brief introduction is not intended by any means to be a history of the changes in Birmingham and the Midlands in the nineteenth century but merely to provide background to the atlas.

We hope, though, that it will help in the understanding of the way development took place and that the atlas itself will make an interesting and useful companion volume to all that has been written in the past and will doubtless be written in the future. With the huge growth of modern cities, it becomes more and more difficult for their inhabitants to have a sense of belonging and clinging to one's roots becomes more and more important. If those roots are now buried under a few hundred acres of cement, this atlas will show where they lay.

Barry Bruff
London, 1989.

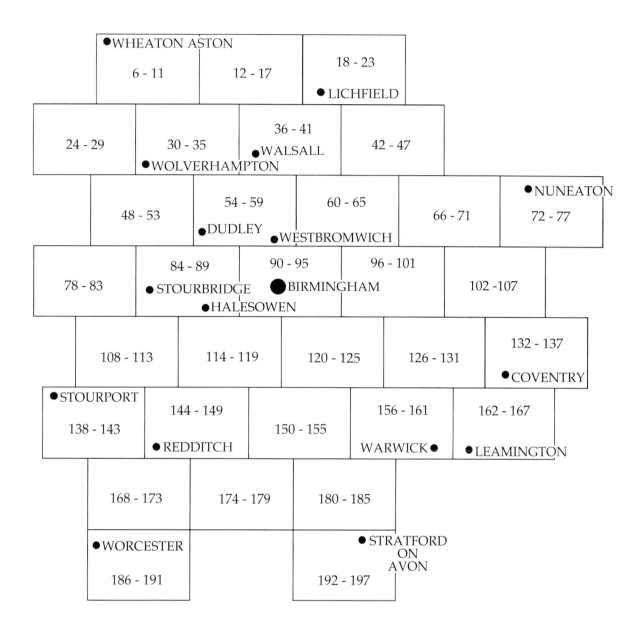

*The Maps*

## Publisher's Note

The maps in this Atlas are based on a scale of two inches to the mile. However, because of the number of different maps involved and the reproduction thereof there may be some minor variations in scale. The age of the maps and the fact that there could be as much as fifteen years difference between the dates of survey of adjoining maps, plus the handling and folding which has taken place over the years, have also meant that there are small differences here and there which are impossible to eradicate.

The publishers have made every effort to minimise these faults and trust the reader will make allowances for any slight imperfections.

6

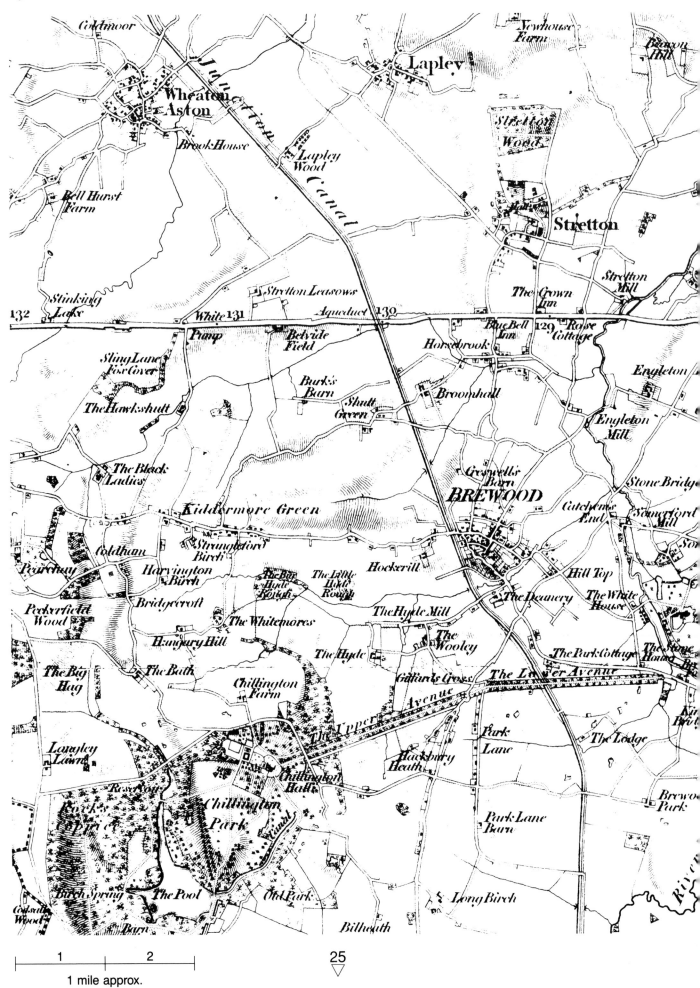

1 mile approx.

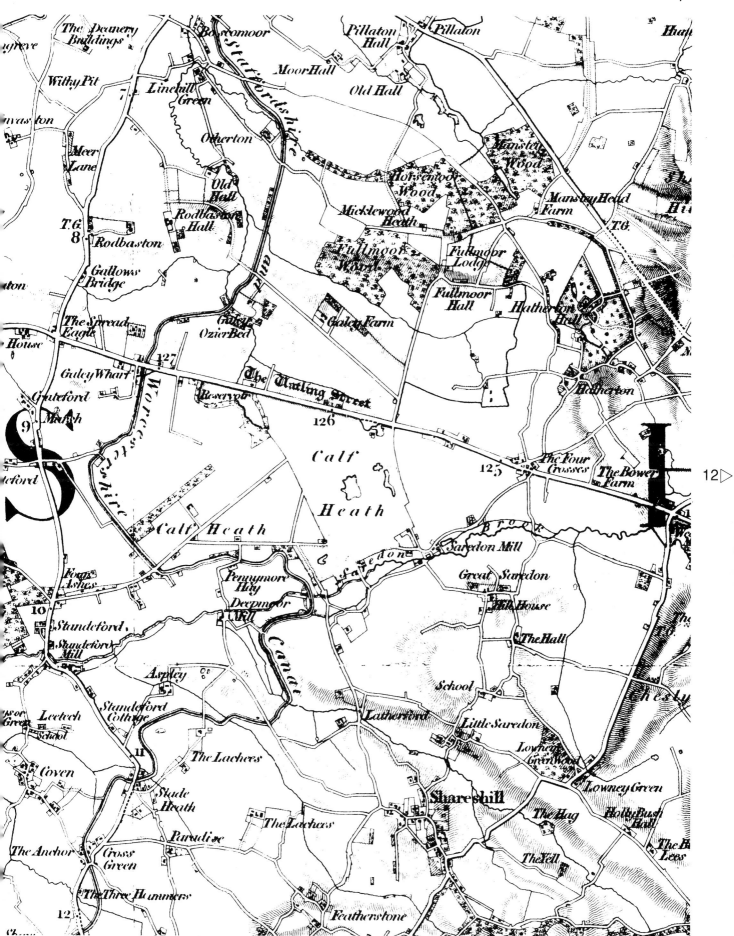

Published 1834.

8

.344

*Caulamore*

*The Lobby*

312

*Ch* ... **Lapley**

Lock

**Wheaton
Aston**

*Stretton
Wood*

360

*Ivy Villa*

*Bell Hurst
Fm*

382

*Lapley Wood
Fm*

*The Hall*

**Stretton**

369

*The Hurst*

464

*The Leasows*

351

*Ivetsey
Bank* 9

*White
Pump*

378

WATLING STREET

314

12

*Horsebroo
Hall*

10

*Ivetsey Fm*

11

400

*Belvide Reservoir*

372

*Broom Hall*

324

*The Hawkshutts*

402

*Shutt
Green*

**Bishop's Wood**

500

*Ch.*

*The Black Ladies*

Gas
Works

*Denns*

**Kiddemore Green**

444

846

**Brewood**

*Pearse Hay
Fm*

*Coldham*

*Oakley*

*Hockerill Fm*

400

*Harvington Birch
Fm*

317

*Royal Oak*

500

*The Whitemoors*

*Mill*

499

*Hungry Hill Fm*

*The Wooller*

484

*Bath Fm*

*Hyde
Fm*

*Park*

*OBEL*

416

*Chillington Fm*

*Horse
Paddock
Wood*

*Giffard's
Cross*

400

400

*Spring
Coppice*

427

*Ackbury
Heath*

385

**Park
Lane**

*Langley
Lawn*

*Chillington Hall*

434

*Renshaw
Wood*

476

400

*Big
Wood*

400

461

*Long Birch Fm*

*The
Pool*

| 1 | | 2 |
|---|---|---|

1 mile approx.

Surveyed 1880 - 86. Published 1895.

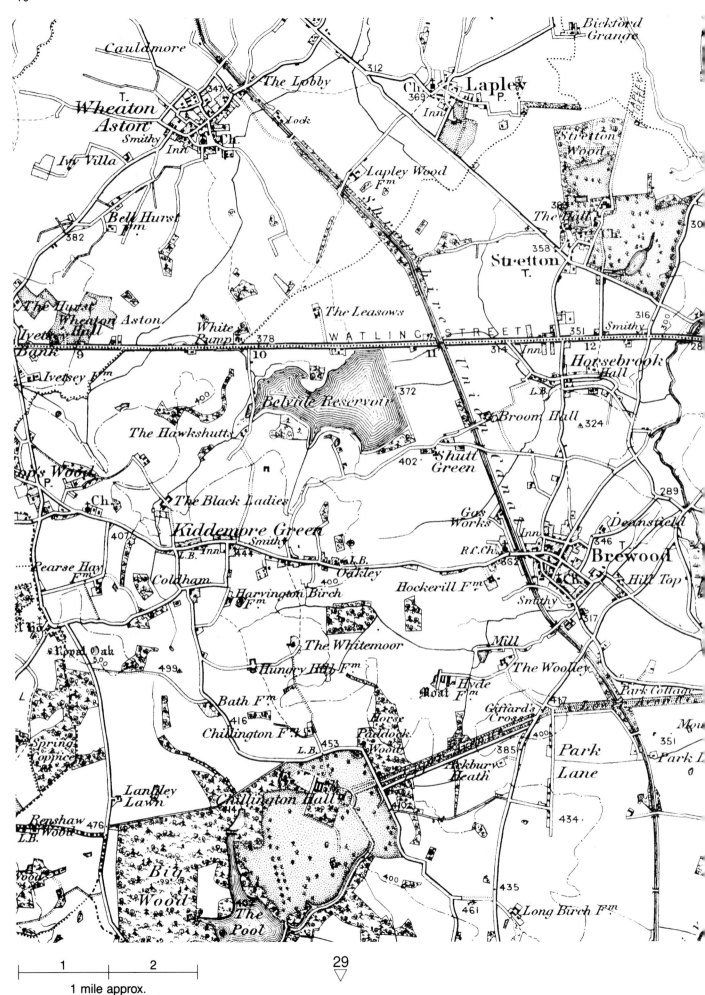

Caualamore

The Lobby

312

Ch. Lapley P.

Bickford Grange

Wheaton Aston T.

347

Inn

369

Stretton Wood

The Hall

30

Smithy Init Ch.

Ivy Villa

Lock

Lapley Wood Fm

358

Stretton T.

Bell Hurst Fm

382

316

300

The Hurst
Wheaton Aston

The Leasows

WATLING STREET

351 Smithy 28

Ivetsey Hall

White Pump

378

10

11

314 Inn

12

Horsebrook Hall

Bank

9

Ivetsey Fm

400

372

L.B.

Belvide Reservoir

Broom Hall

324

The Hawkshutt

402

Shutt Green

289

n's Wood P.

Gas Works

Deanstield

Ch.

The Black Ladies

Kiddemore Green

407

Smithy

R.C.Ch.

Inn

346 T.

Brewood

L.B. Inn

444

L.B.

862

Pearse Hay Fm

Oakley

Hill Top

Coldham

400

Hockerill Fm

Smithy

317

Harvington Birch Fm

The Whitemoor

Mill

The Woolley

Royal Oak

499

Hungry Hill Fm

Park Cottage

L

Hyde Fm

Giffard's Cross

417

Spring Coppice

Bath Fm

Moat

385

Park Lane

416

Chillington F.

Horse Paddock Wood

Pckbury Heath

400

351

Park L

Langley Lawn

L.B.

453

402

434

Renshaw Wood

476

Chillington Hall

414

L.B.

400

435

Wood

Big Wood

The Pool

461

Long Birch Fm

1      2

1 mile approx.

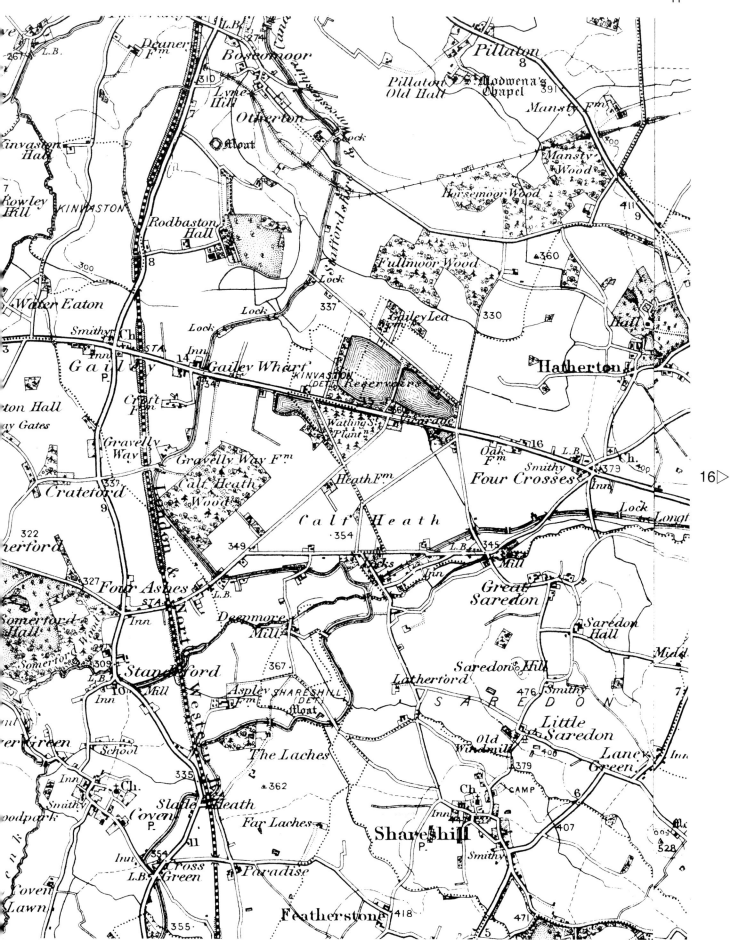

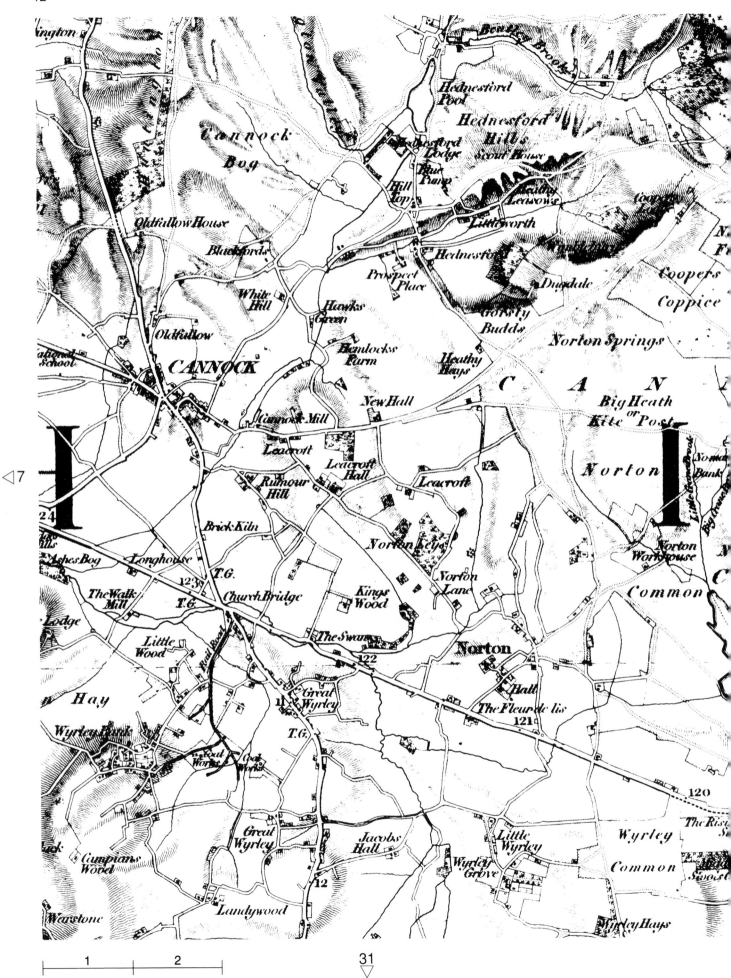

◁31▽

1 mile approx.

Published 1834.

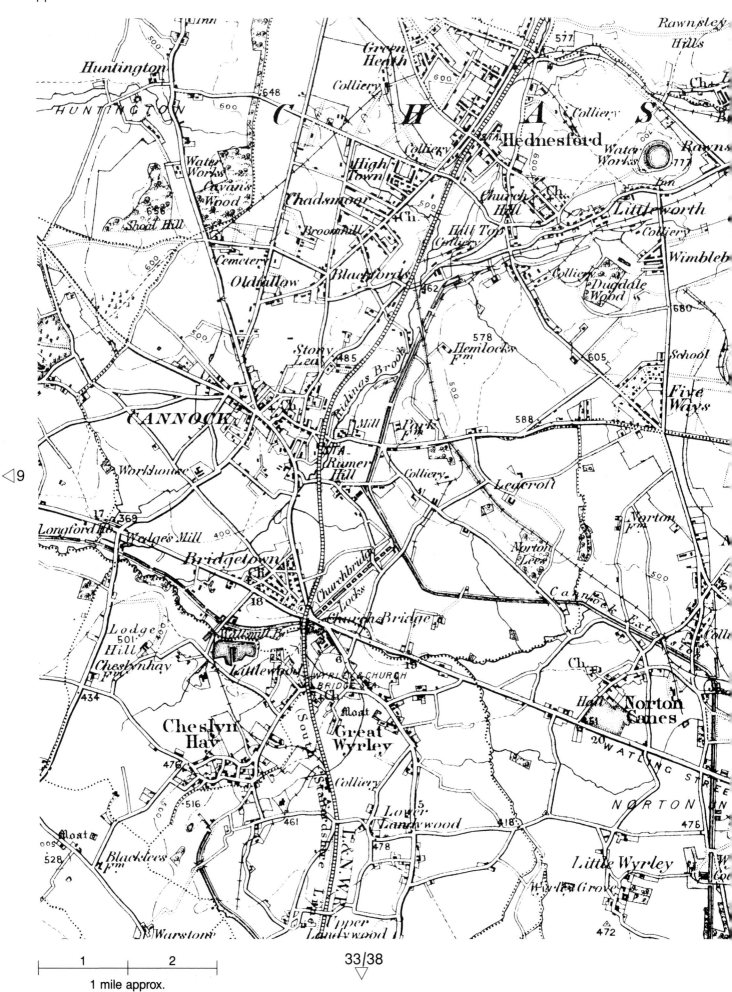

1 mile approx.

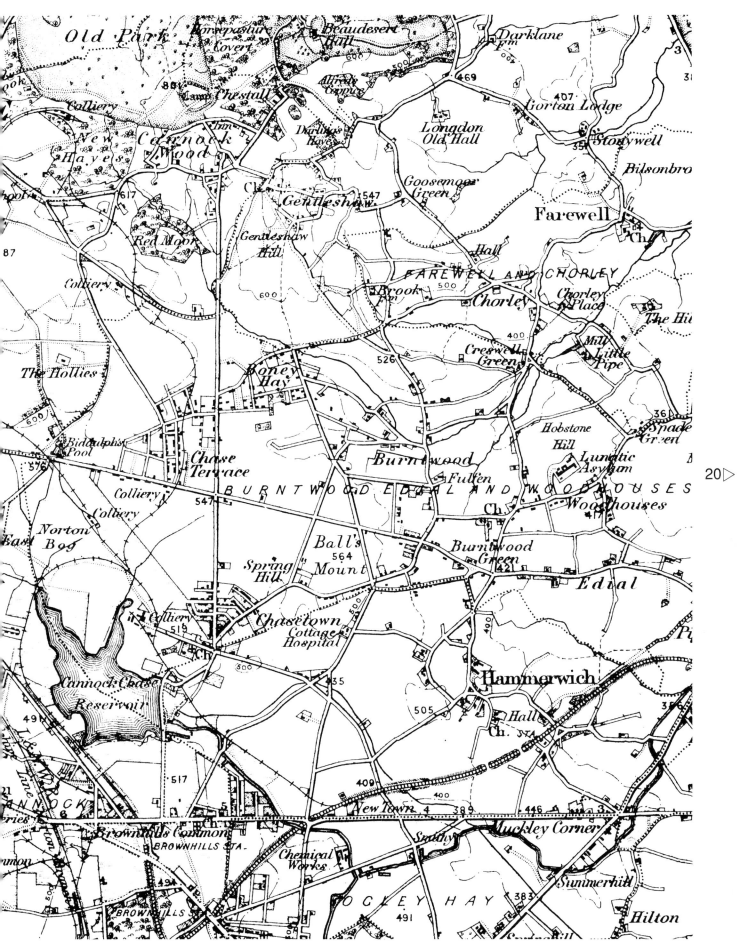

Old Park
Horsepasture Covert
Beaudesert Hall
Darklane Fm
469
Gorton Lodge
407
Stowell
Bilsonbro
Longdon Old Hall
35
Farewell
Ch
Colliery
New Cannock Wood Hayes
Lamp The stall
Alfred's Coppice
Darling's Hayes
Goosemoor Green
617
Cha Gentleshaw
547
Hall
FAREWELL AND CHORLEY
Colliery
Red Moor
Gentleshaw Hill
500
Chorley
Chorley Place
The Hi
600
Brook Fm
526
Creswell Green
Mill Little Pipe
Boney Hay
The Hollies
400
36
Spade Green
Hobstone Hill
Lunatic Asylum
20
Biddulph's Pool
576
Chase Terrace
BURNTWOOD EDIAL AND WOODHOUSES
Burntwood
Fulfen
Ch
Woodhouses
547
Colliery
Colliery
Norton Bog
East
Ball's Mount
564
Burntwood Green
42
Edial
Spring Hill
Colliery
519
Chasetown
Cottage Hospital
500
Hammerwich
500
Cannock Chase Reservoir
491
435
505
Hall
Ch
517
409
400
New Town 4 389
446
Muckley Corner
CANNOCK
eries
Brownhills Common
BROWNHILLS STA.
Smithy
Summerhill
49
Chemical Works
BROWNHILLS
OCLEY HAY
491
383
Hilton

Surveyed 1880 - 87. Published 1895.

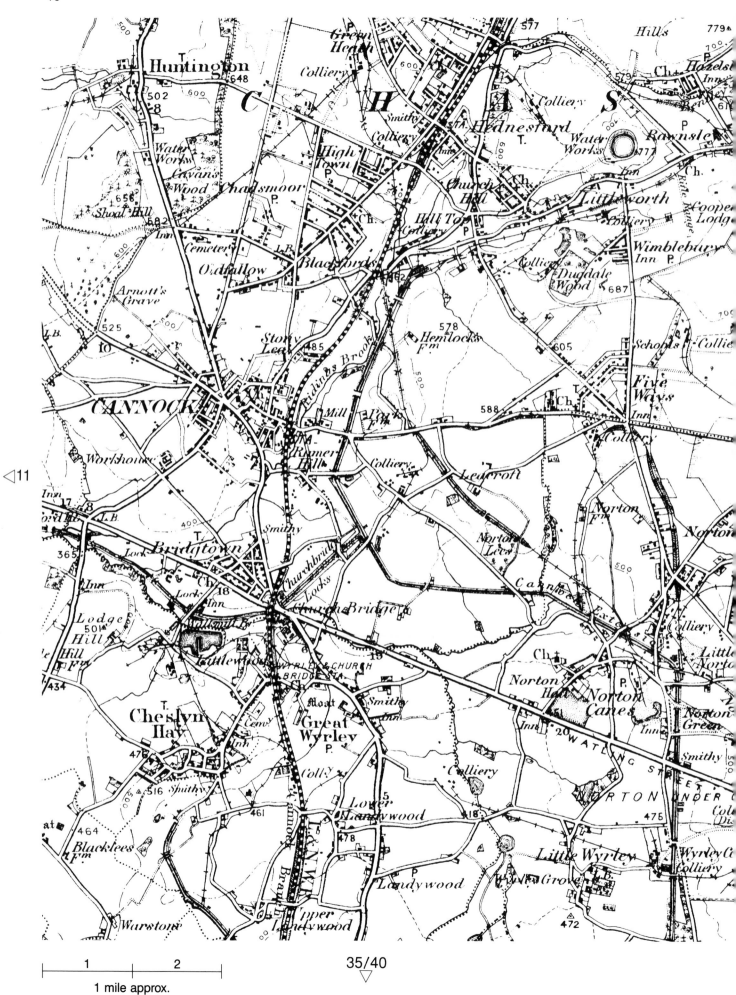

1      2

1 mile approx.

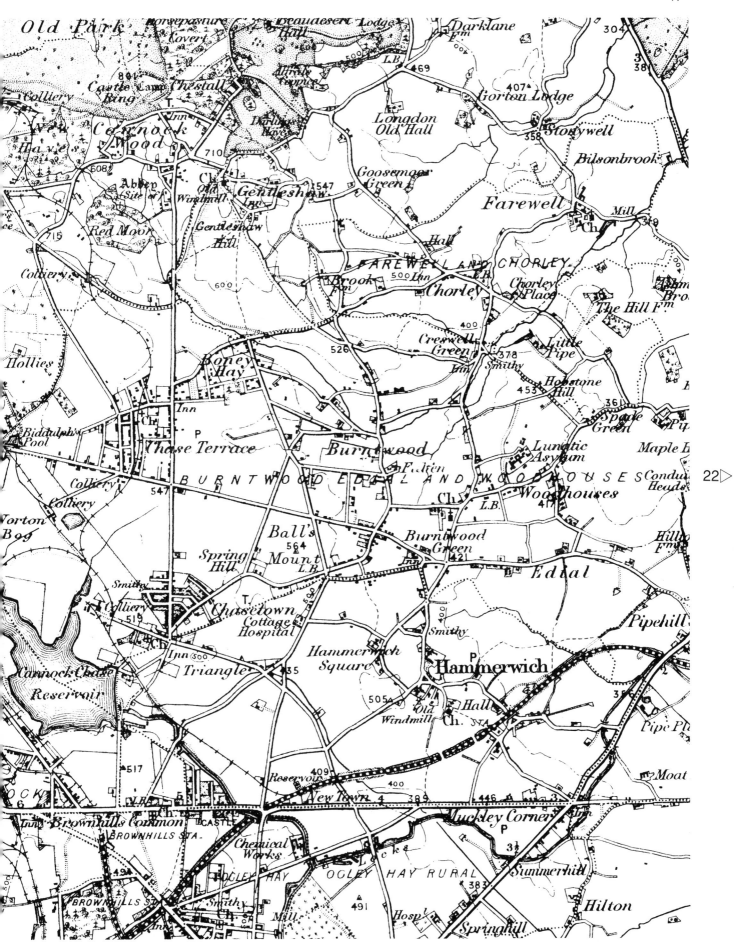

Surveyed 1878 - 86. Revised 1905. Published 1907.

◁13

37 ▽

1 mile approx.

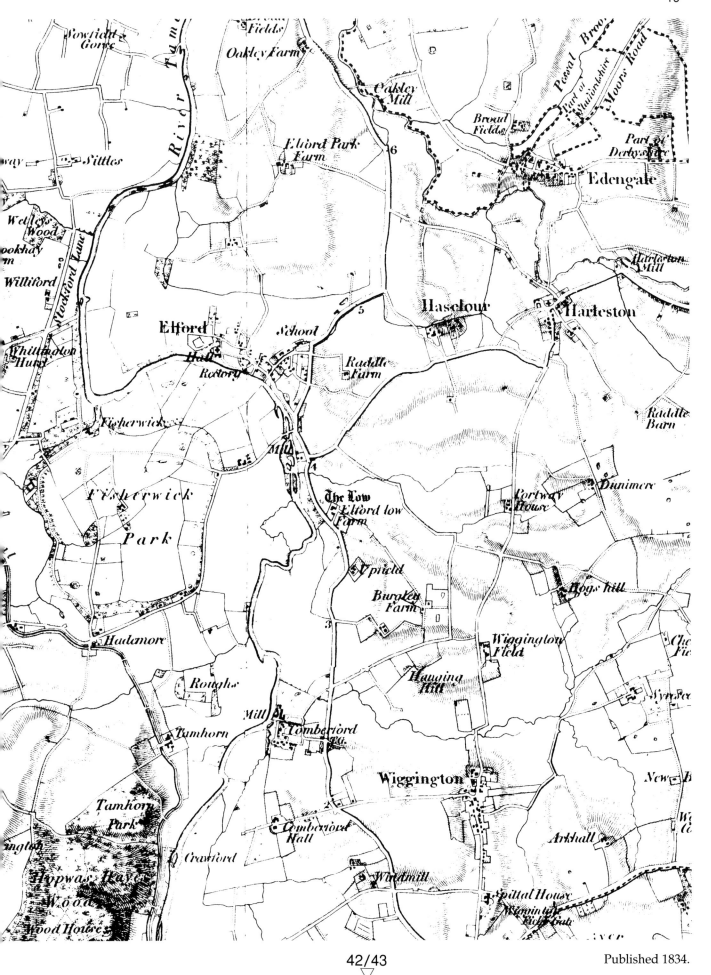

Published 1834.

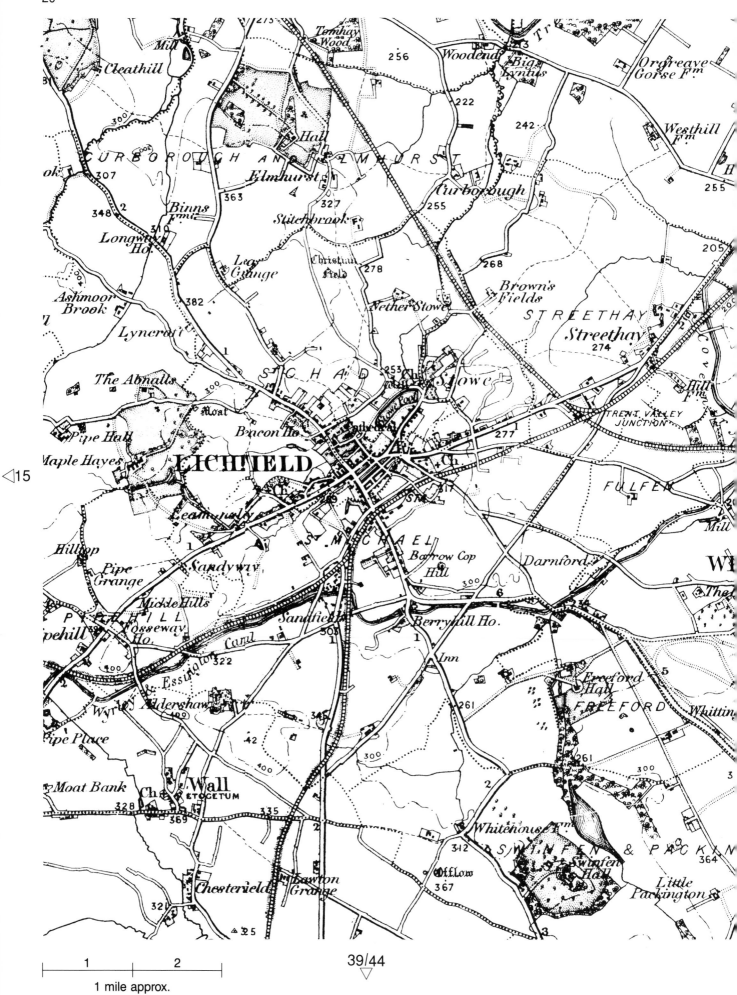

◁15

1 mile approx.

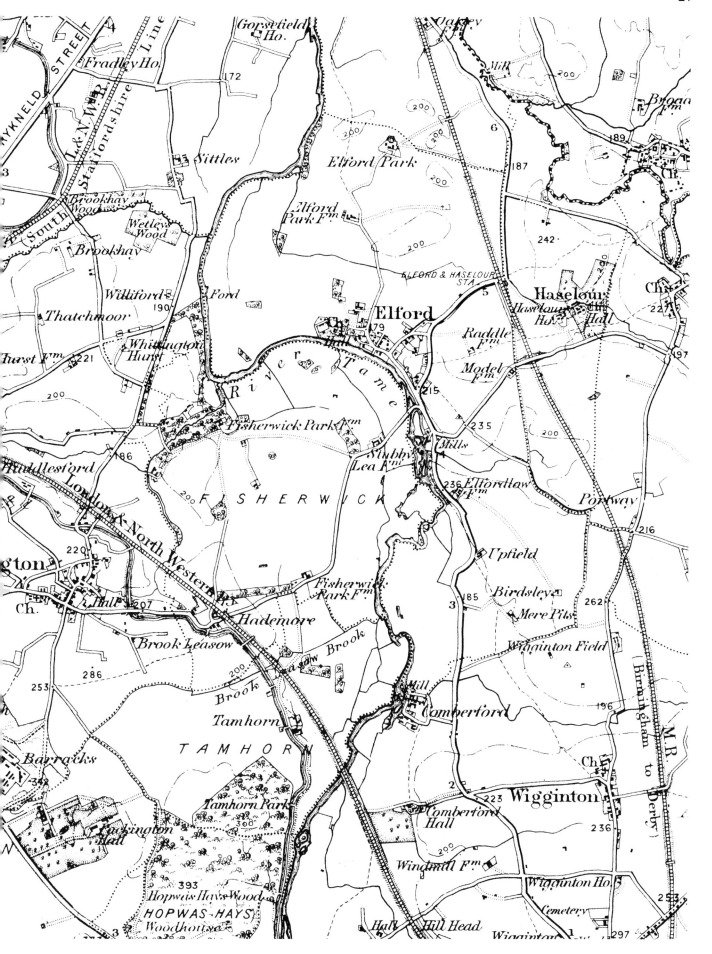

Surveyed 1880 - 87.  Published 1895.

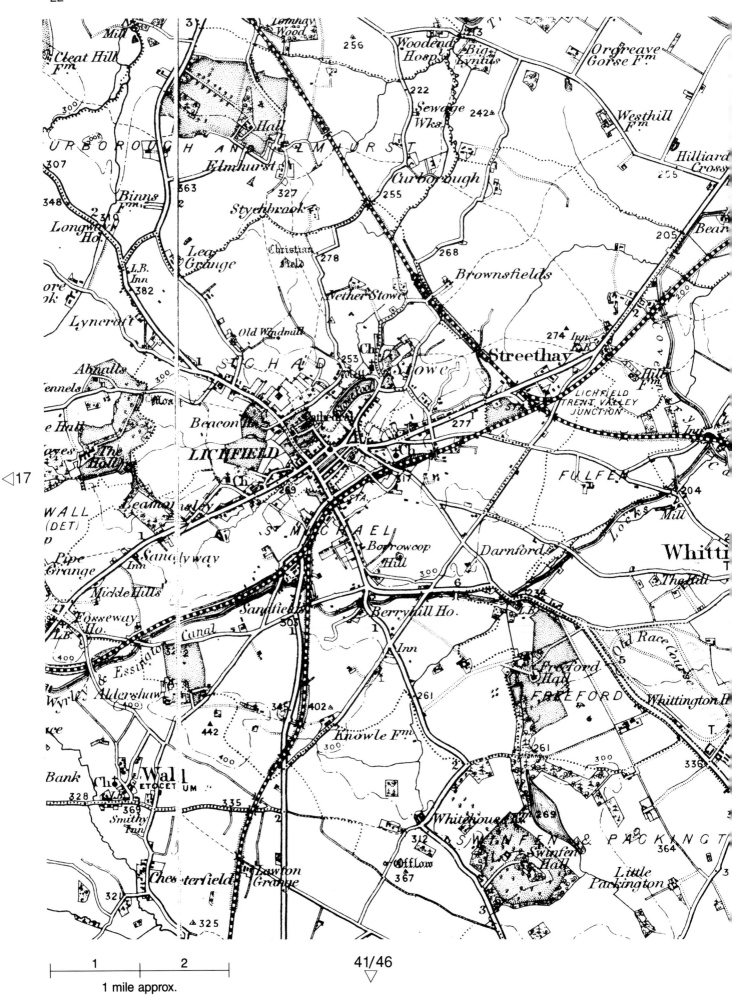

41/46

1 — 2

1 mile approx.

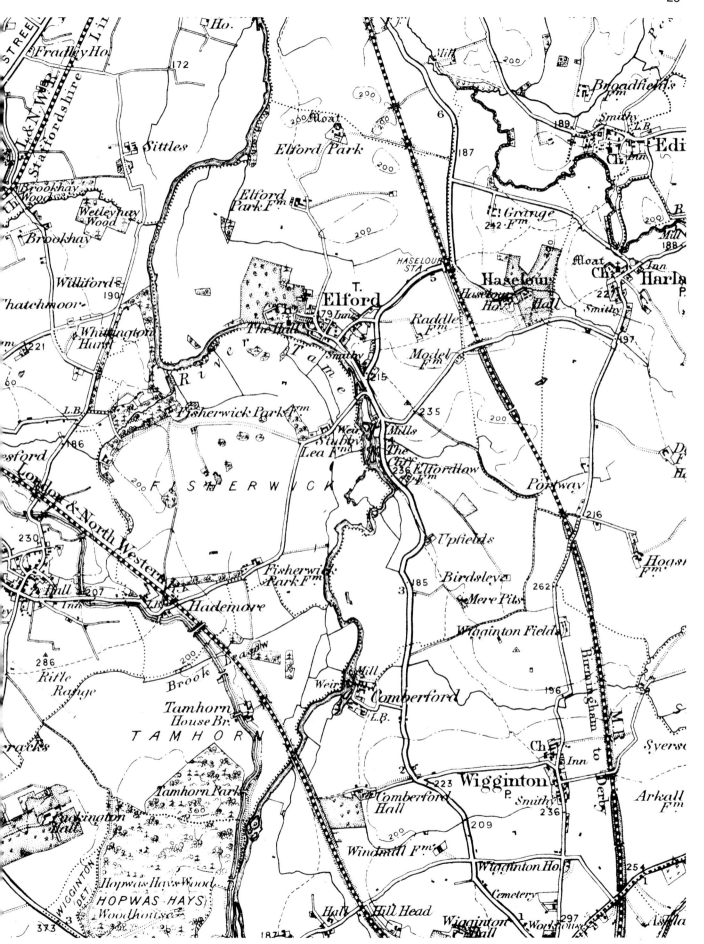

Surveyed 1878 - 86.  Revised 1905.  Published 1907.

24

1 mile approx.

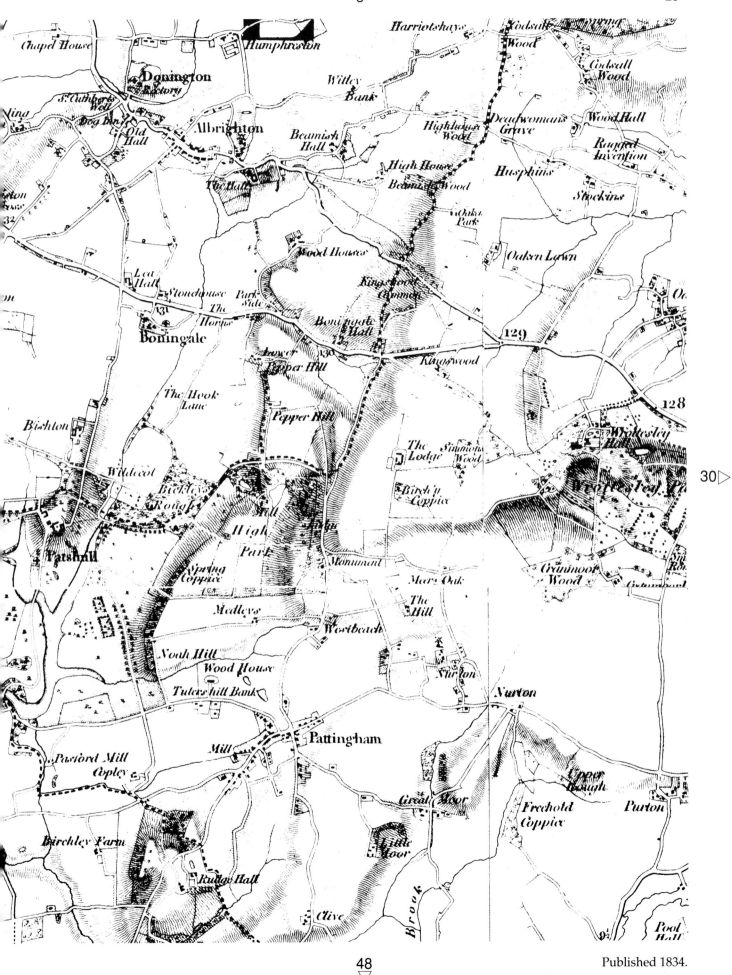

Published 1834.

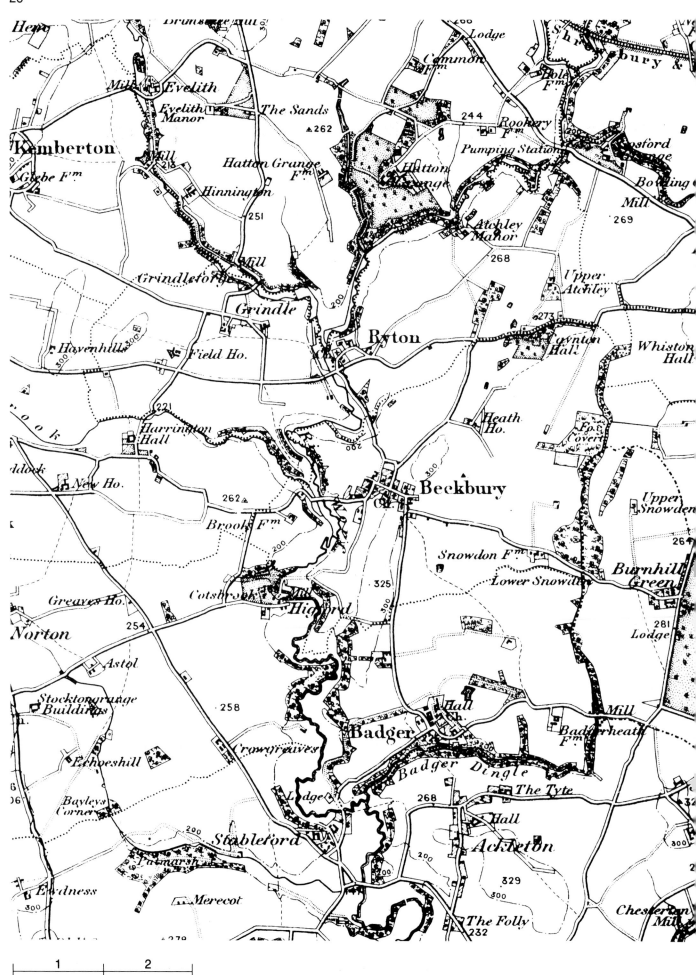

1 mile approx.

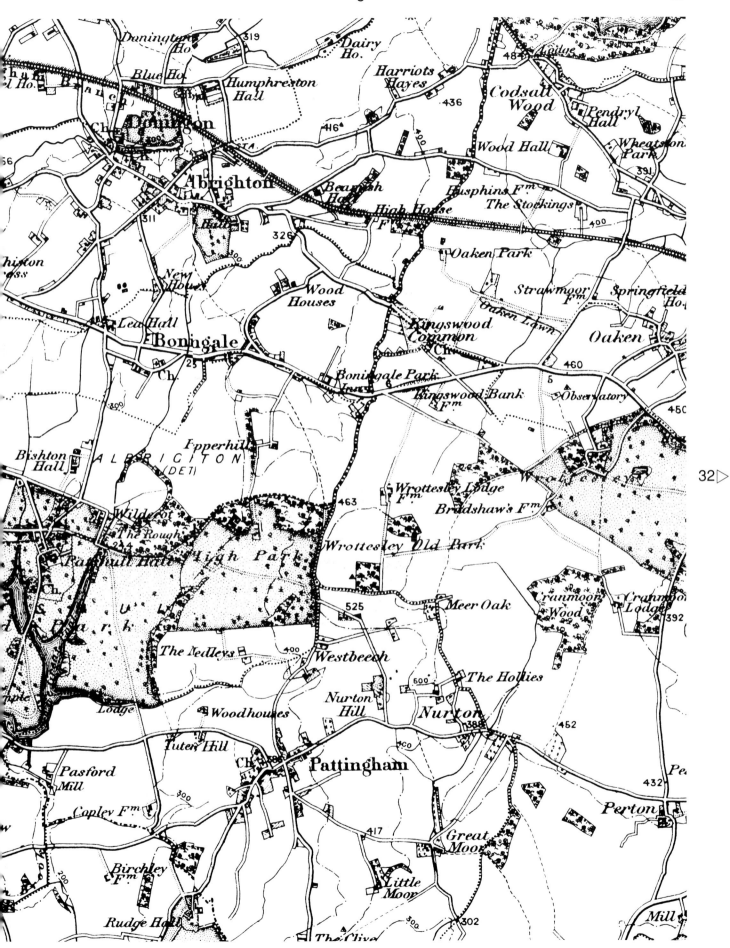

Surveyed 1880 - 86. Published 1895.

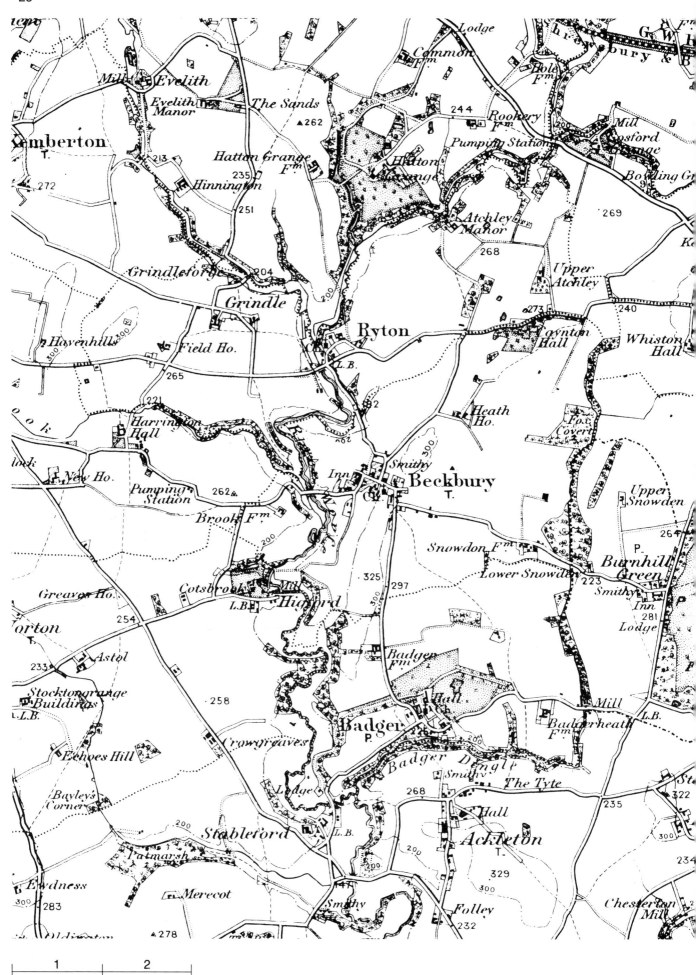

1 mile approx.

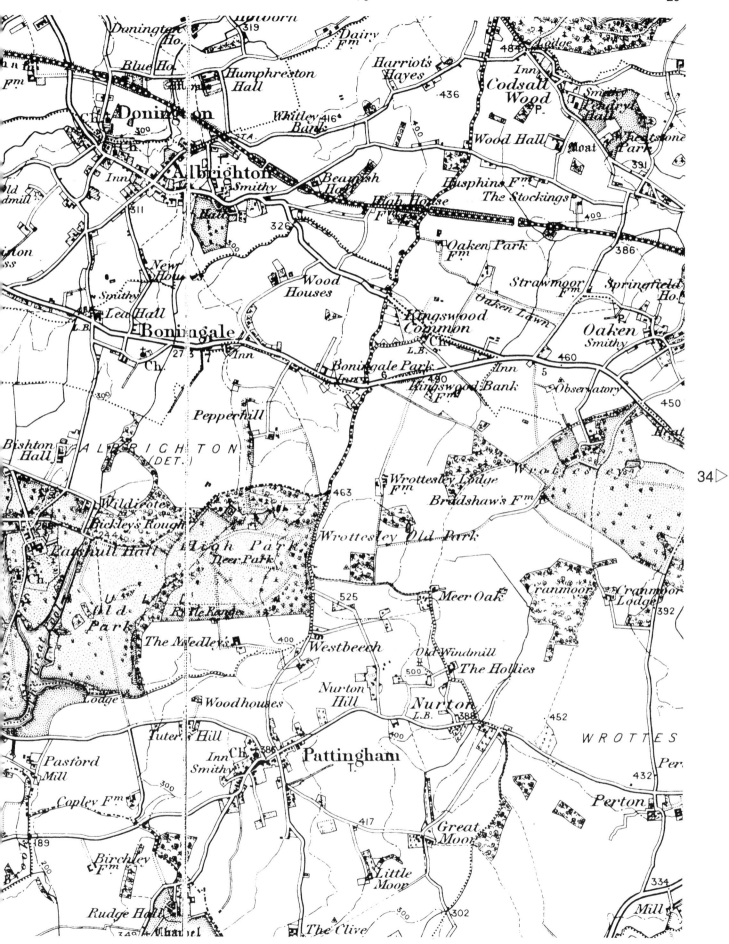

Surveyed 1878 - 85. Revised 1905. Published 1907.

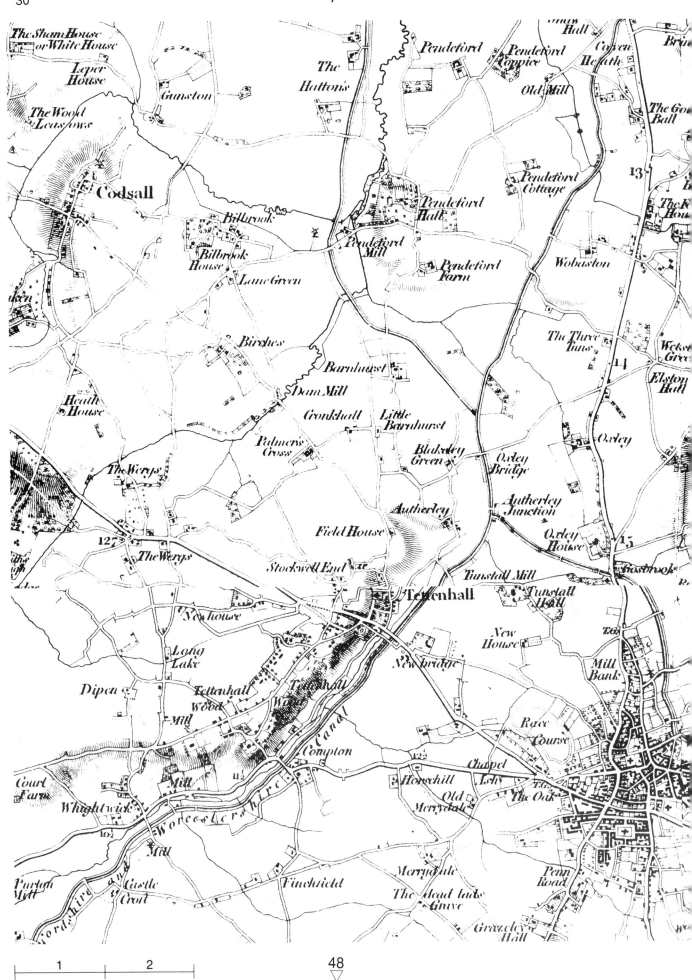

◁25

```
1          2
```
1 mile approx.

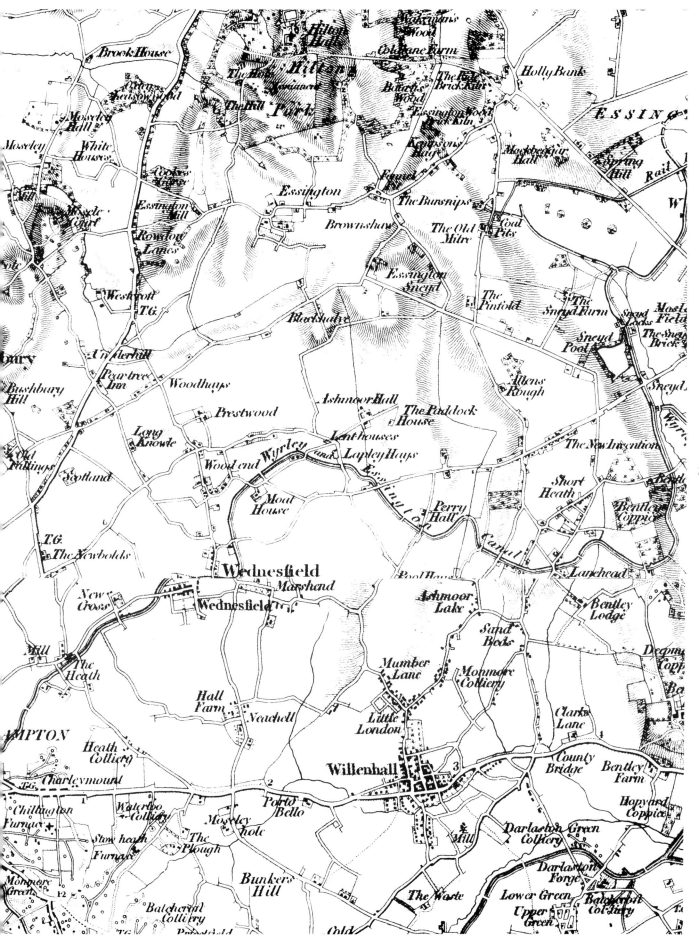

Published 1834.

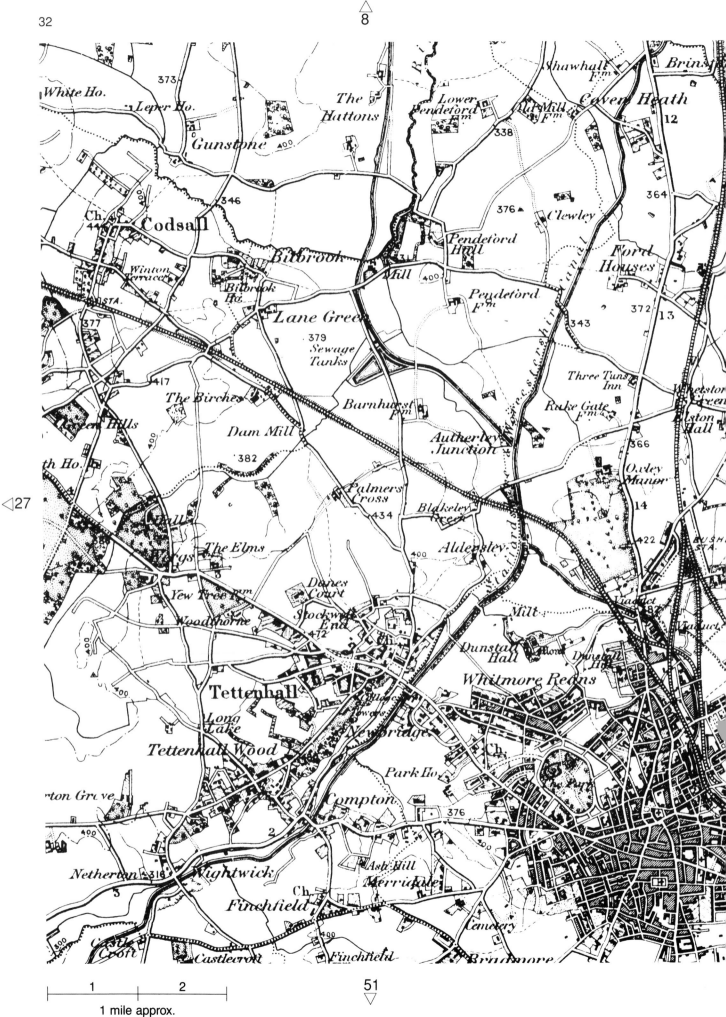

27

1     2

1 mile approx.

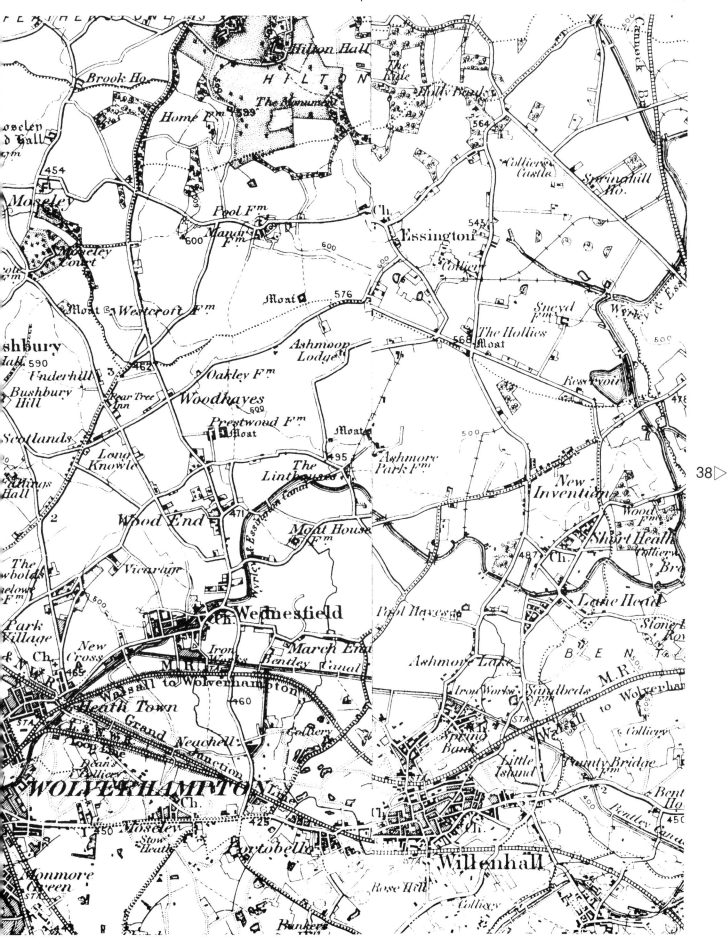

38▷

Surveyed 1880 - 86. Published 1895.

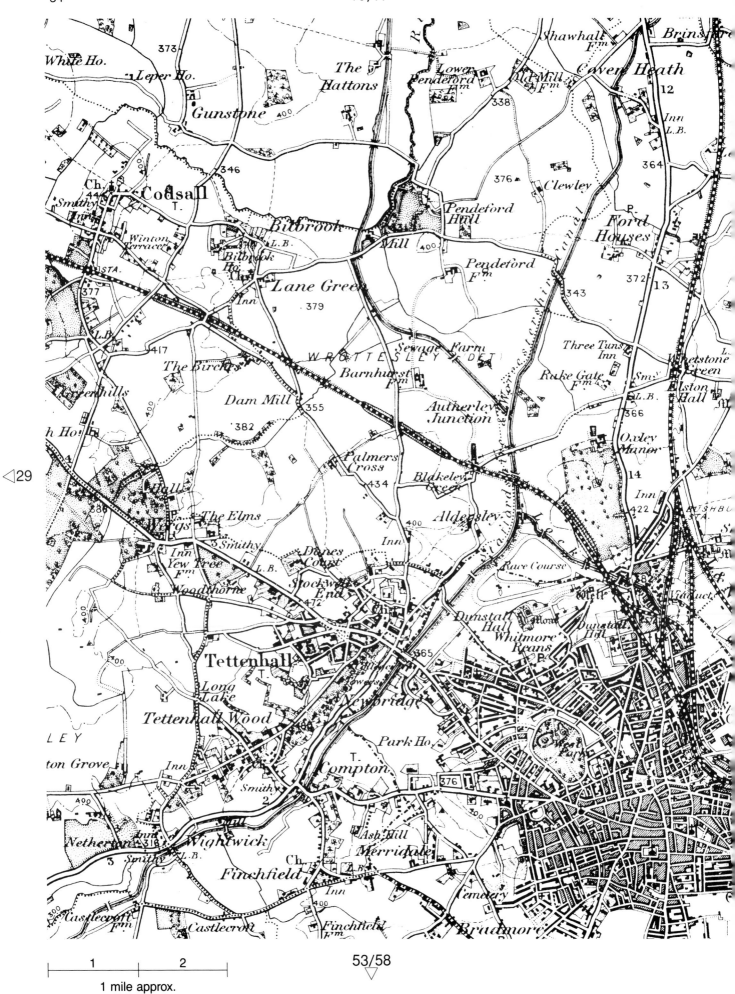

1     2

1 mile approx.

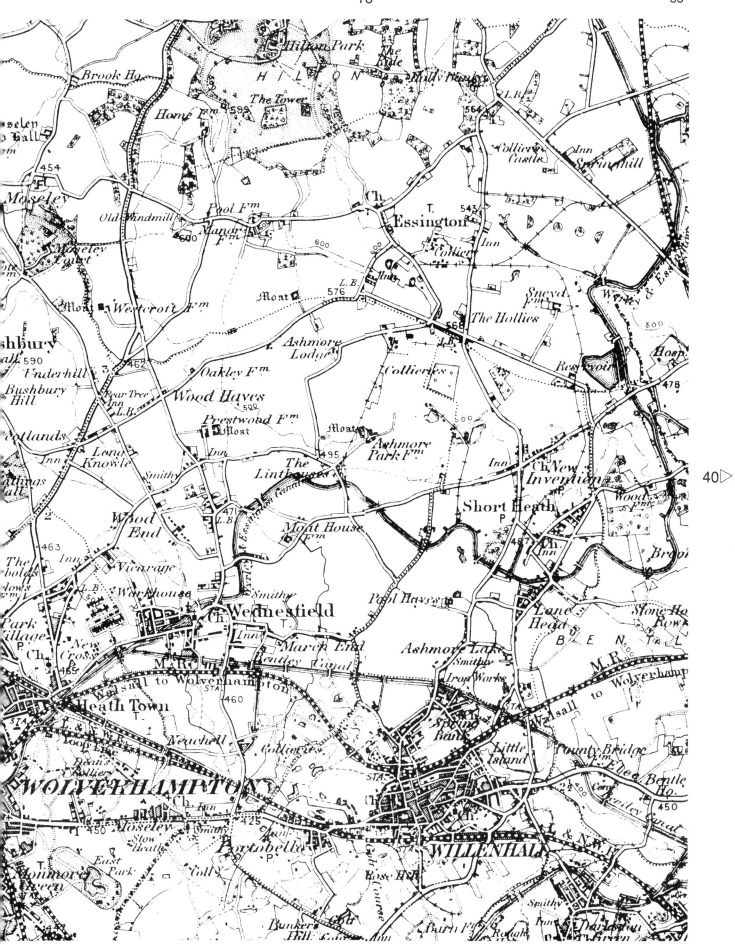

Surveyed 1878 - 86. Revised 1905. Published 1907.

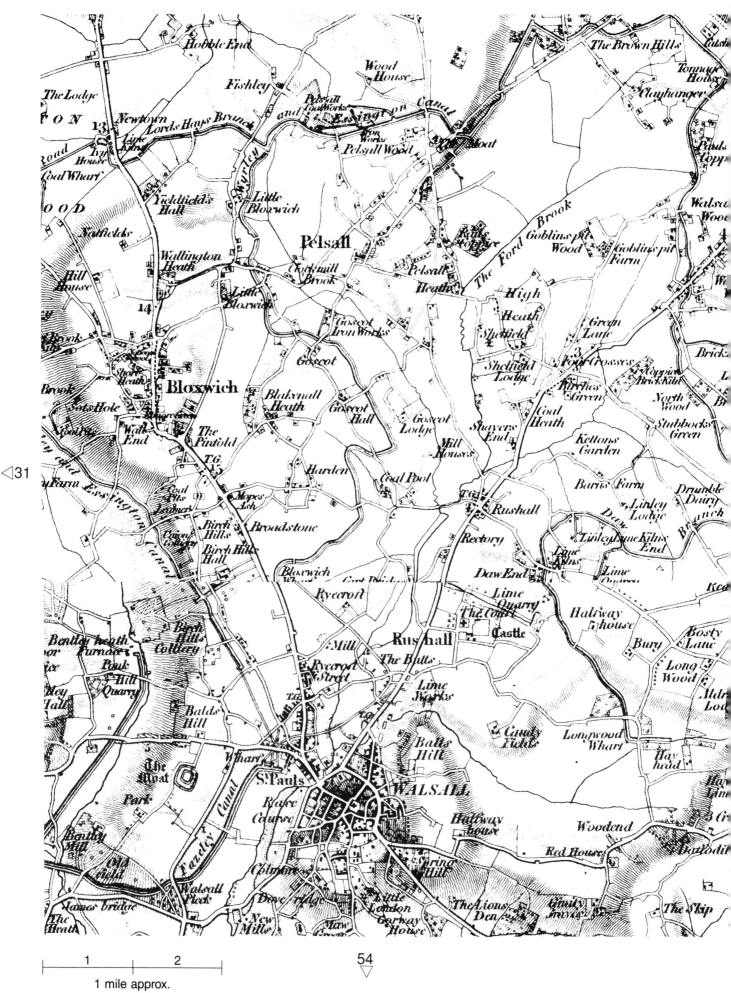

1 mile approx.

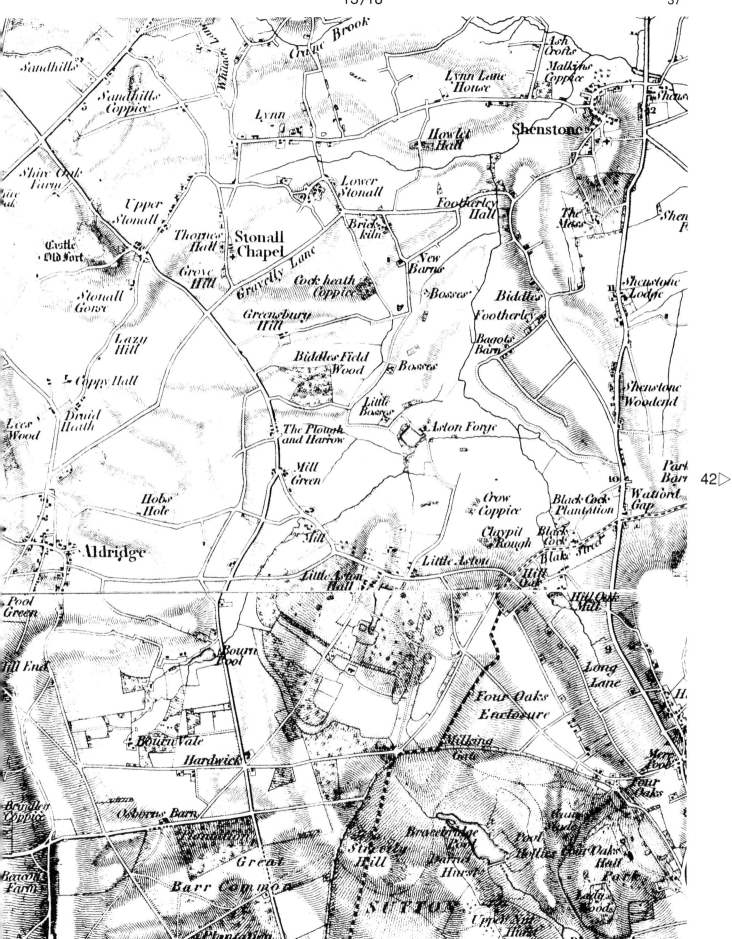

42 ▷

Published 1834.

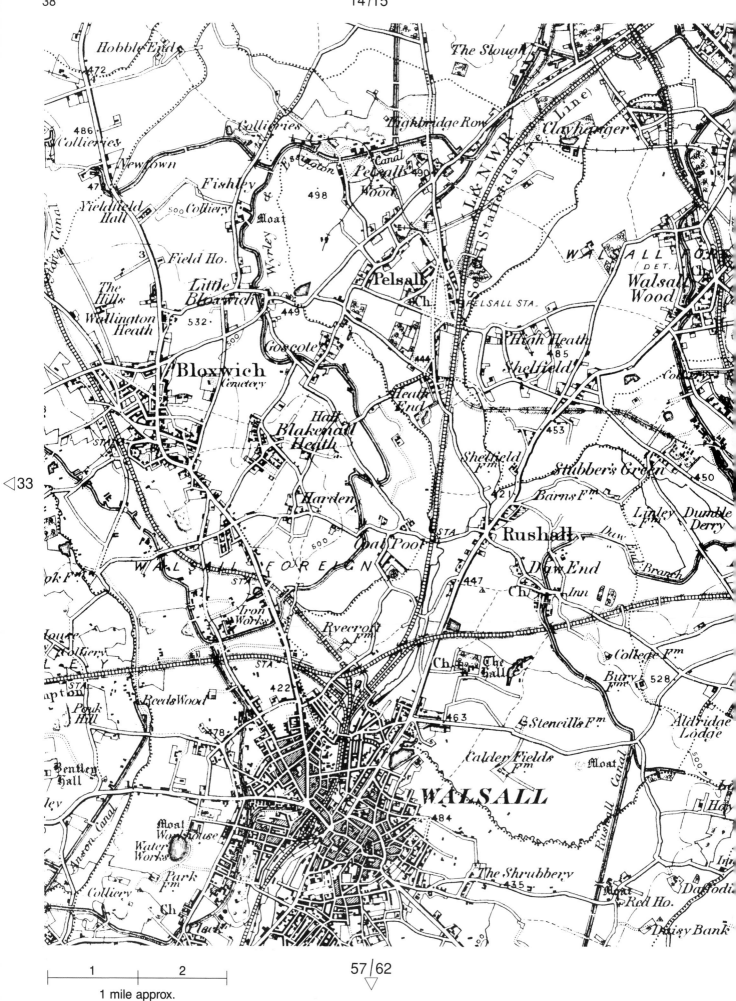

◁33

1 mile approx.

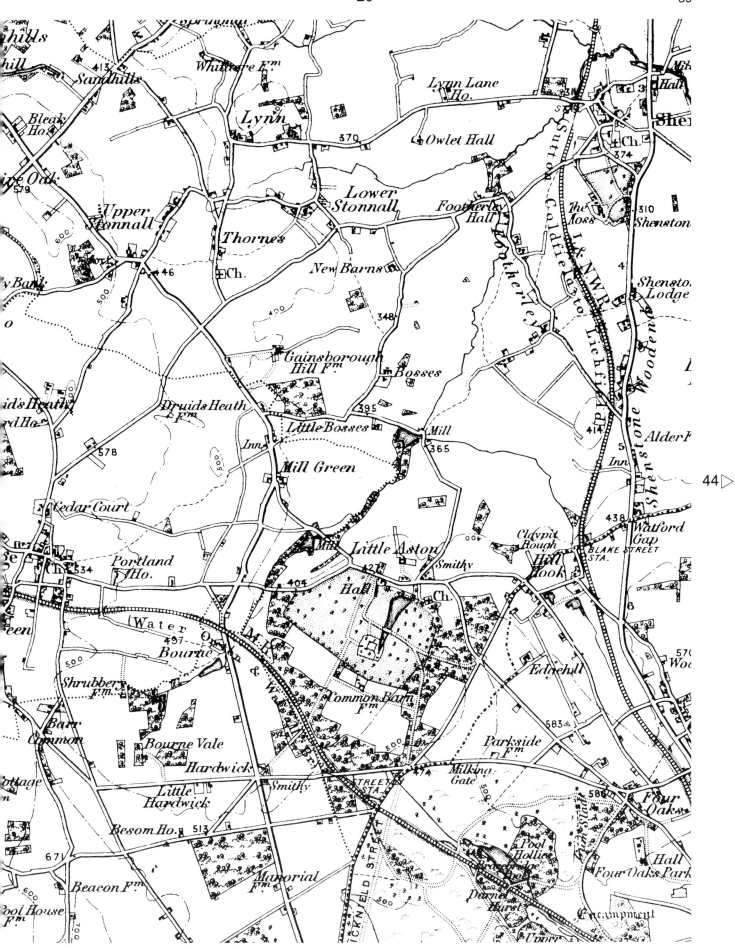

Surveyed 1880 - 87. Published 1895.

1 mile approx.

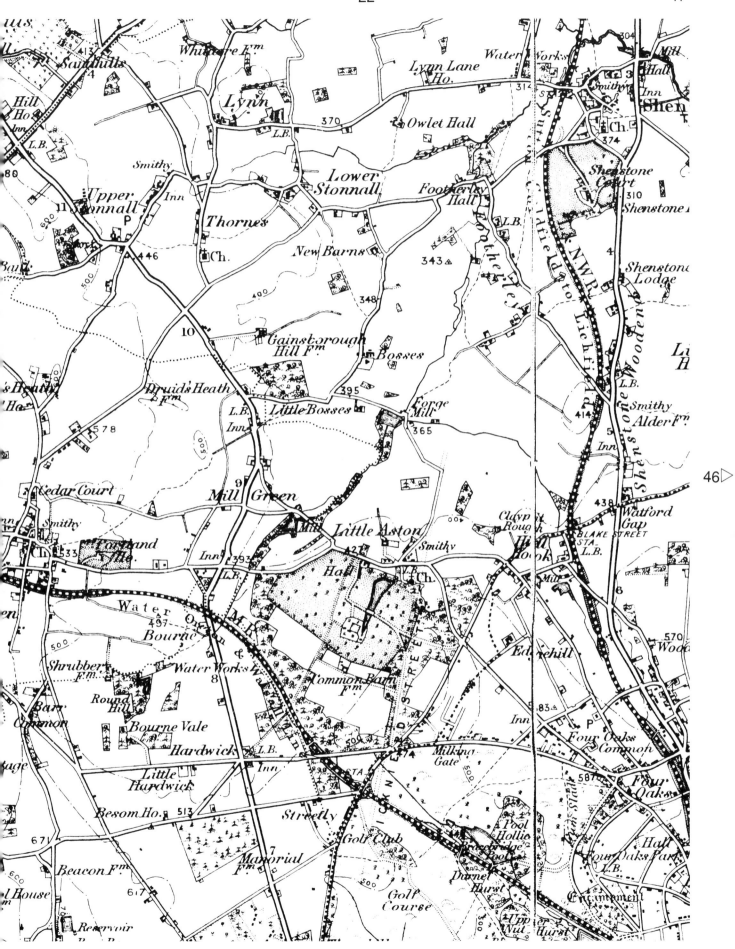

Surveyed 1878 - 86. Revised 1905. Published 1907.

1 mile approx.

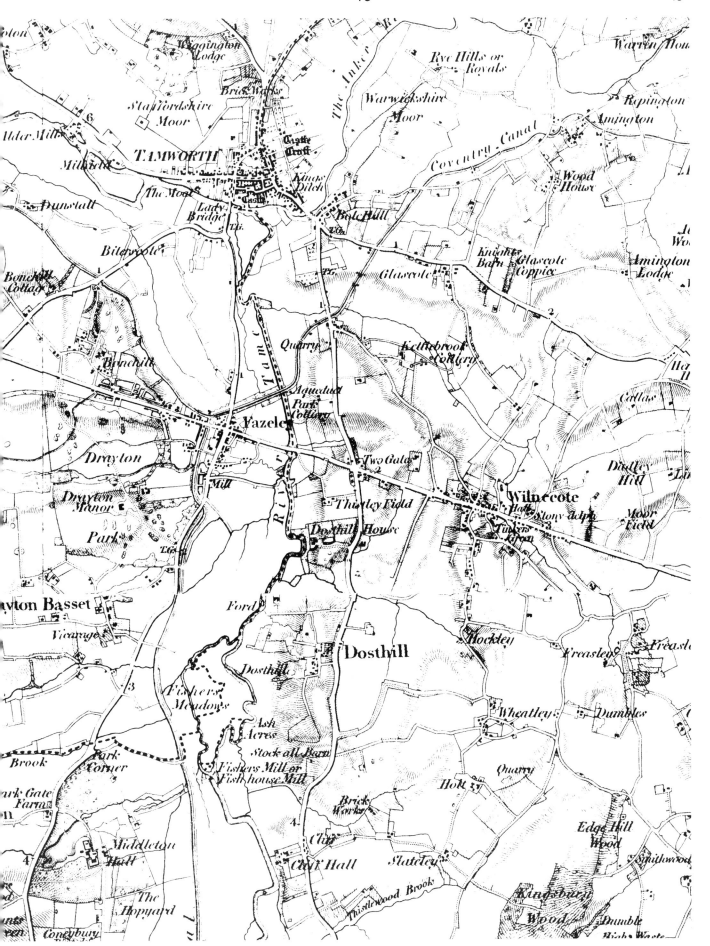

Published 1834.

315

313 Streetway Ho.

343

326 Weeford

304 Smithy Ch. Buck's Head F<sup>m</sup>

Common Barn 501

The Devil's Dressing Room

225

Hopwa F<sup>m</sup>

400

300

e Park Manley Hall

Rectory

300 Black Brook

300

The Bodnets

498

Kendall's Wood

365

Little Hay

427

TUMULUS

Old Hall Hints Hill

285

Hints Bangle H

Green Barn

259 ord

Bangley F<sup>m</sup>

300

ne

300

m 497

ourne Brook

Hints Forge

Moneymore

300

Lower Bangley 232

△39

529 Weeford Park

Brockhurst F<sup>m</sup>

300

Hints F<sup>m</sup>

3

Hill

421 Camp F<sup>m</sup>

5

Stockfields

400

Great Bangley

400

Weeford Park F<sup>m</sup>

524 6

Canwell Hall

Site of Priory

400 437

Oak F<sup>m</sup>

Springhill F<sup>m</sup>

4

Manorial F<sup>m</sup>

305

426

Hill Wood 534

Canwell Gate

500

Shirrall Hall

dfield Ho.

500

Lamb F<sup>m</sup>

School

Hill

7 479 Upper Ho

Marlpit Hall

Roughley

Bassett's Pole

Trickley Coppice

Slade F<sup>m</sup>

Muffin's Den

Ch. 590

Mere Green

Little Sutton

Fox Hill House F<sup>m</sup>

455

400

315

Middleton Wood F<sup>m</sup>

300 Ch

ley Hill

Moorhall

oor Hall

Ashfurlong Hall

New Park Wood

Langley Brook

Doe Bank

464

Wheatmoor

High Heath

Littleworth End

Ash End F<sup>m</sup>

344

Collet's Brook

1 2

1 mile approx.

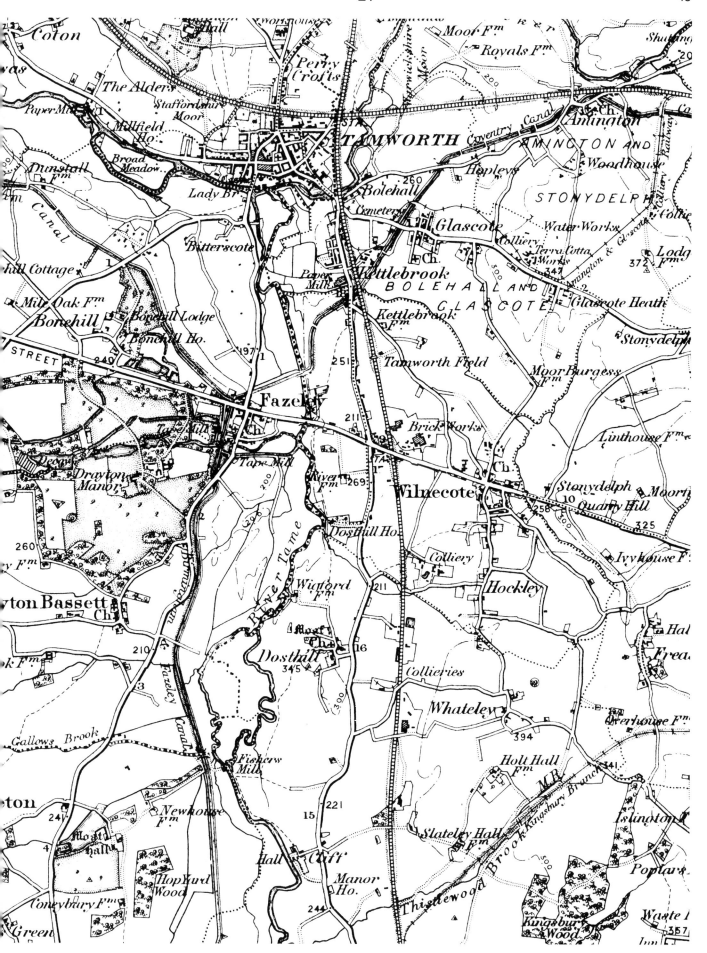

Surveyed 1880 - 87.  Published 1895.

313
Streetway Ho.
343
1305
4 326
◁stone
▲304
Weeford
Smithy
L.B
Buck's Head Fm
Blackbrook
Black Brook
Common Barn 501
The Devil's Drawing Room
Hopwas Fm
225
Manley Hall
300
Water Works
Packington Fm
The Bodnets
300
498
Kendall's Wood
5
Hints Hill
285
427
TUMULUS
365
Hints
259
Bangley Ho.
6
Inn
Smithy
▲497
Hints Forge
Bangley Fm
Bourne Brook
300
ttle ay
Green Barn
Windmill
Moneymore
Lower Bangley 232
▲529
WA
◁41
▲421
Camp Fm
Weeford Park
Brockhurst Fm
Stockfields
Hints Fm
Great Bangley
300
3
Loo
Hill F
Weeford Park Fm
6
▲437
Manorial Fm
Cot
426
534
Springhill Fm
524
Canwell Hall
Site of Priory
400
400
Oak Fm
Hill Wood
Canwell Gate
L.B
Carroway Head
305
field Ho.
567
Shirrall Hall
Hill
Lamb Fm
School
479
7
Routhley
Bassetts Pole P.H.
Trickley Coppice
Upper Hous
Marlpit Hall Fm
Slade Fm
455
281
Muffin's Den
315
Inn
L.B
Fox Hill House Fm
400
Middleton Wood Fm
Mere Green
Little Sutton
Smithy
New Park Wood
Smithy
M Ch
Inn
Hill
Moorhall Fm
oor Hall
Amington Hall
Langley Brook
256
Collets Brook
Lindworth End
8
Doe Bank
457
416
46
High Heath
344
Ash End Fm
457
Wheatmoor
Withy Hill Fm
Hill Fm
300
Whitehouse Common
Langley Mill Fm

1     2
1 mile approx.

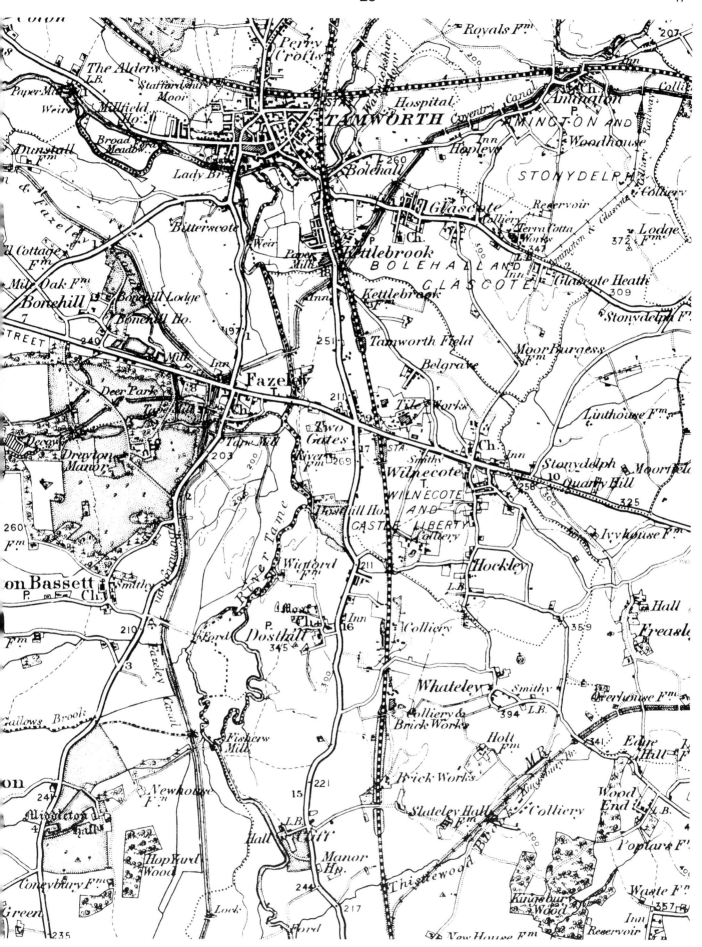

1 mile approx.

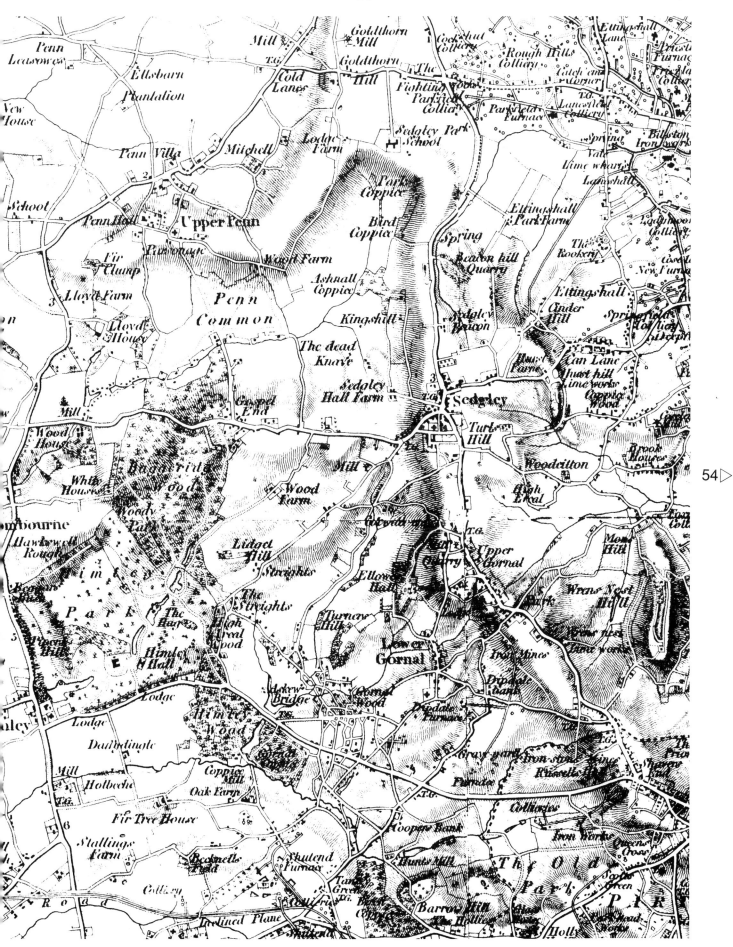

Alder
Coppice

367

400

400

400

E

300

400

300

300

Trescott

294

282

5

321

300

293

4

Furnace Grange

365

L O W E R

316

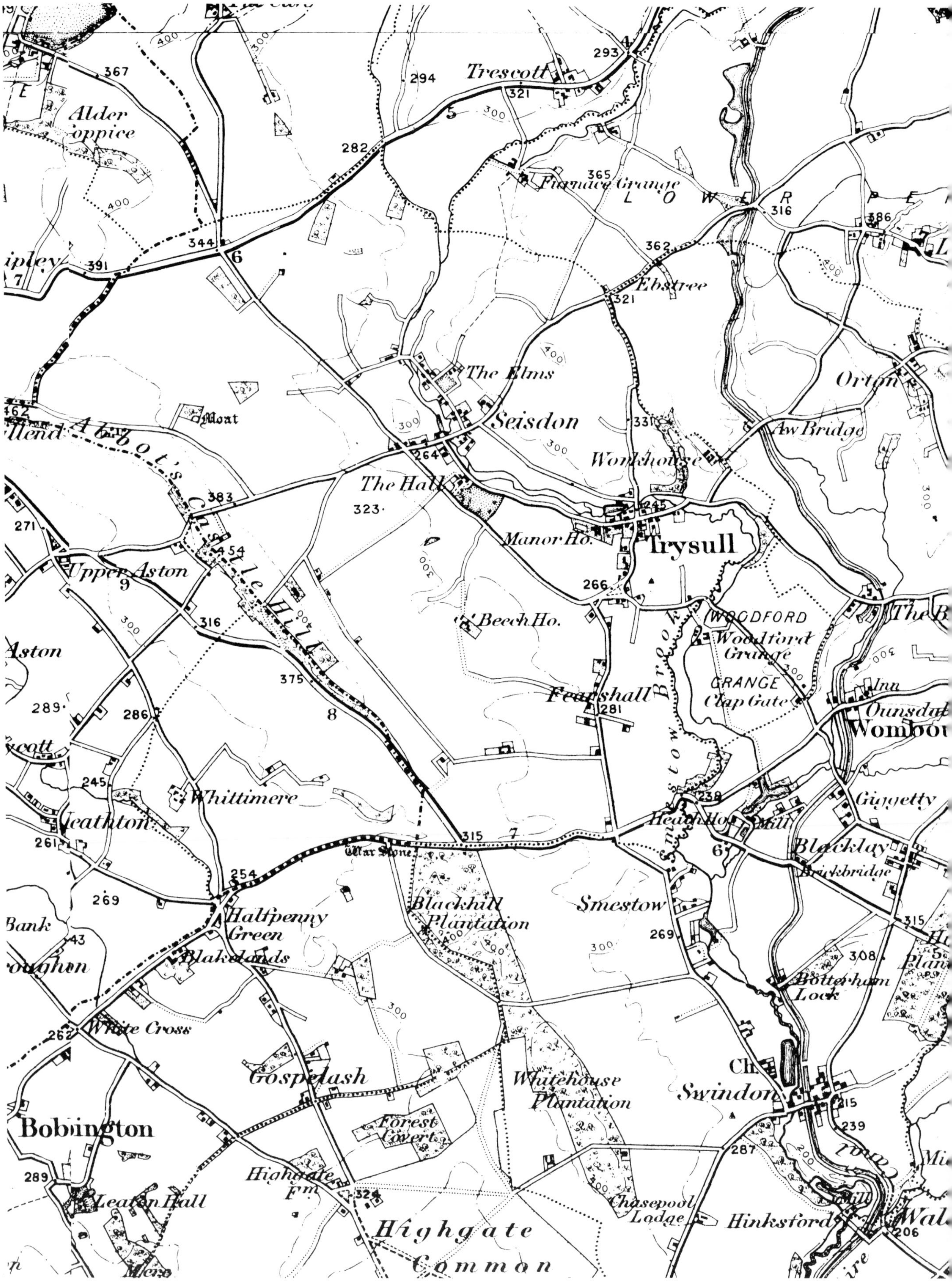

362

Ebstree

321

The Elms

400

300

Seisdon

264

331

300

Aw Bridge

Orton

462

Abbot's

Moat

Wonthouse

300

Manor Ho.

Irysull

245

ellend

383

The Hall

323

266

Castle

Upper Aston

9

300

454

271

Beech Ho.

300

Woodford Grange

WOODFORD

The B

Aston

316

375

Fearshall

281

GRANGE
Clap Gate

Inn

Ounsda

289

286

8

300

Wombou

Scott

245

Whittimere

261

269

315

7

Head Ho Mill

Smestow

269

6

Blacklay

Brickbridge

Giggetty

315

308

Botterham
Lock

Bank

43

254

Halfpenny
Green

269

Blakelands

Blackhall
Plantation

300

300

White Cross

262

Gospelash

300

Whitehouse
Plantation

Ch

Swindon

315

239

Forest
Covert

287

Bobington

289

Leaton Hall

Highgate
Fm

324

Chasepool
Lodge

Hinksford
Wal

206

Highgate

Mere

Common

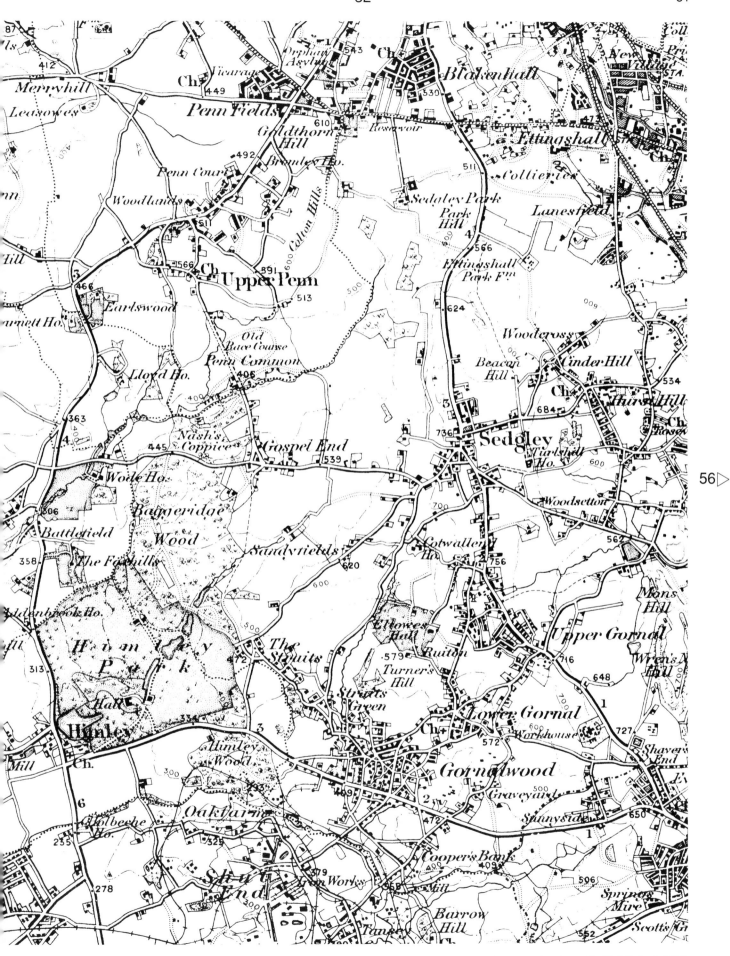

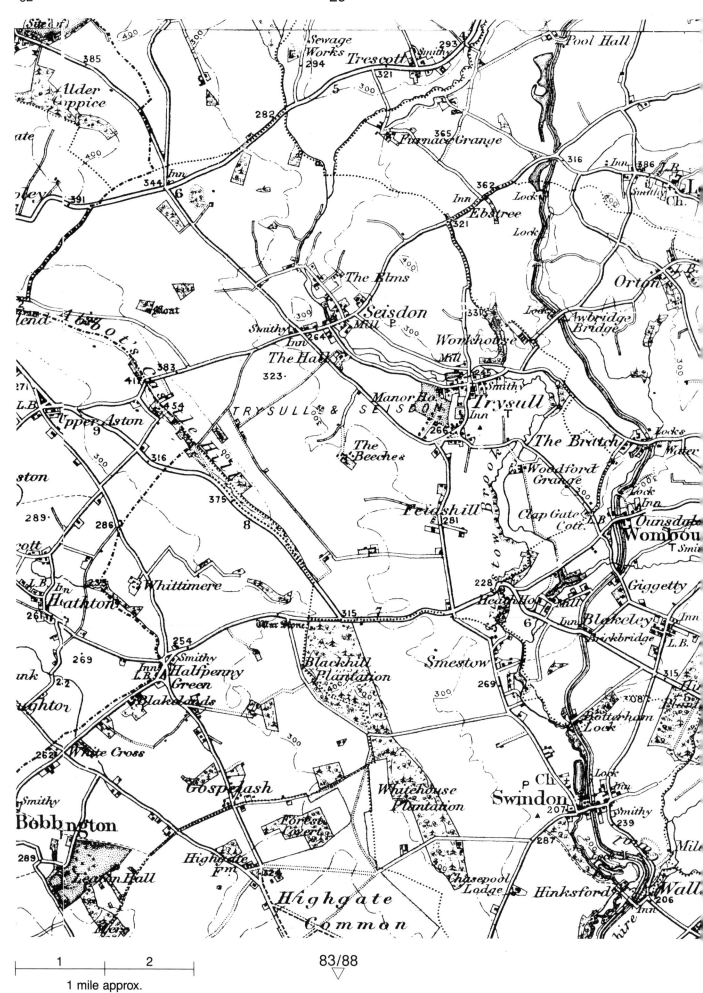

1 mile approx.

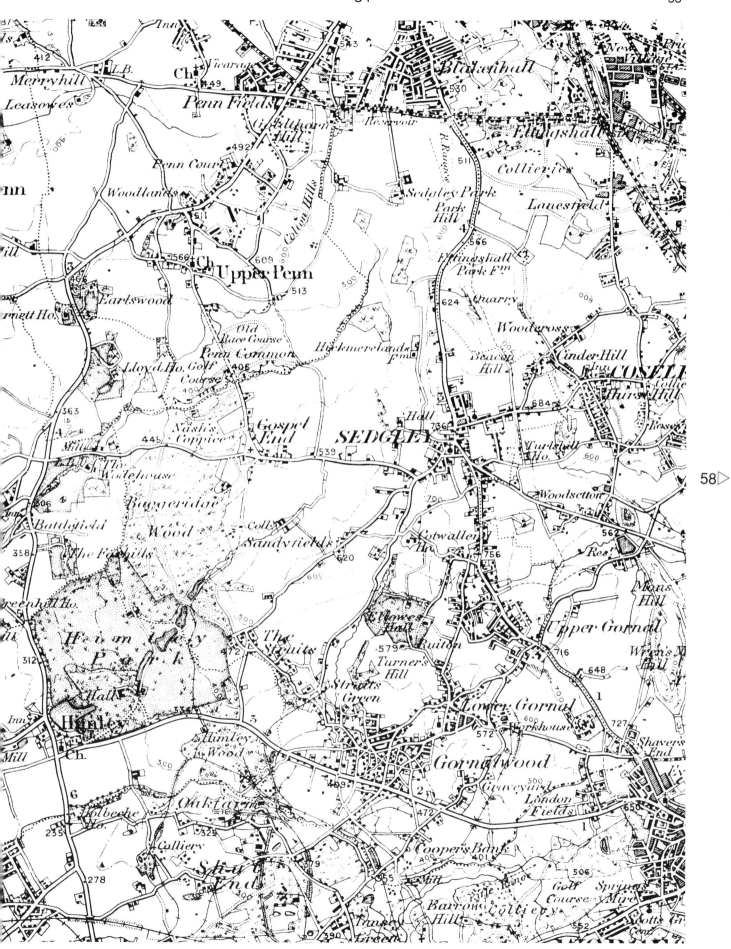

Surveyed 1881 - 83.  Revised 1906.  Published 1908.

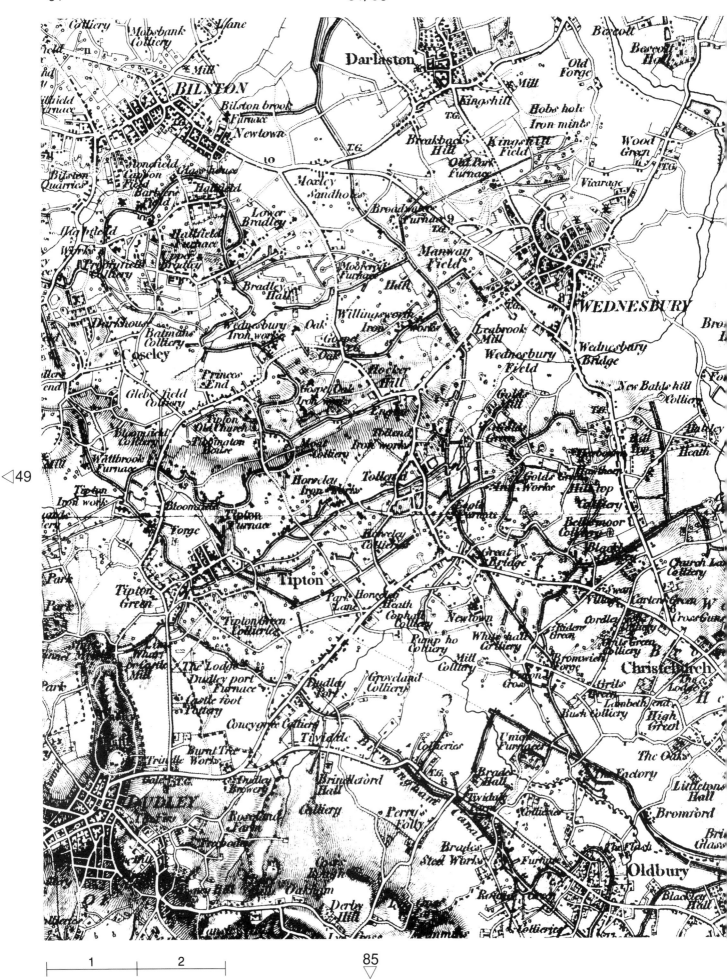

1 — 2

1 mile approx.

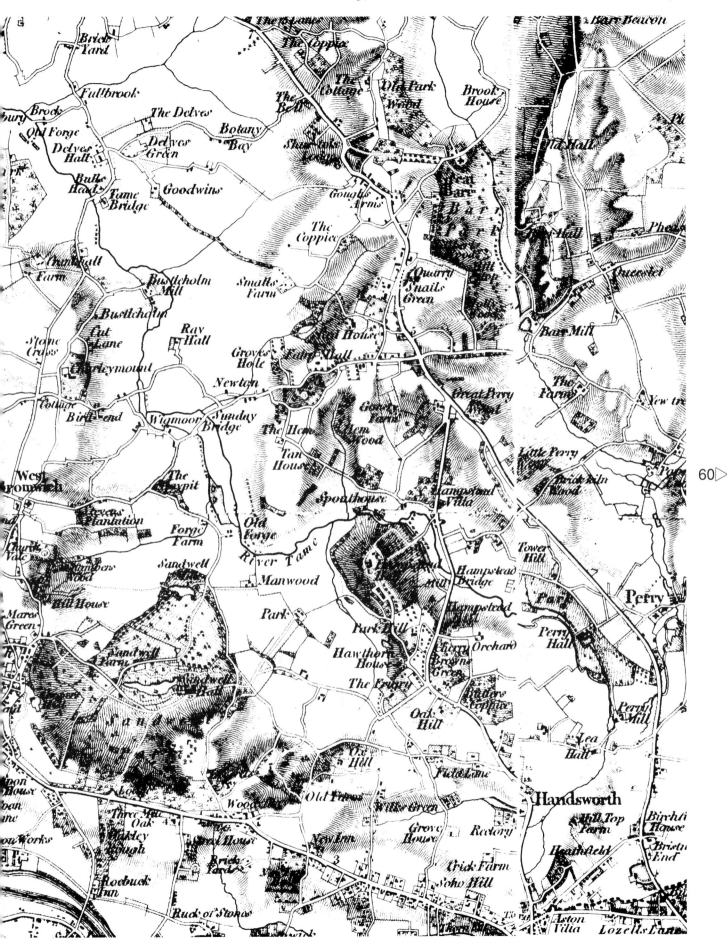

Published 1834.

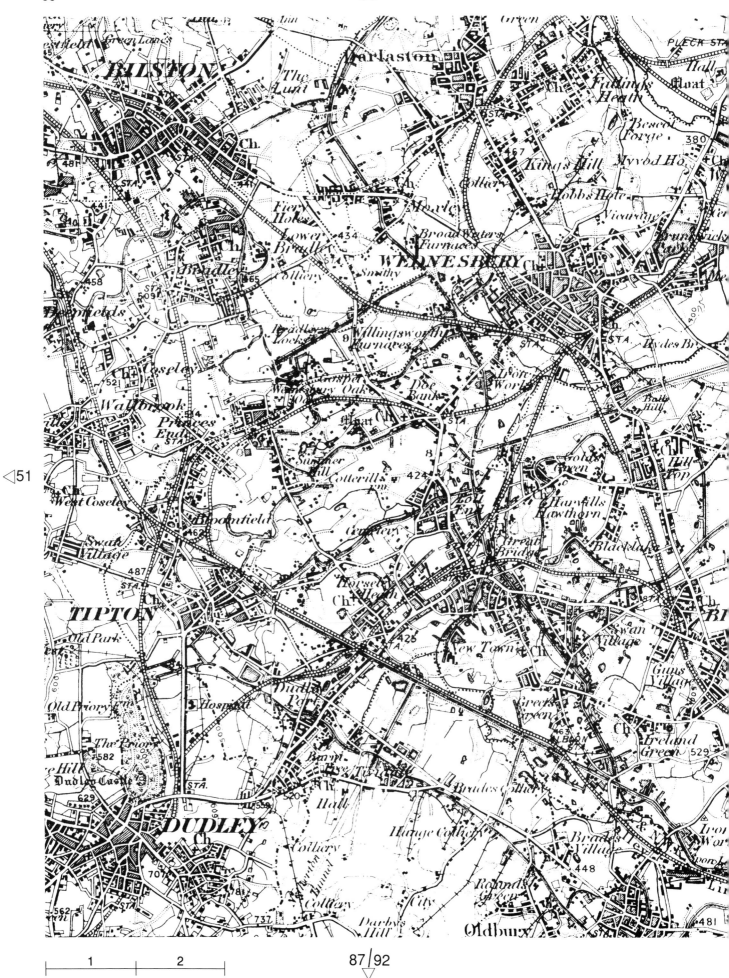

◁ 51

1     2

1 mile approx.

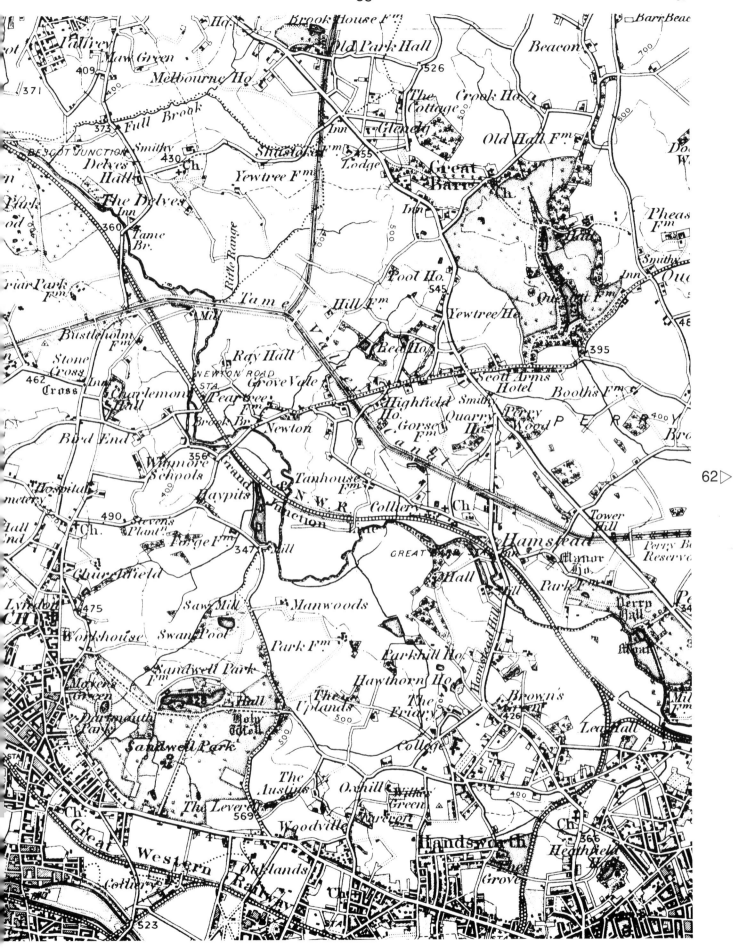

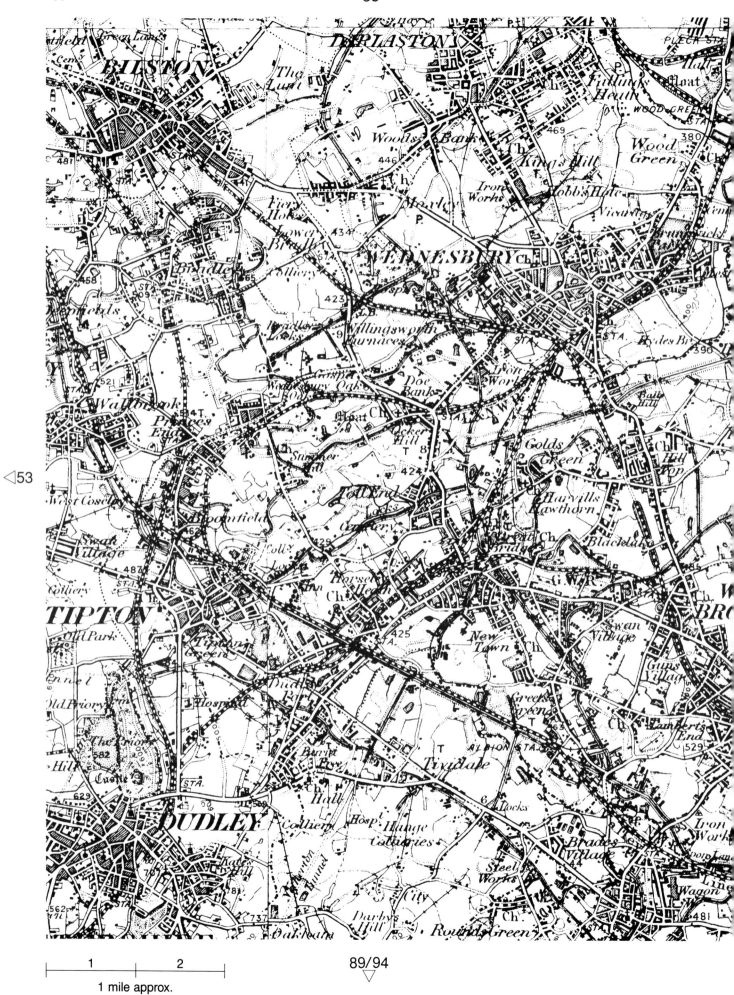

1 mile approx.

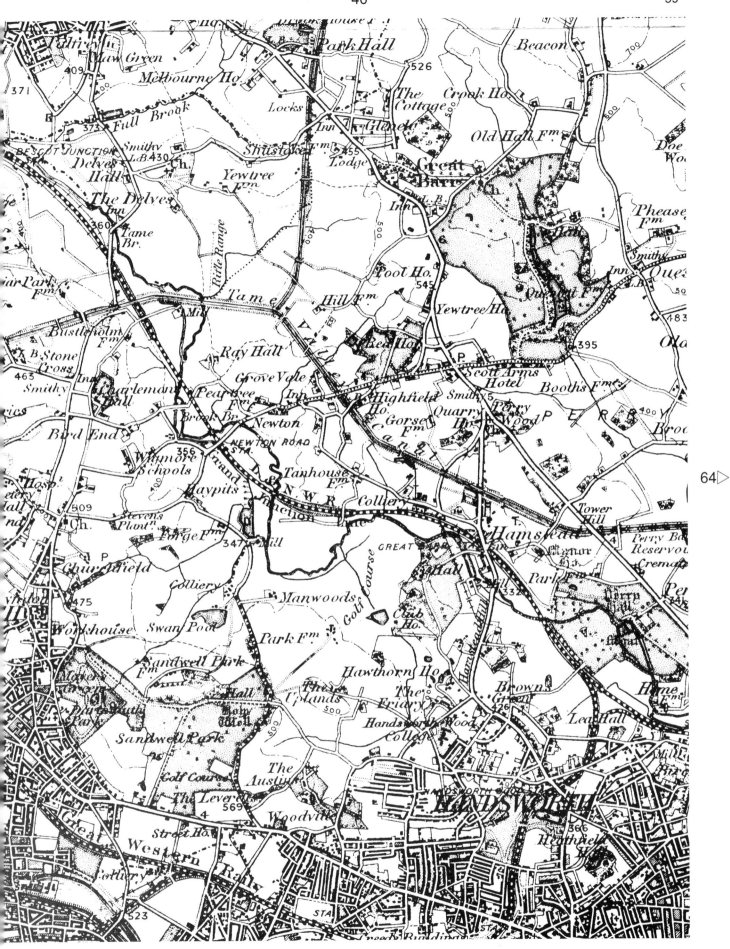

Surveyed 1881 - 88. Revised 1906. Published 1908 - 09.

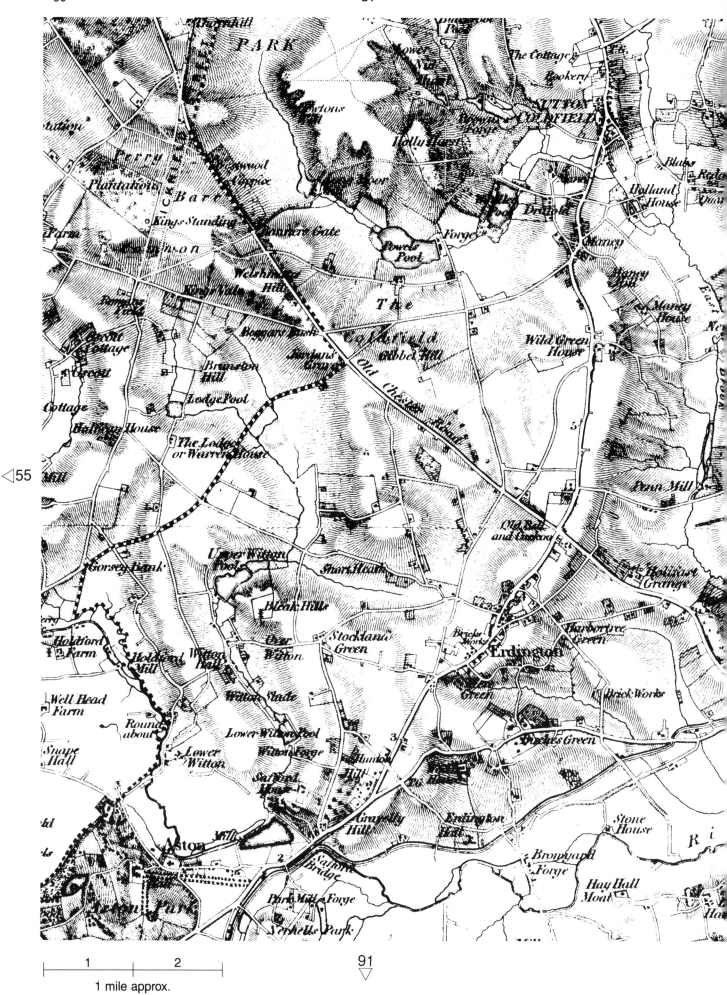

PARK

SUTTON COLDFIELD

Kings Standing

The Lodge
or Warren House

Old Chester Road

Gorsey Bank

Upper Witton
Pool

Short Heath

Black Hills

Erdington

Stockland
Green

Over
Witton

Brick
Works

Brick Works

Holdford
Farm

Holdford
Mill

Witton
Hall

Well Head
Farm

Witton Slade

Round
about

Lower Witton Pool

Pinkes Green

Snape
Hall

Lower
Witton

Witton Forge

Erdington
Hall

Salford
Mill

Gravelly
Hill

Stone
House

Aston

Salford
Bridge

Bromyard
Forge

Hay Hall
Moat

Aston Park

Park Mill Forge

1          2

1 mile approx.

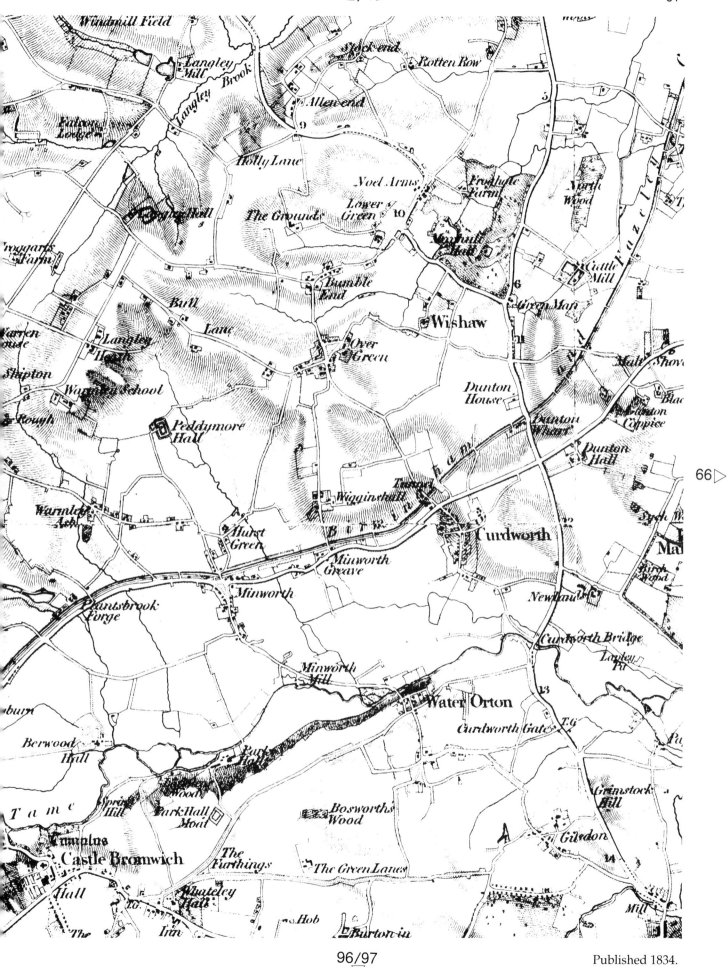

66▷

Published 1834.

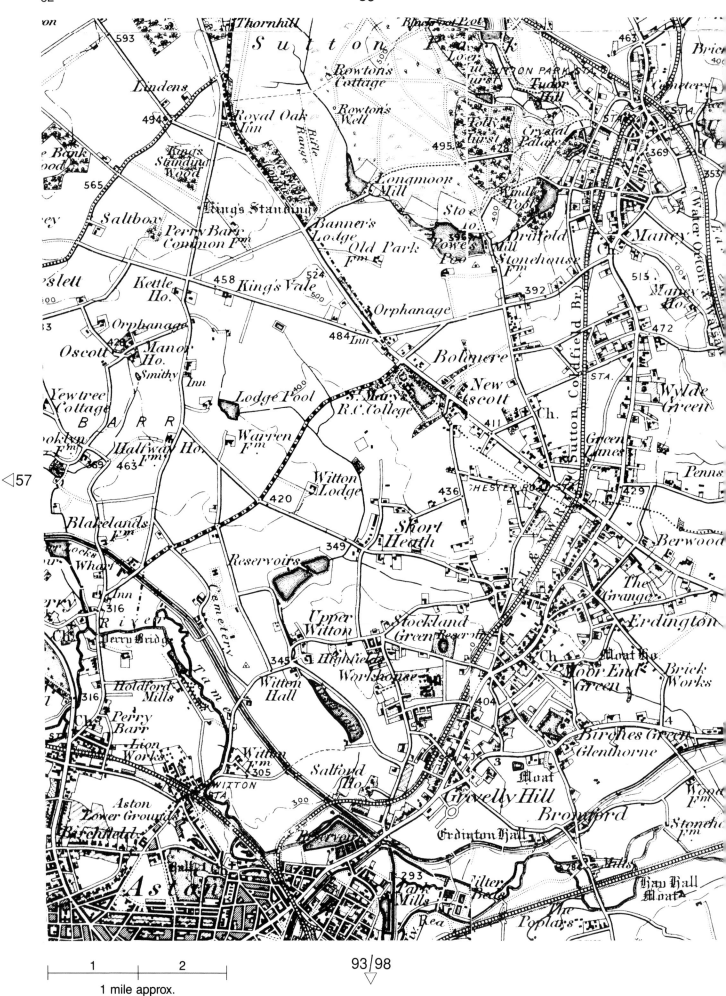

1 mile approx.

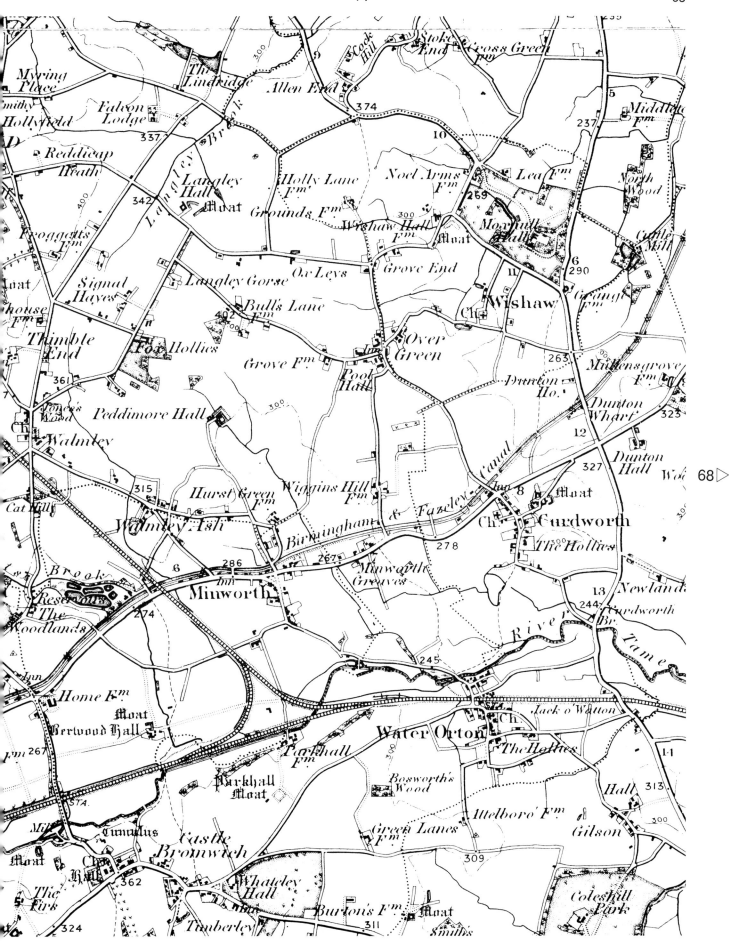

Surveyed 1881 - 88.  Published 1895.

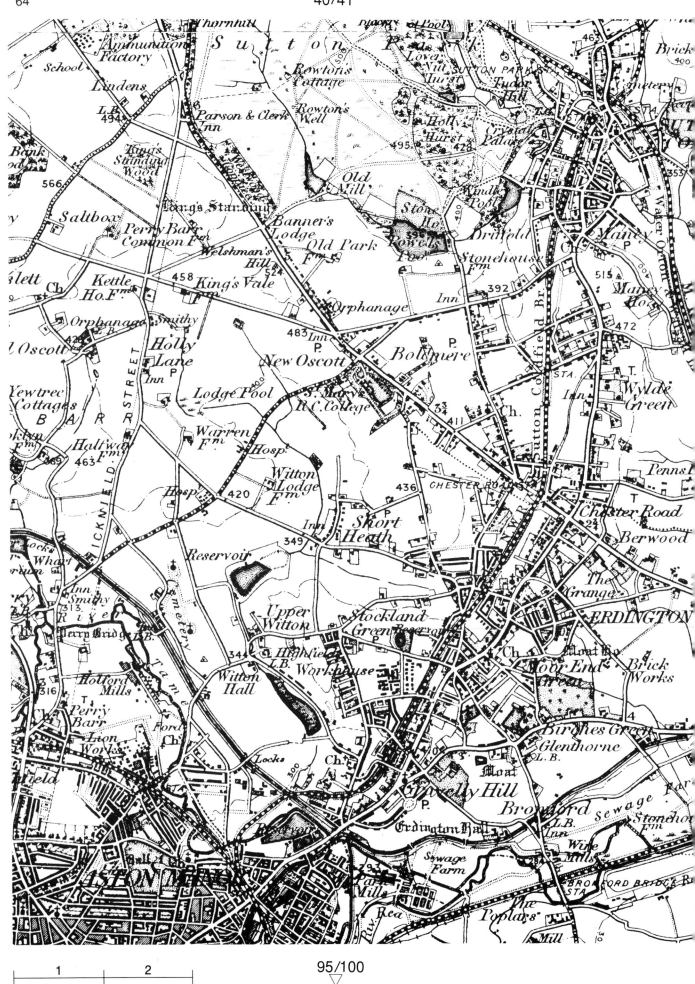

1     2

1 mile approx.

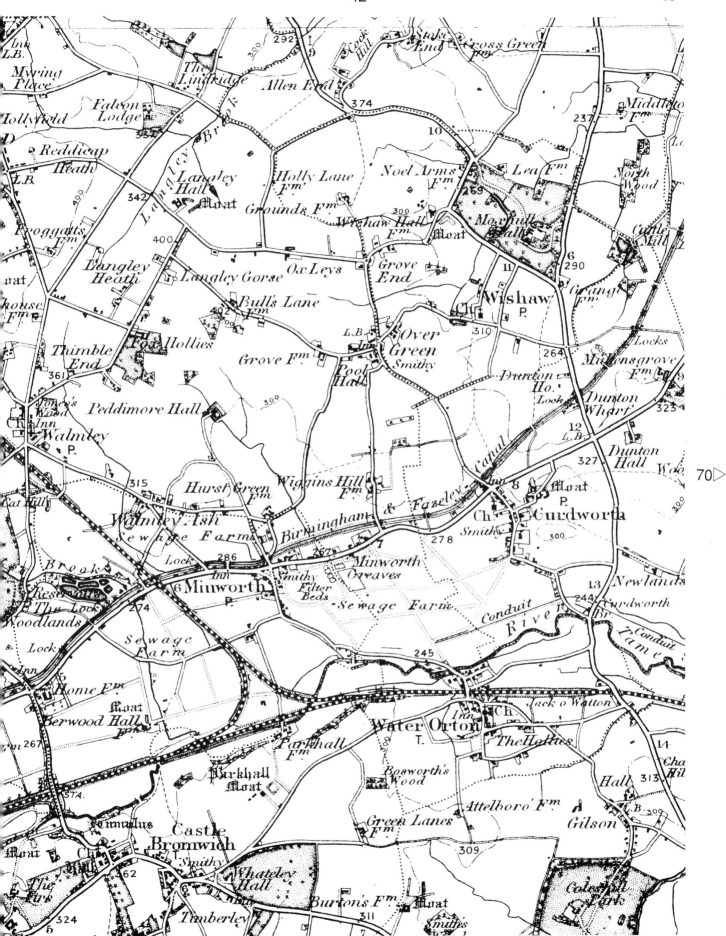

Surveyed 1881 - 88. Revised 1906. Published 1909.

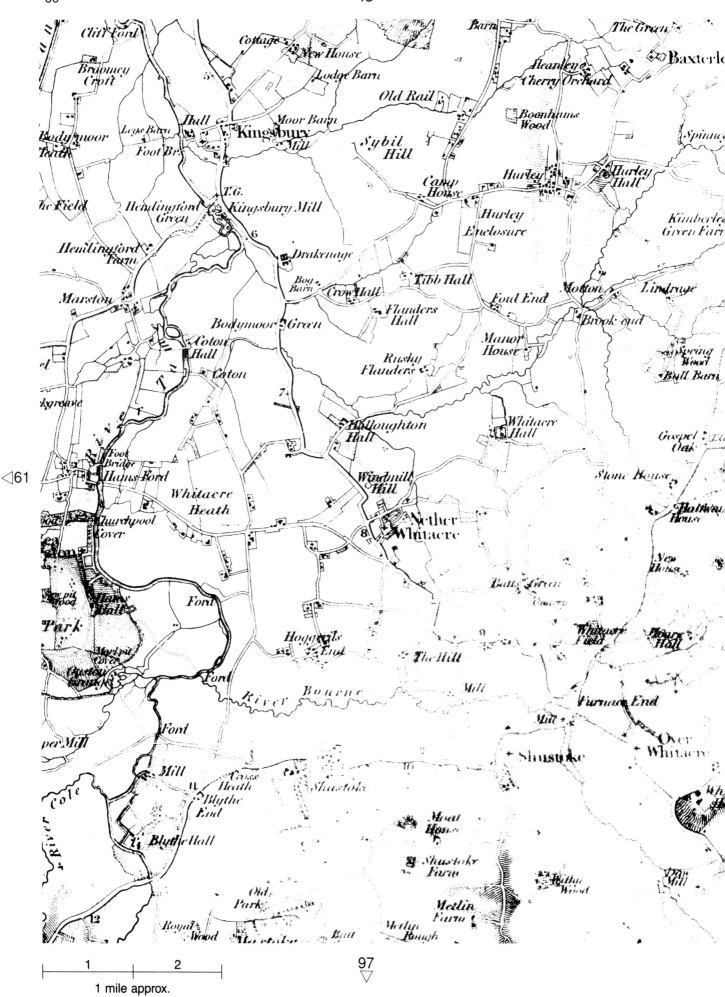

1 mile approx.

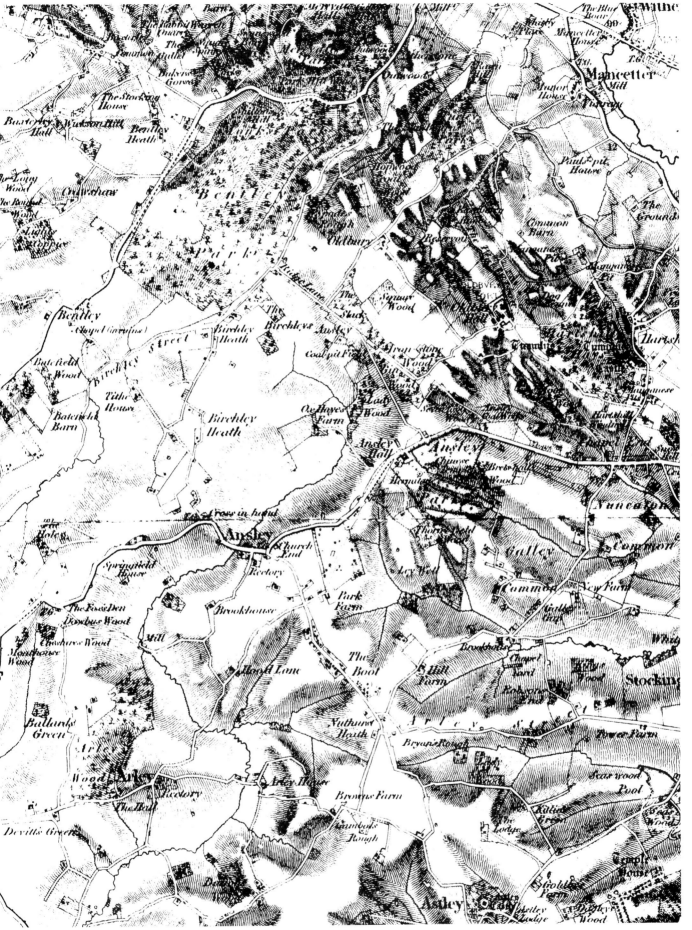

72▷

Published 1834.

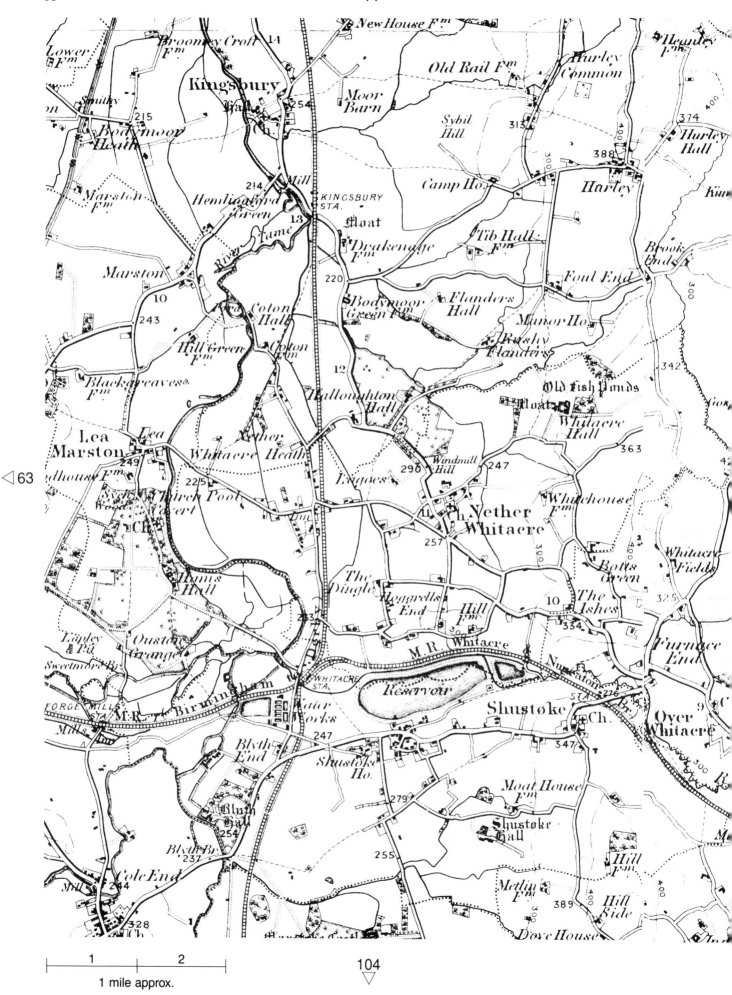

1      2

1 mile approx.

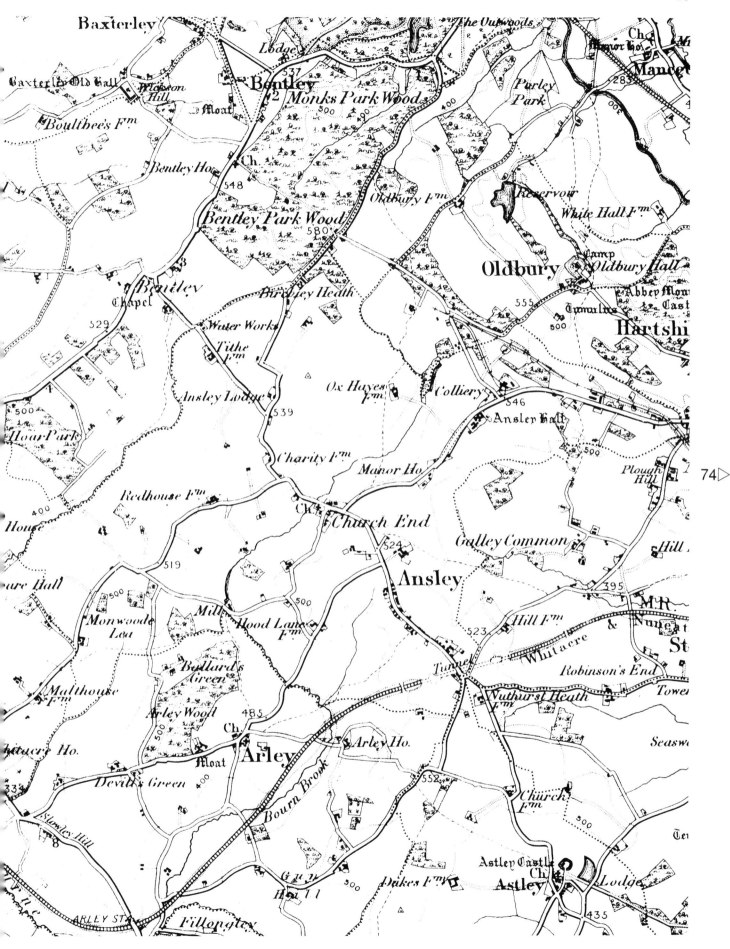

74▷

Surveyed 1881 - 88. Published 1892 / 1895.

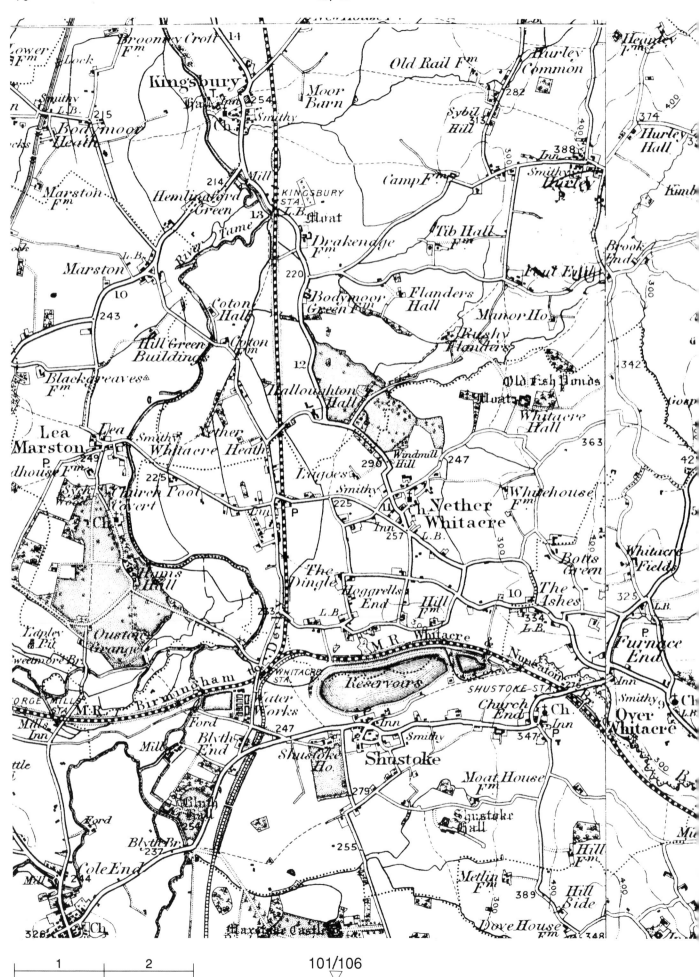

|---1---|---2---|

1 mile approx.

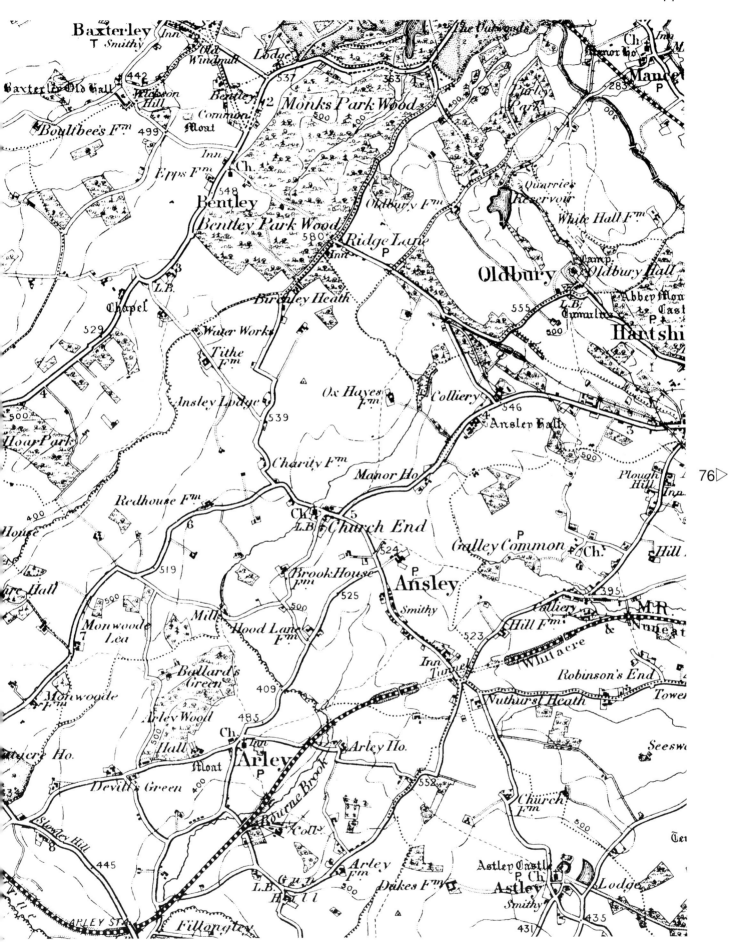

76 ▷

Surveyed 1881 - 88.  Revised 1906.  Published 1908 - 09.

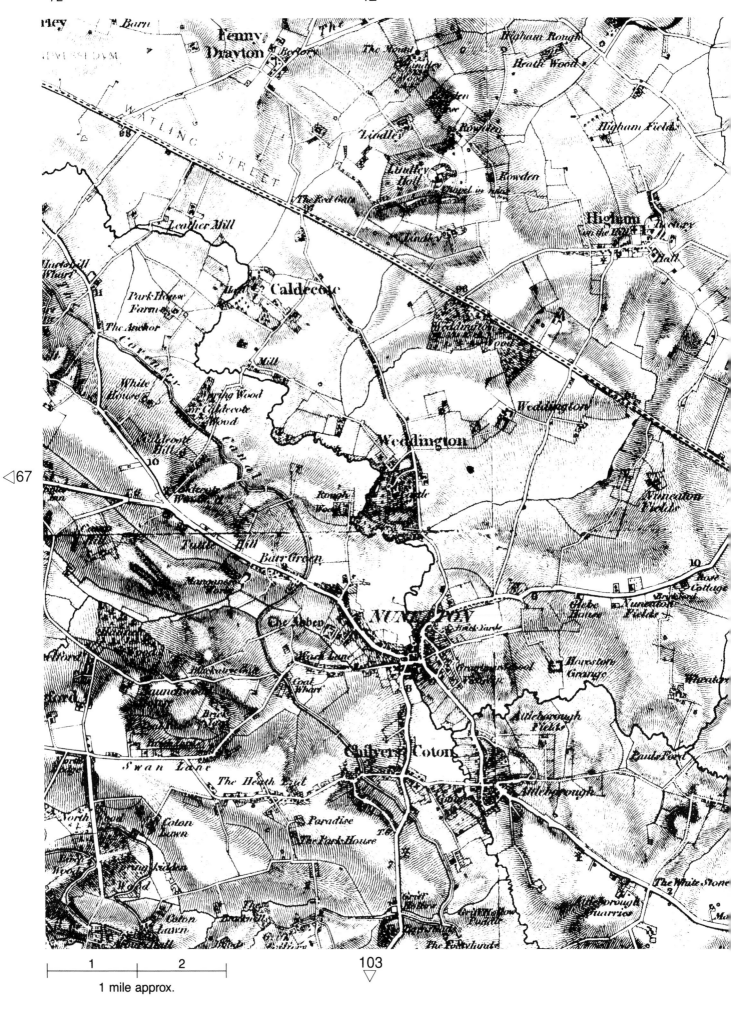

1          2

1 mile approx.

Published 1835.

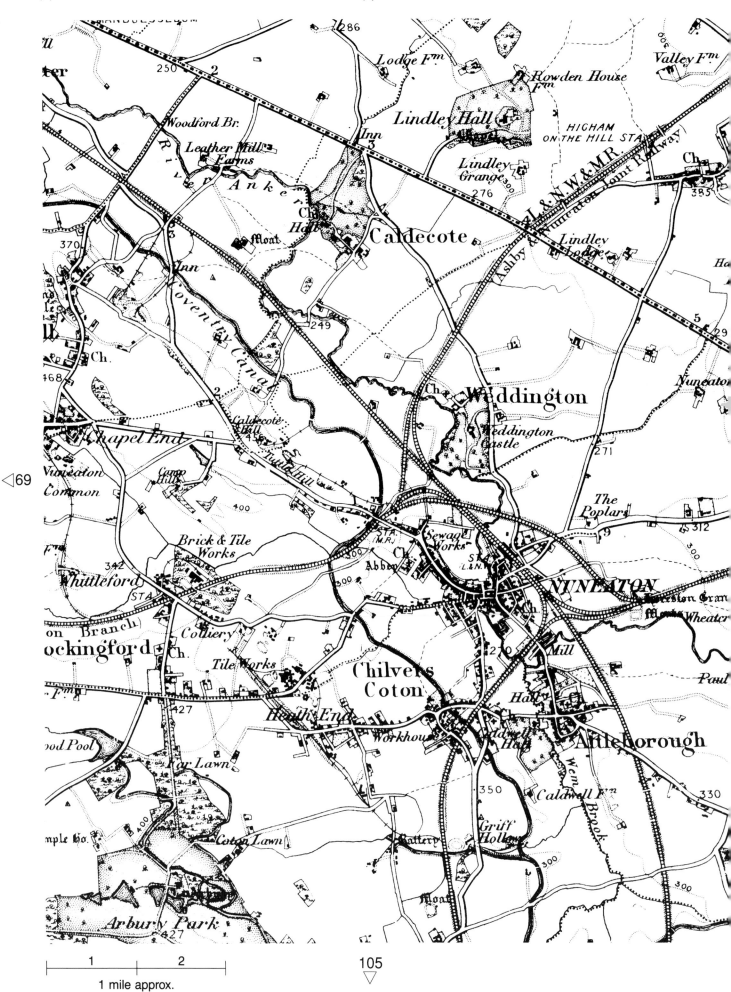

1     2

1 mile approx.

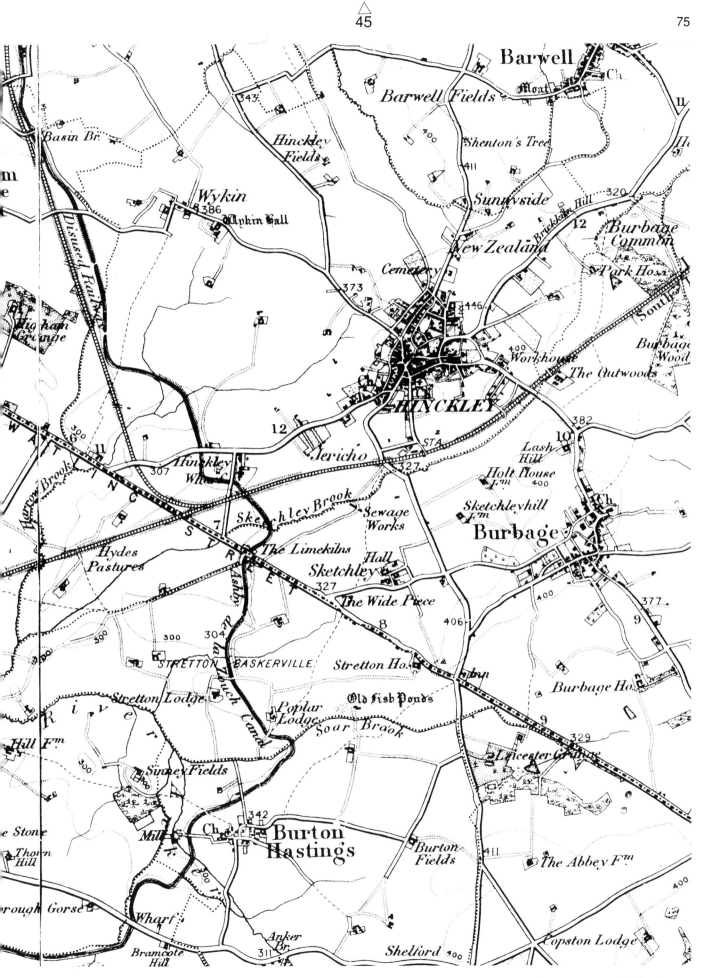

Surveyed 1885 - 86.  Published 1892.

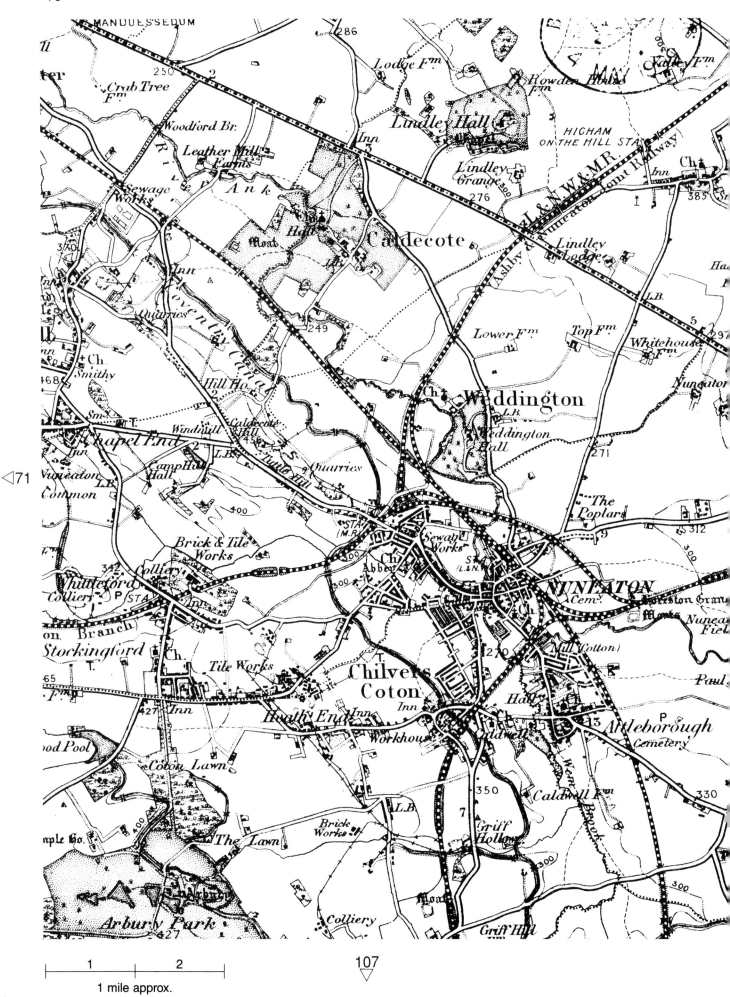

MANDUESSEDUM

Crab Tree Fm

Woodford Br.

Leather Mill Farms

Lindley Hall

Rowden House Fm

Lodge Fm

HIGHAM ON THE HILL STA

Sewage Works

River Anker

Caldecote

Lindley Grange

Lindley Lodge

Hall

Moat

Quarries

Inn

Lower Fm

Top Fm

Whitehouse Fm

Nuneaton

Smithy

Ch.

Hill Ho.

Weddington

Weddington Hall

Windmill

Caldecote Hill

Chapel End

Camp Hill Hall

Tuttle Hill

Quarries

The Poplars

Nuneaton Common

Brick & Tile Works

STA (M.R)

Sewage Works

STA (L.N.W)

Colliery

Abbey

NUNEATON

Cem.

Whittleford Colliery

STA

Stockingford

Tile Works

Chilvers Coton

Mill (Cotton)

Heath End

Inn

Workhouse

Attleborough Cemetery

Wood Pool

Coton Lawn

Caldwell Fm

Griff Hollow

The Lawn

Brick Works

Arbury Park

Colliery

Griff Hill

1    2

1 mile approx.

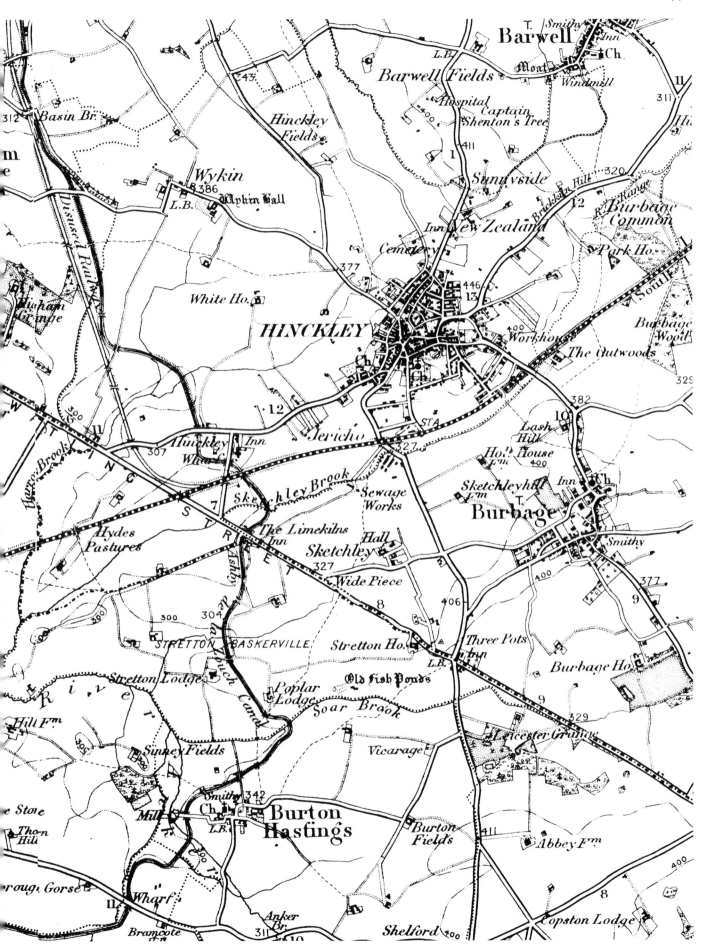

Surveyed 1885 - 86. Revised 1906. Published 1908.

1 mile approx.

Published 1834.

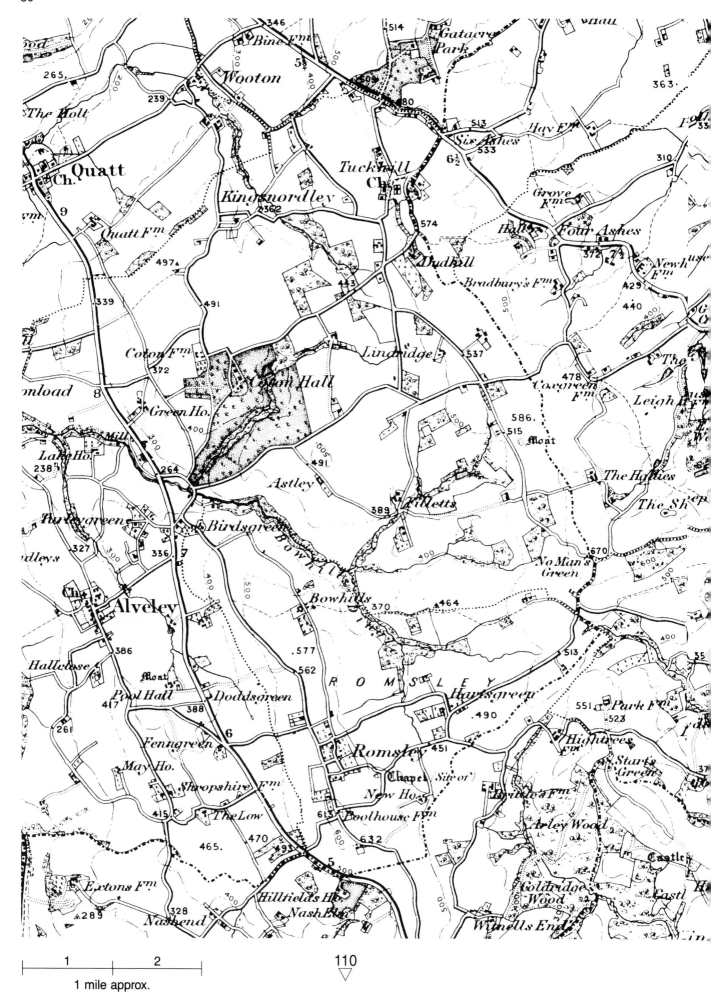

1 mile approx.

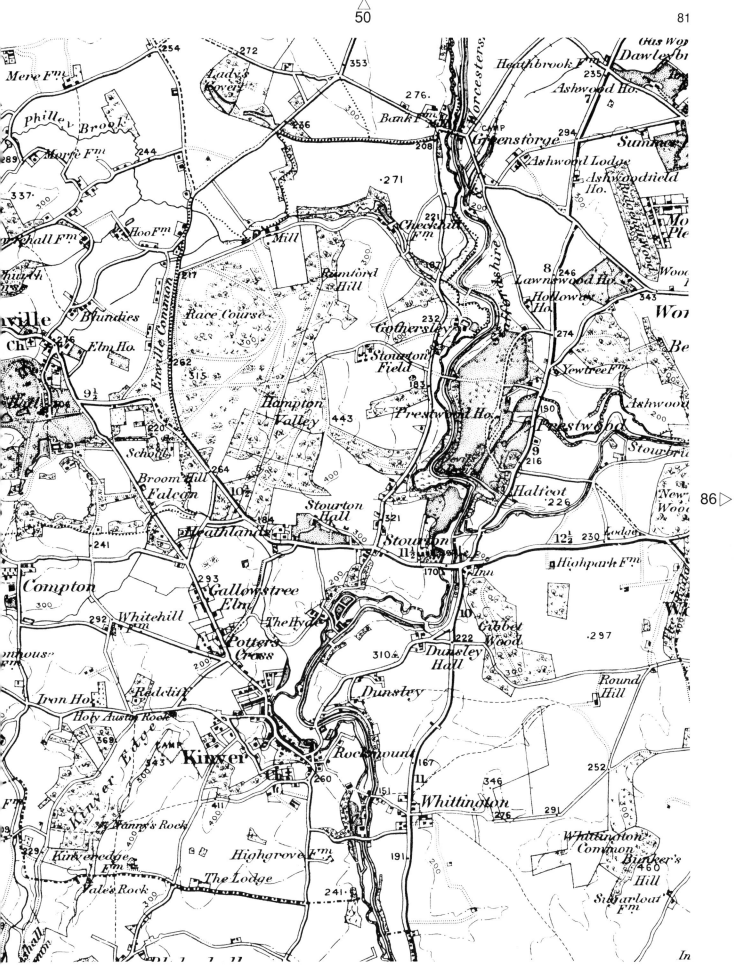

Mere F<sup>m</sup>

philley Brook

Morre F<sup>m</sup>

337

rehall F<sup>m</sup>

hurch

ville

Ch

Blundies

Elm Ho.

9½

Enville Common

217

262

315

Race Course

254

272

353

Lady's Covert

236

Bank F<sup>m</sup>

Mill

Ramford Hill

Greensforge

208

271

276.

Checkhill F<sup>m</sup>

221

Gothersley

Stourton Field

232

183

Staffordshire

Worcestershire

Heathbrook F<sup>m</sup>

Dawley

235

Ashwood Ho.

294

Ashwood Lodge

Ashwoodfield Ho.

Lawnswood Ho.

Holloway Ho.

Yewtree F<sup>m</sup>

Summe

Mo Ple

Wood

Wor

Be

246

343

274

Hampton Valley

443

Prestwood Ho.

Prestwood

Ashwood

150

180

216

9

200

Stourbri

Stourbr

Broom Hill Falcon

School

220

264

10½

184

Stourton Hall

321

Heathlands

241

Compton

300

293

Gallowstree Elm

Whitehill F<sup>m</sup>

292

Potters Cross

200

Iron Ho.

Redcliff

Holy Austin Rock

369

543

CAMP

Kinver

Ch

Stourton

11½

170

Halfcot

226

12½ 230 Lodge

Highpark F<sup>m</sup>

Inn

The Hyde

10

Gibbet Wood

222

310

Dunsley Hall

Dunsley

Rockmount

260

151

167

346

252

291

86 ▷

297

Round Hill

W

Kinver Edge

Nanny's Rock

Kinveredge F<sup>m</sup>

429

The Lodge

Vale's Rock

400

Highgrove F<sup>m</sup>

400

411

241

191

200

11

Whittington

276

Whittington Common

Bunker's Hill

460

Sugarloaf F<sup>m</sup>

In

Surveyed 1881 - 85.  Published 1895.

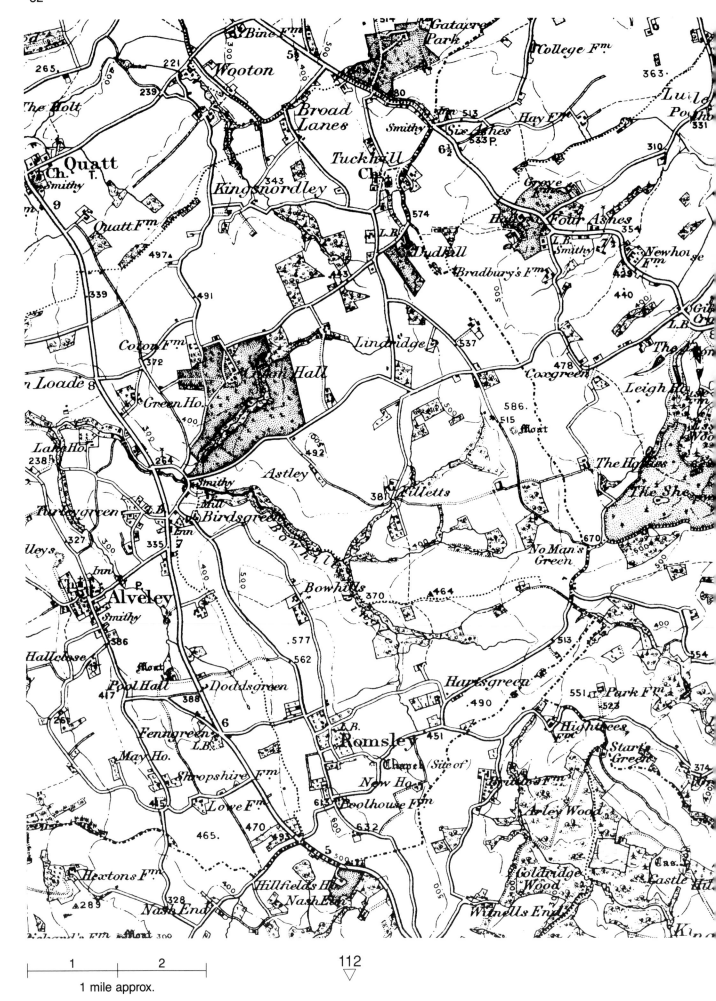

1 mile approx.

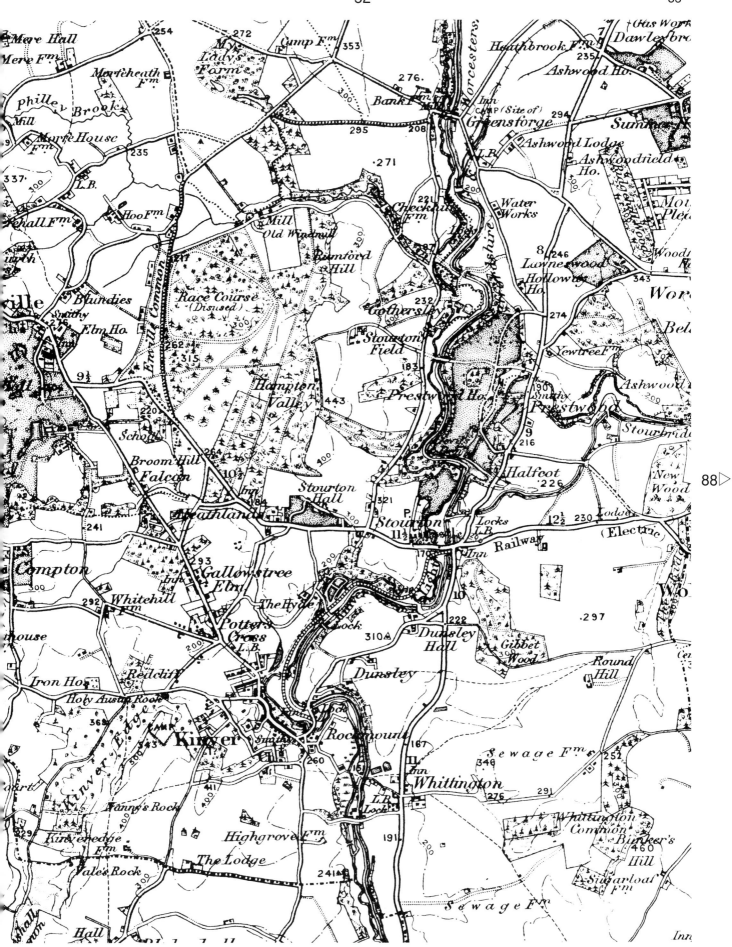

Surveyed 1881 - 83. Revised 1906. Published 1908.

| 1 | 2 |

1 mile approx.

Published 1834.

90▷

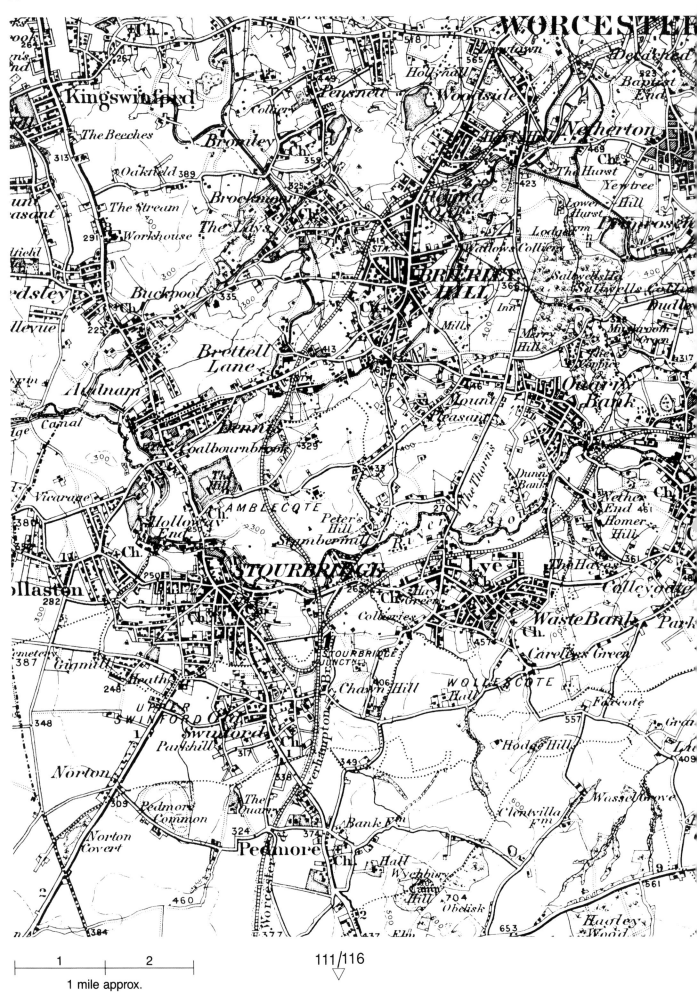

1          2

1 mile approx.

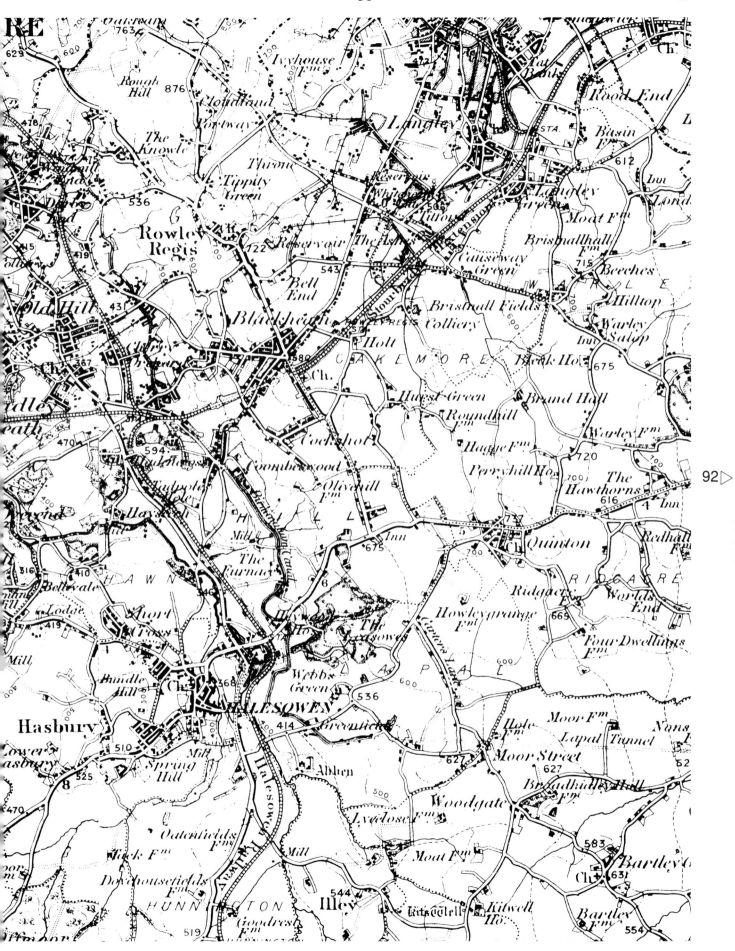

Surveyed 1881 - 88. Published 1895.

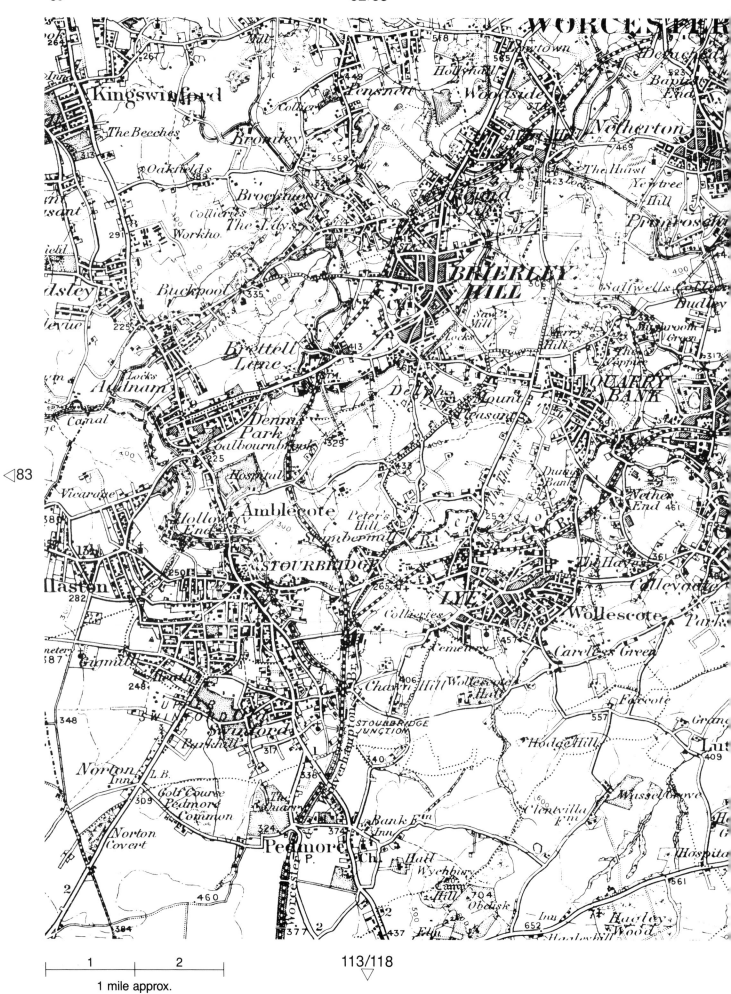

1 mile approx.

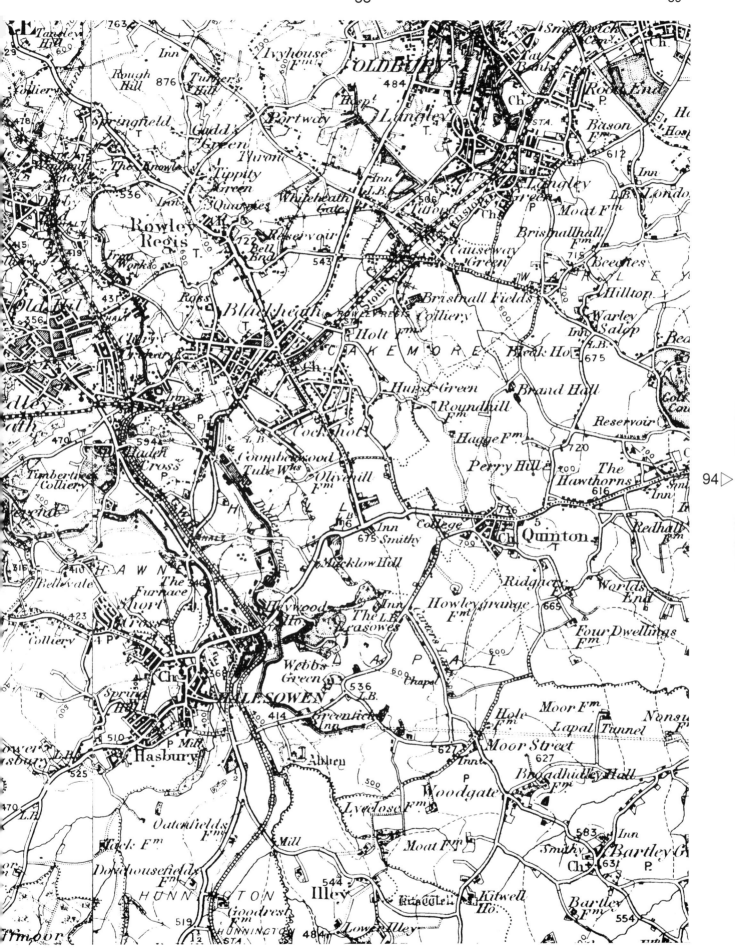

94 ▷

Surveyed 1881 - 88. Revised 1906. Published 1908 - 09.

85

1 mile approx.

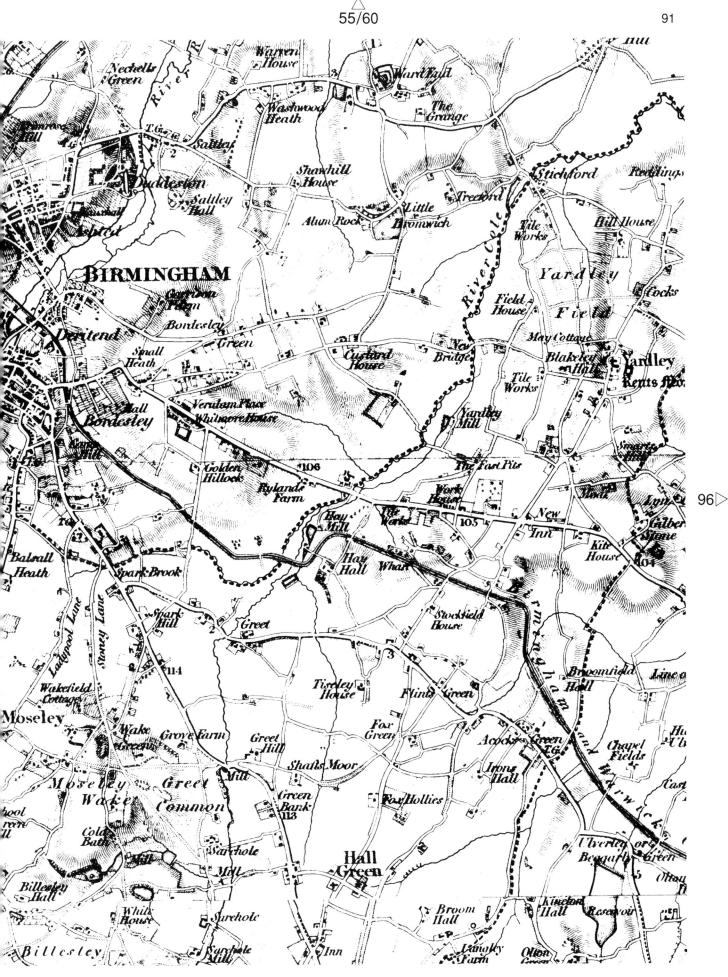

Published 1834.

1 mile approx.

Surveyed 1881 - 88. Published 1895.

1 mile approx.

100▷

Surveyed 1881 - 88.  Revised 1906.  Published 1909.

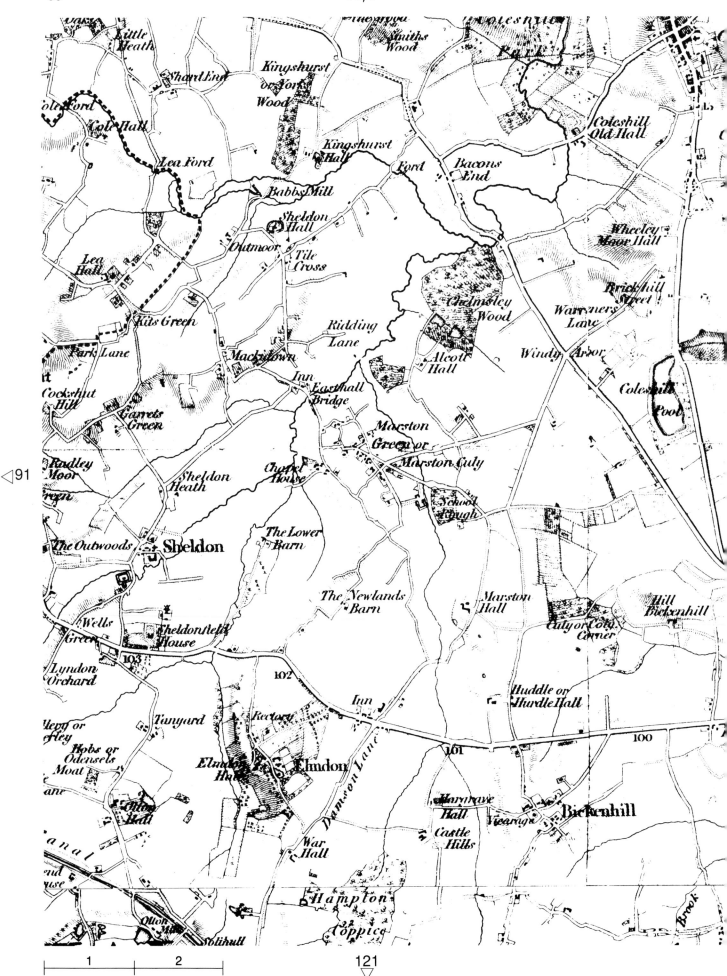

91

| 1 | 2 |
|---|---|

1 mile approx.

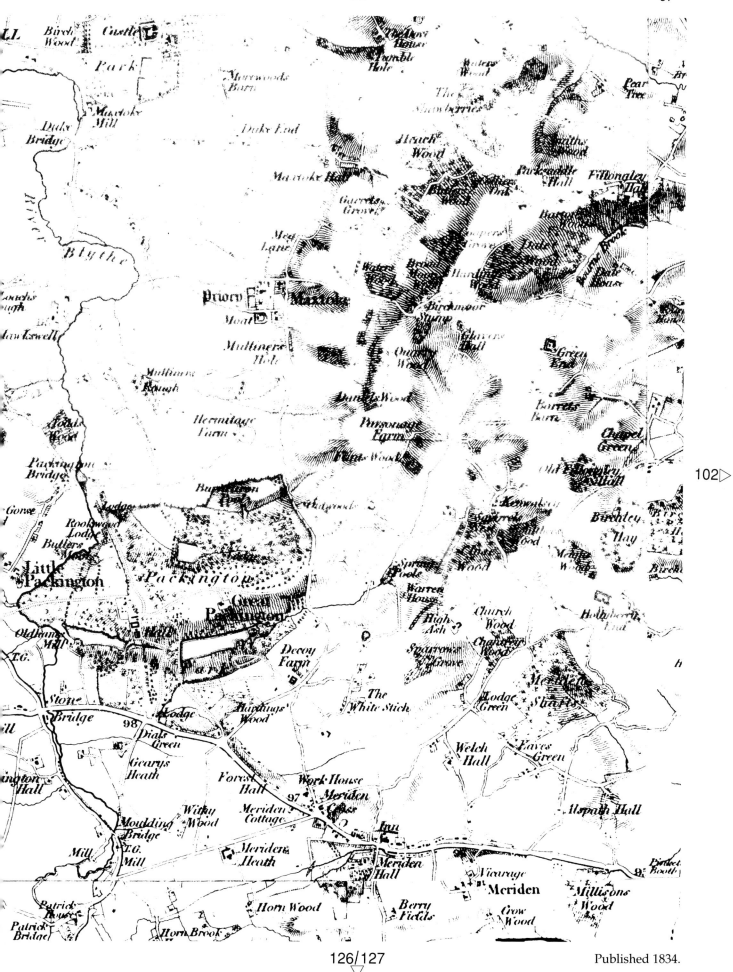

102 ▷

Published 1834.

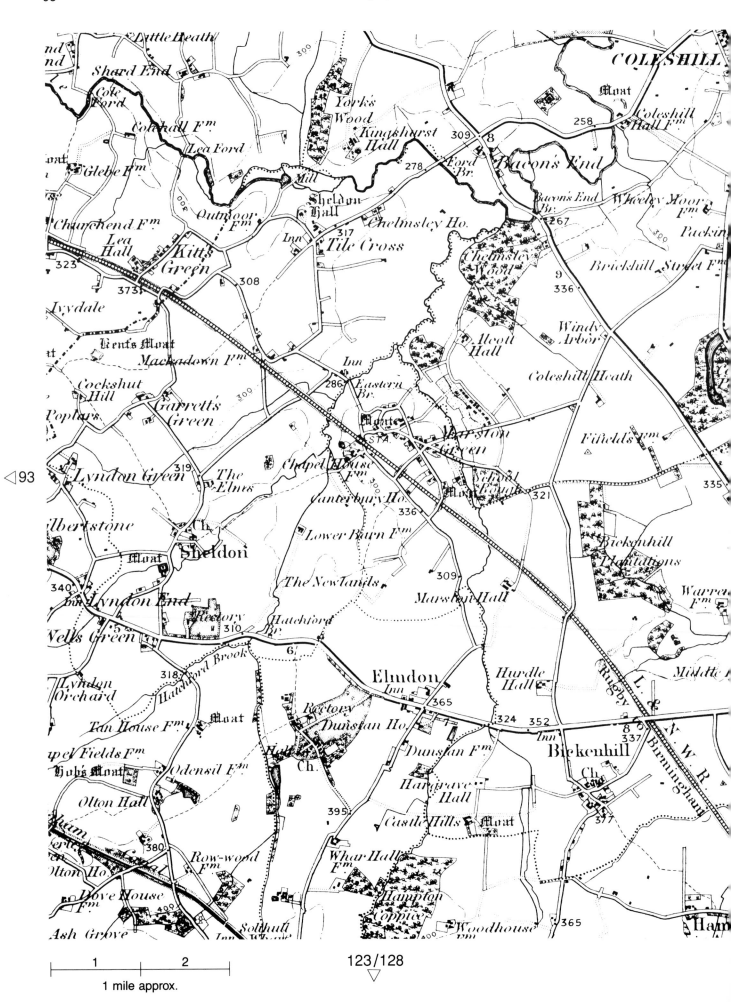

◁93

```
|----1----|----2----|
1 mile approx.
```

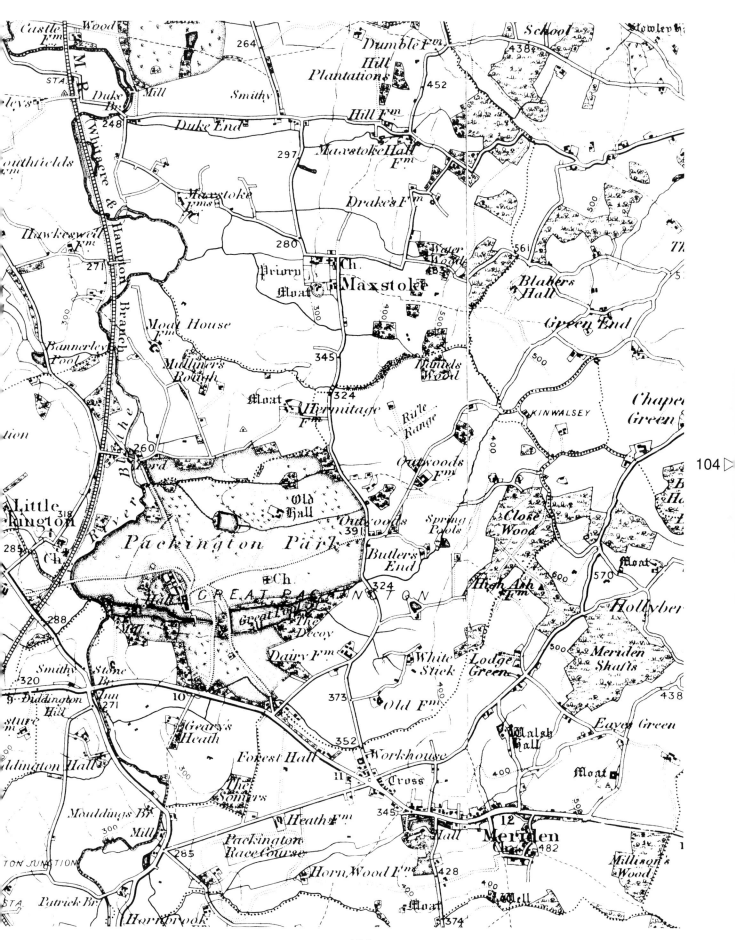

104 ▷

Surveyed 1881 - 88.  Published 1895.

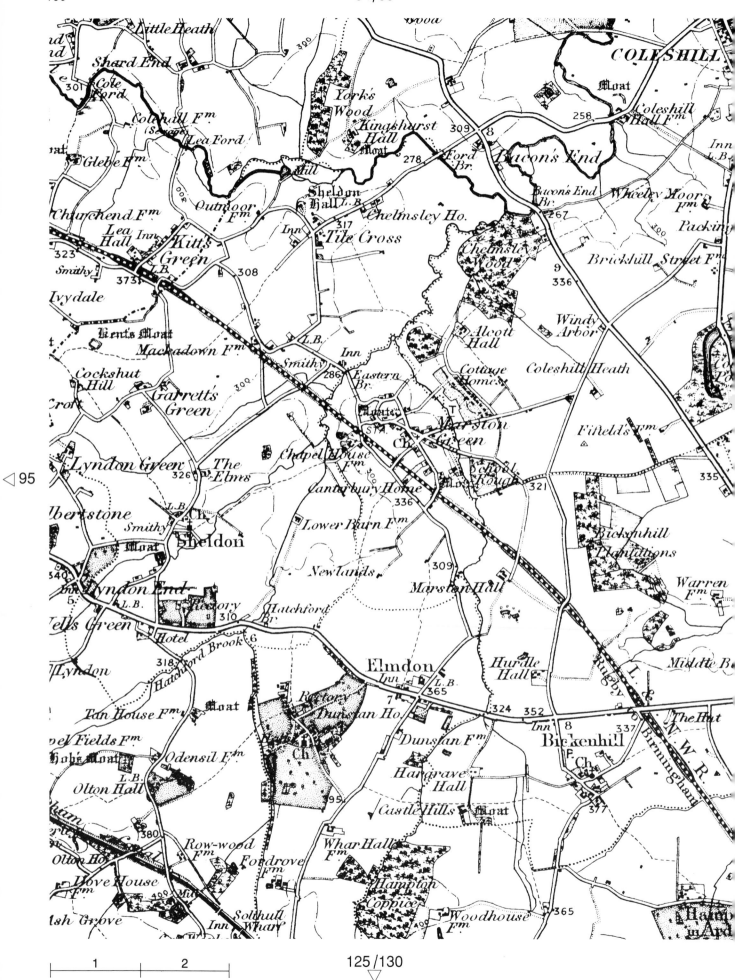

1 mile approx.

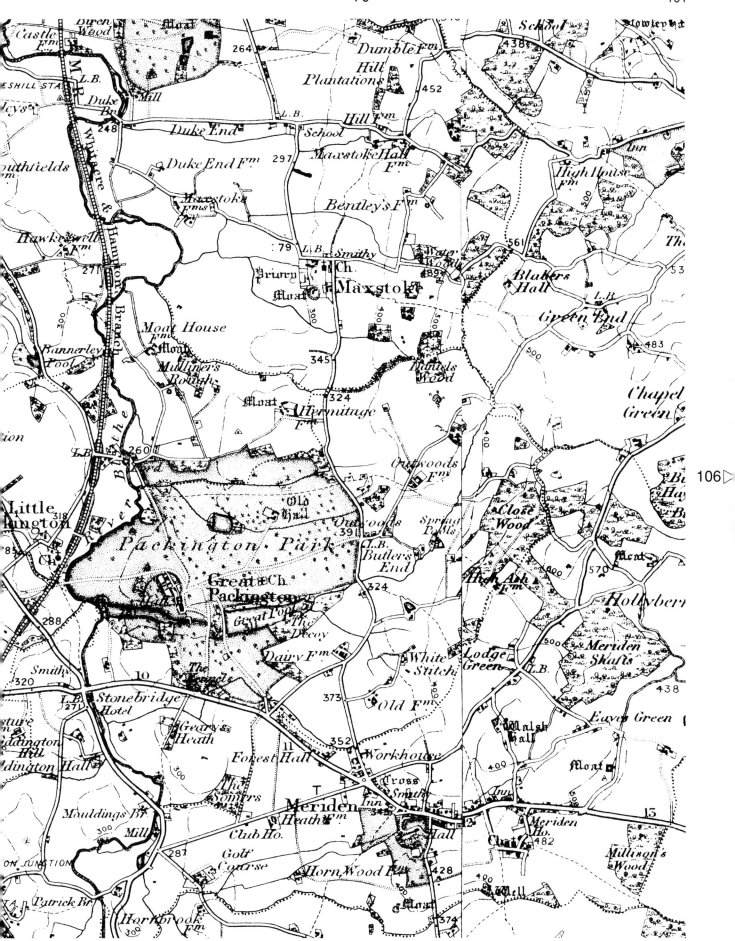

Surveyed 1881 - 88. Revised 1906. Published 1908 - 09.

◁97

1     2

1 mile approx.

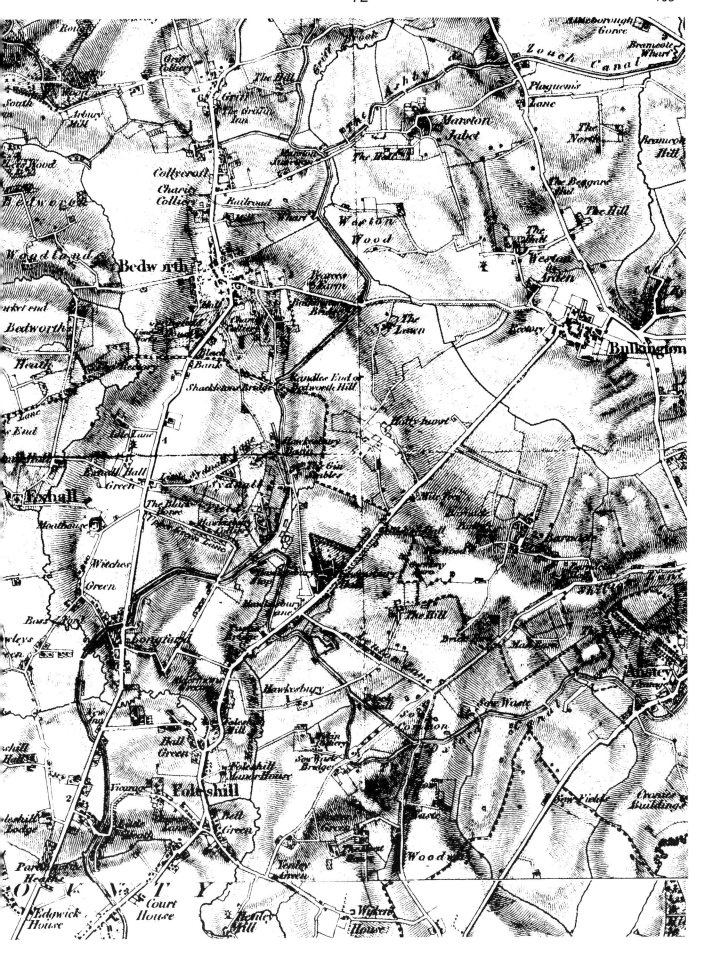

Published 1835.

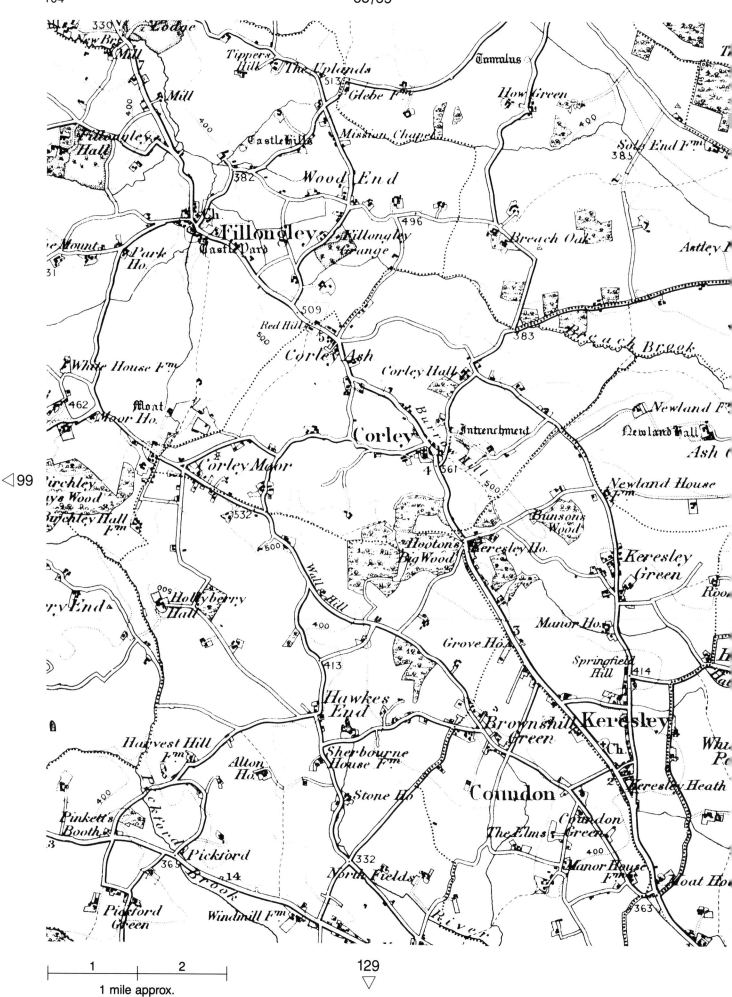

◁99

1

2

1 mile approx.

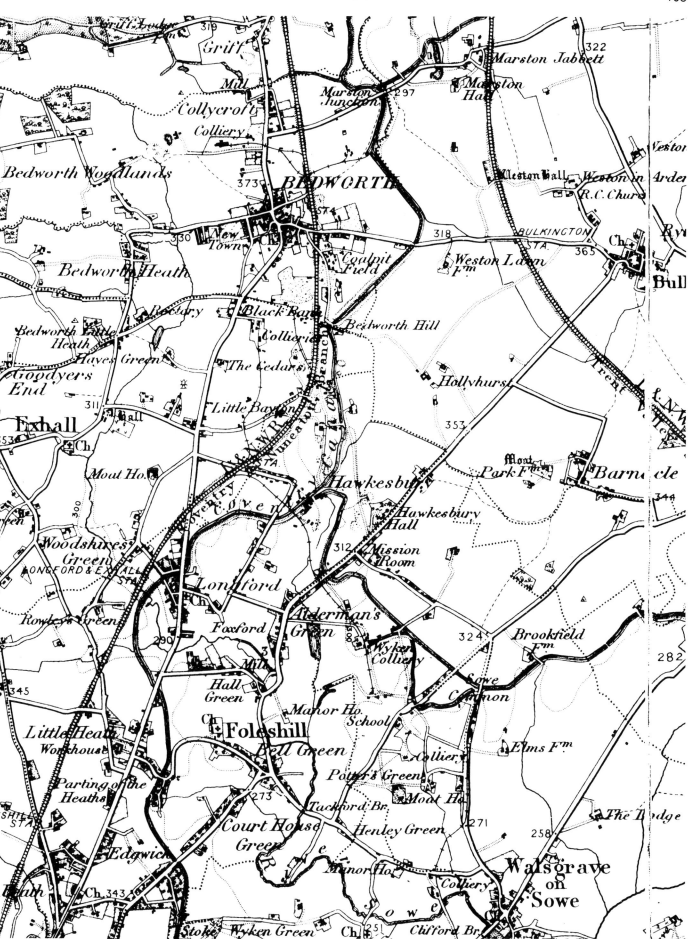

Surveyed 1881 - 88.  Published 1892 / 1895.

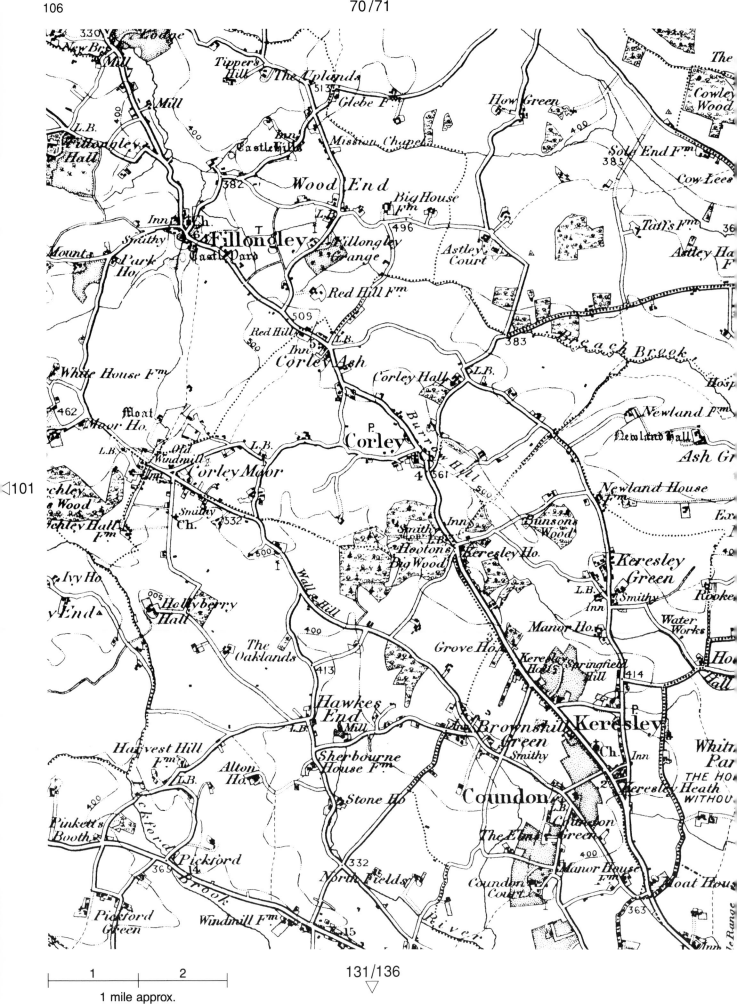

1    2

1 mile approx.

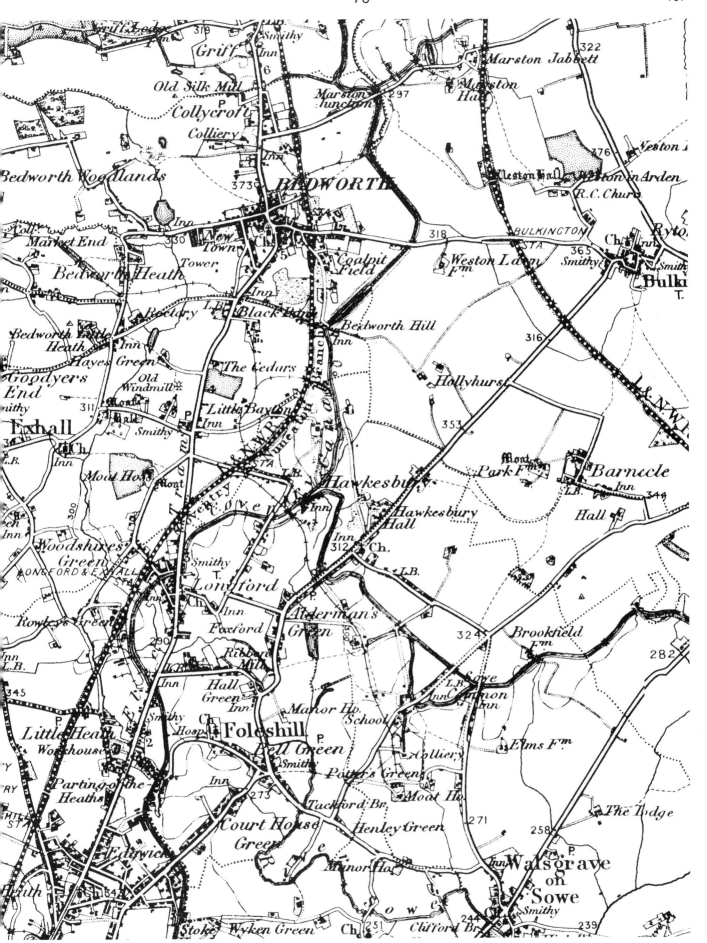

Surveyed 1885 - 86.  Revised 1906.  Published 1908.

1 2

1 mile approx.

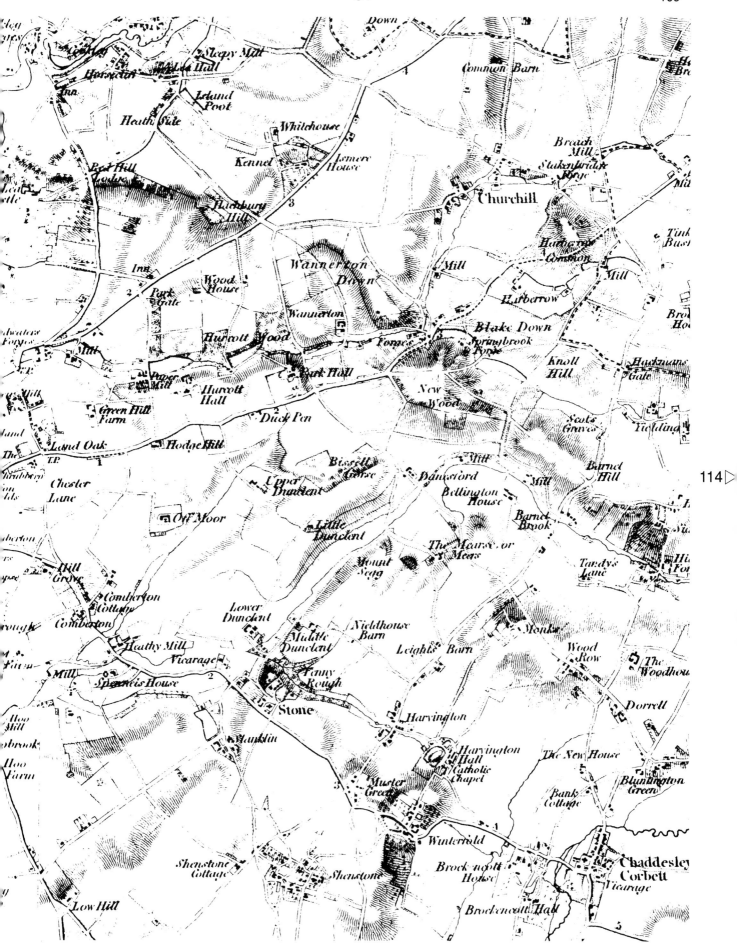

Published 1832.

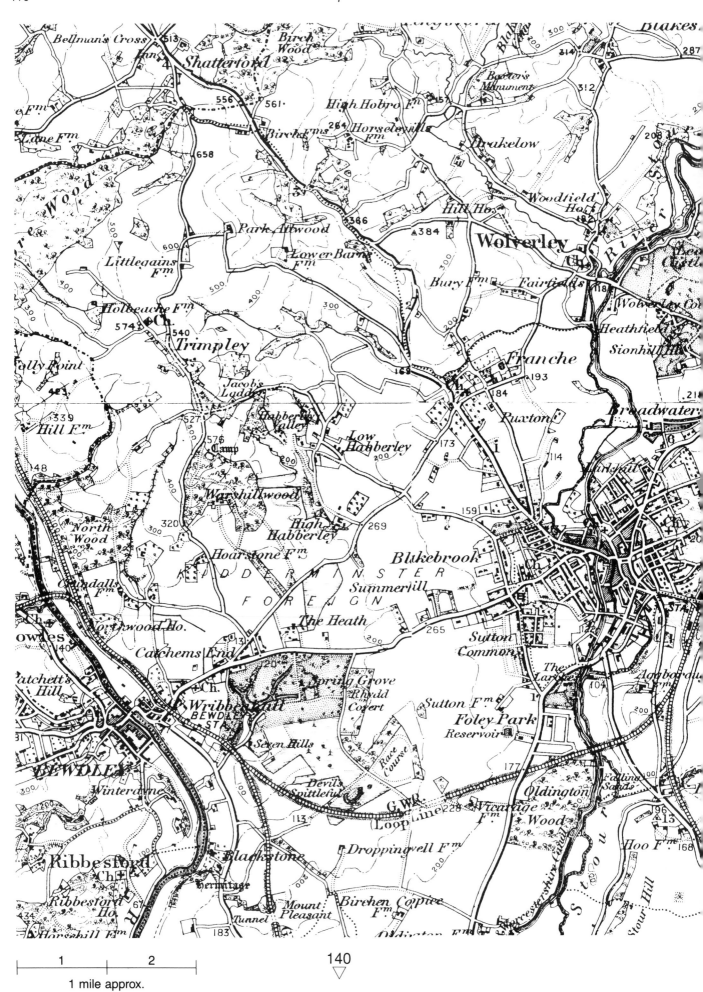

1 mile approx.

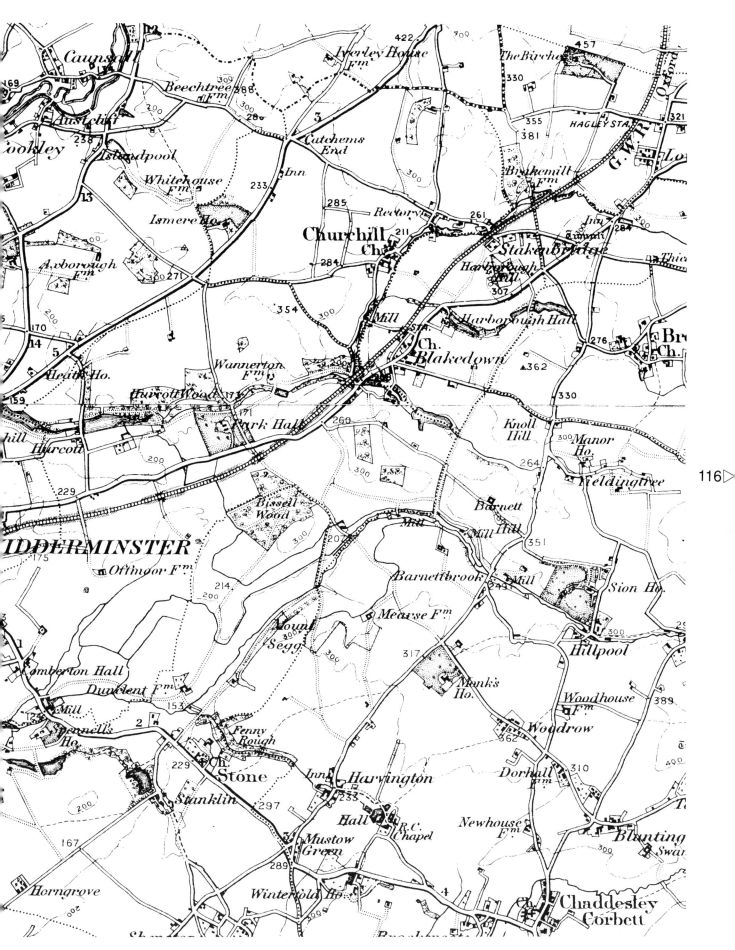

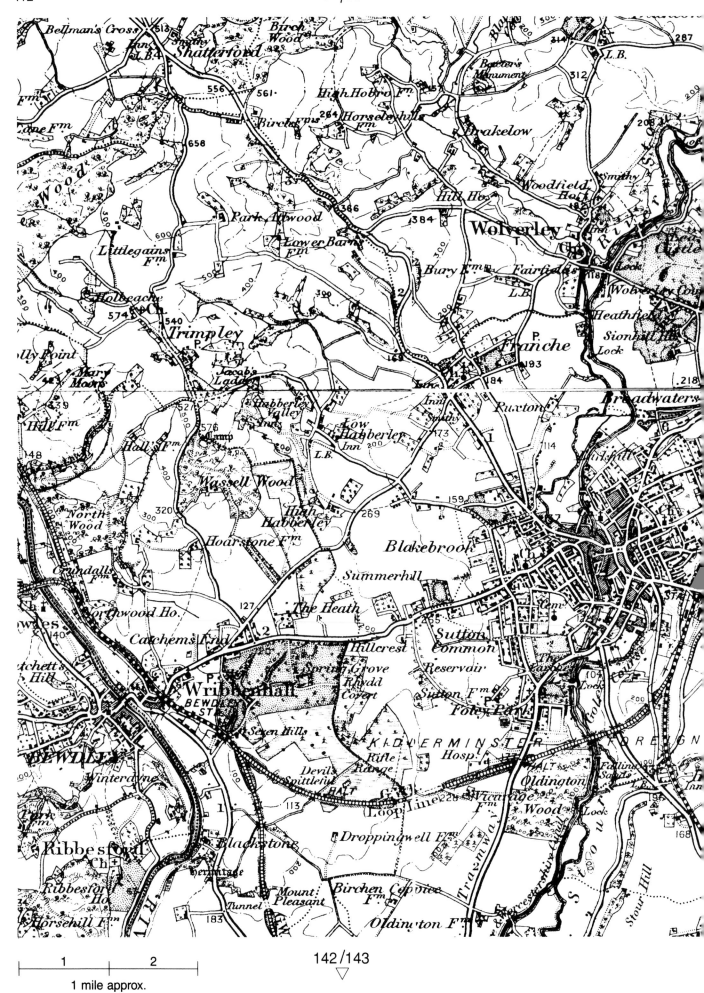

1    2

1 mile approx.

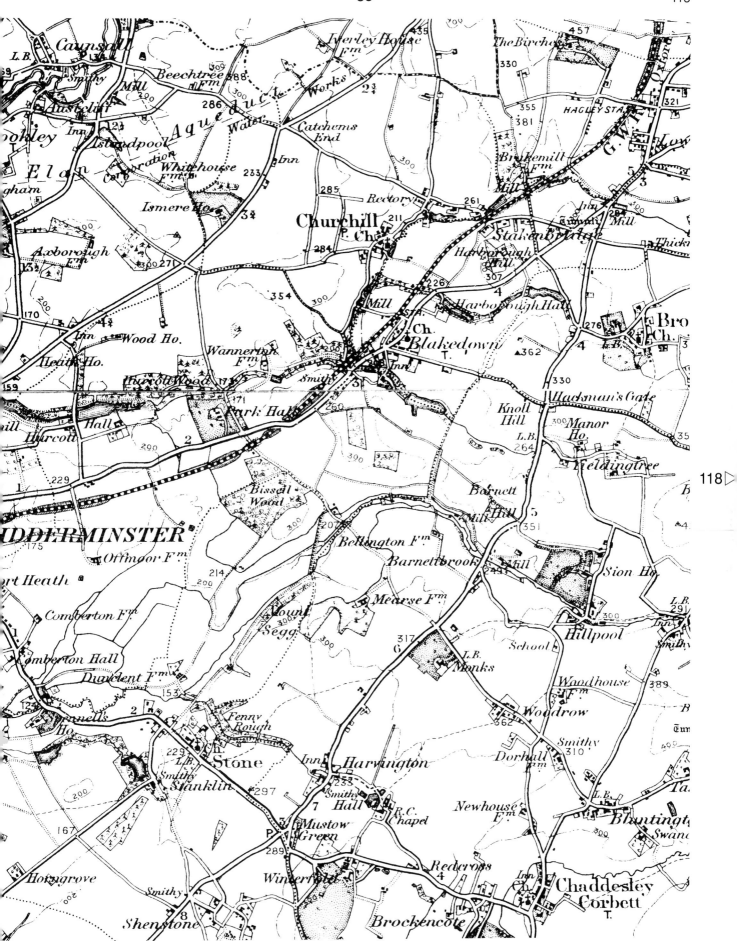

118 ▷

Surveyed 1881 - 84. Revised 1906 - 7. Published 1908 - 09.

◁109

145
▽

1      2

1 mile approx.

Published 1832.

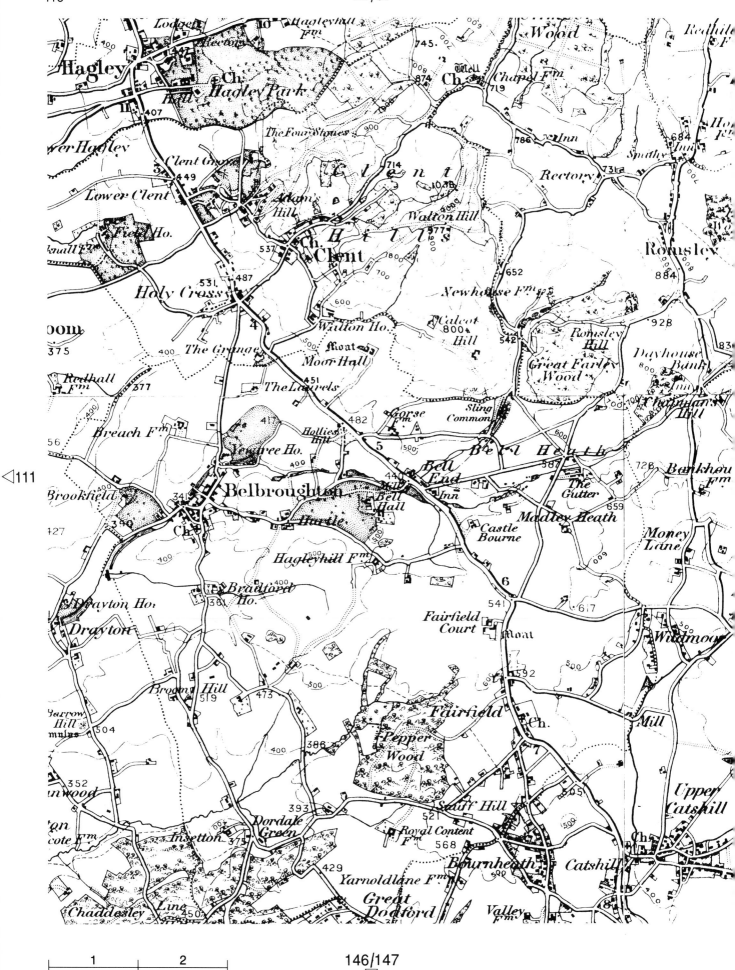

⊲111

1      2

1 mile approx.

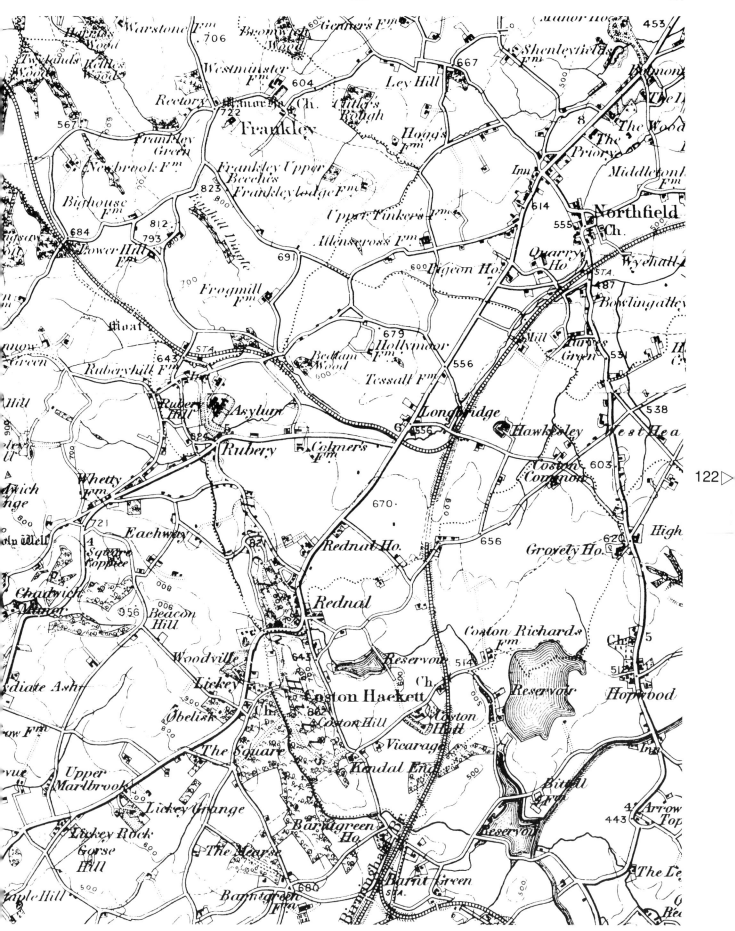

Surveyed 1881 - 88. Published 1895.

◁113

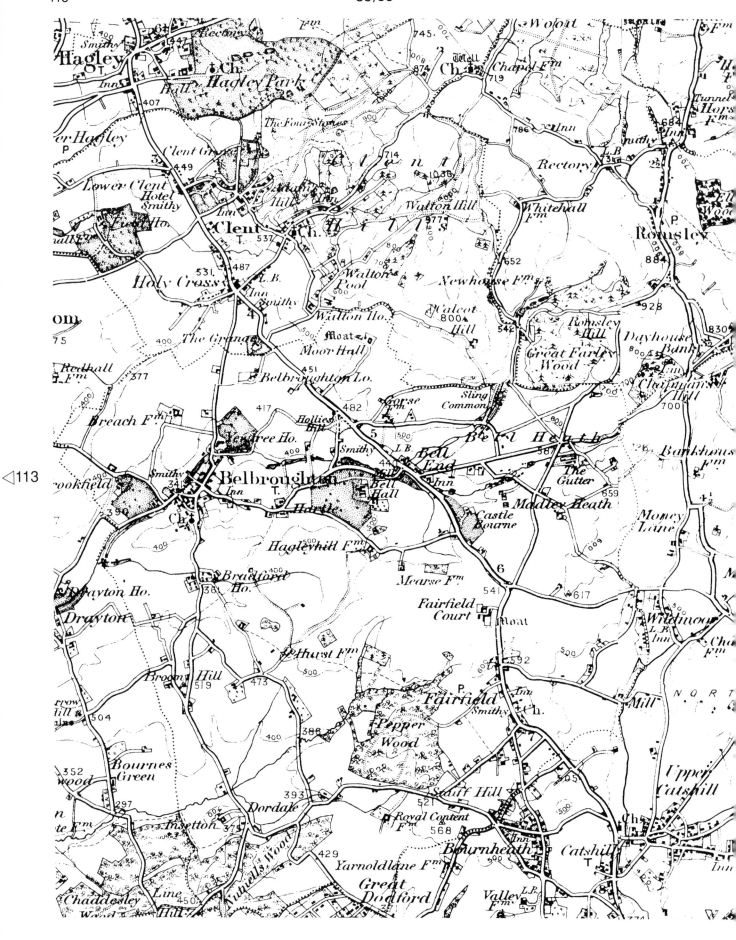

1 mile approx.

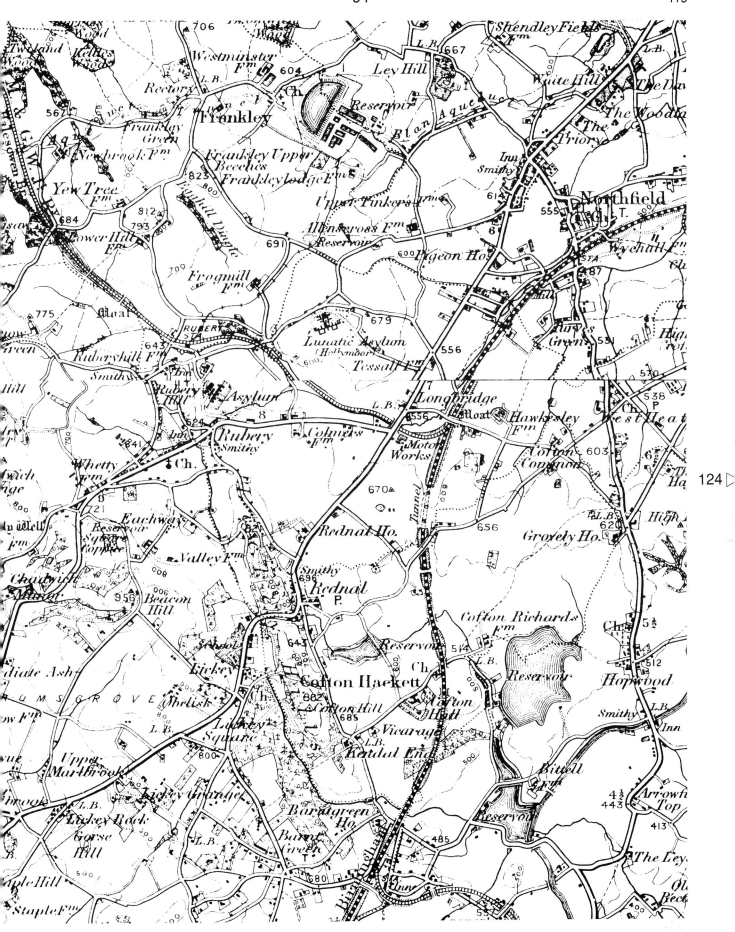

Surveyed 1881 - 86. Revised 1906 - 7. Published 1908 - 09.

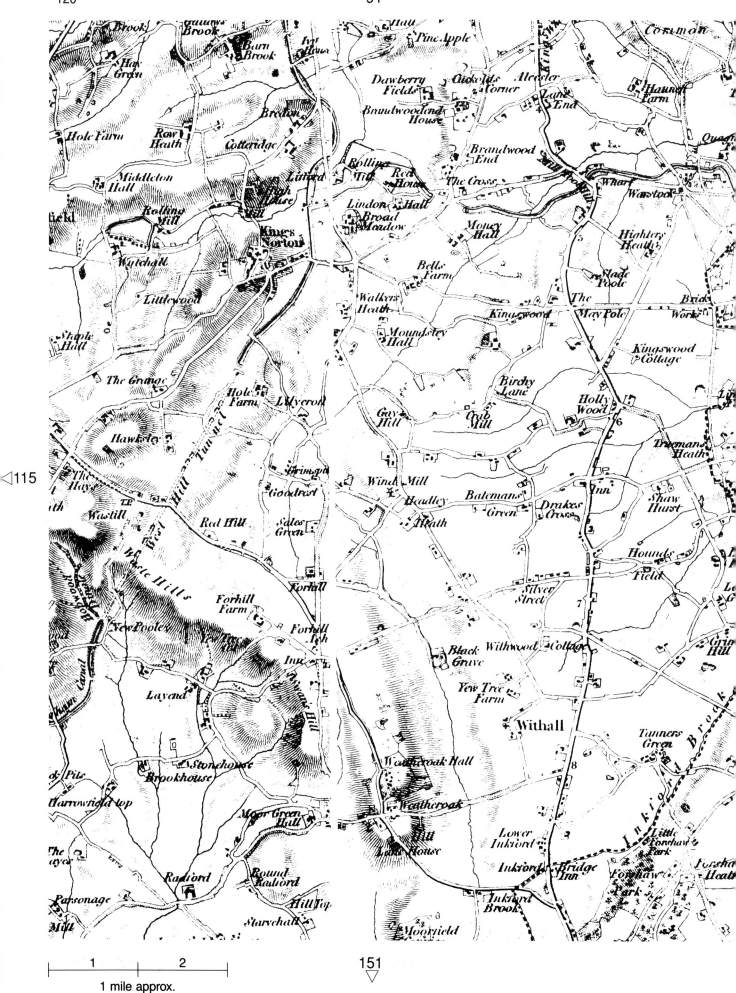

115

1   2

1 mile approx.

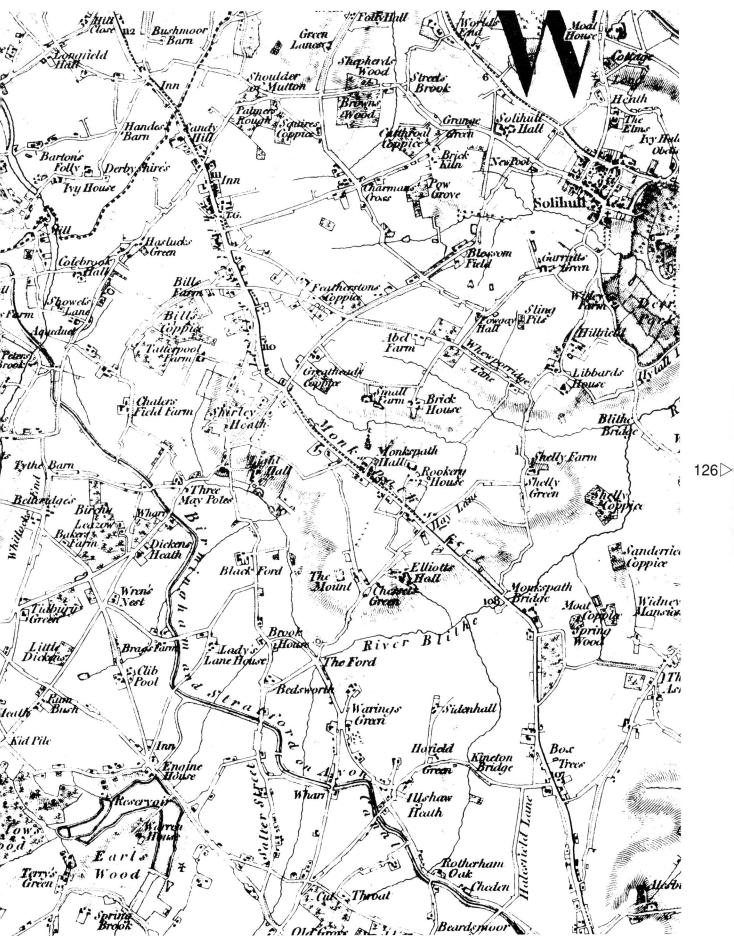

126▷

Published 1831.

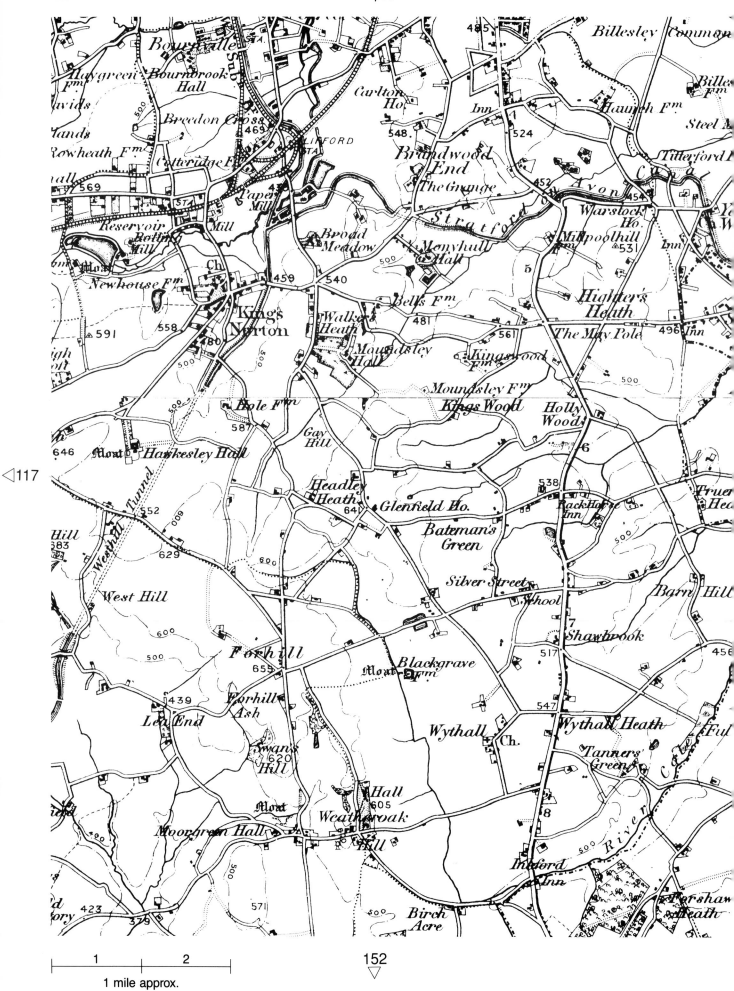

1     2

1 mile approx.

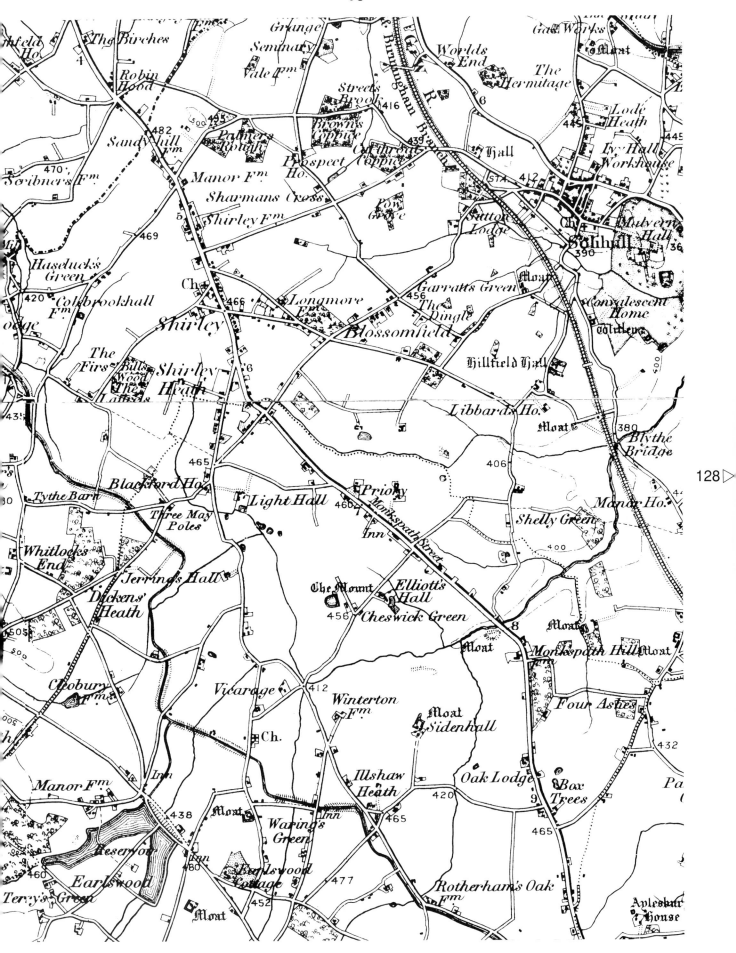

128 ▷

Surveyed 1881 - 88.  Published 1895.

◁119

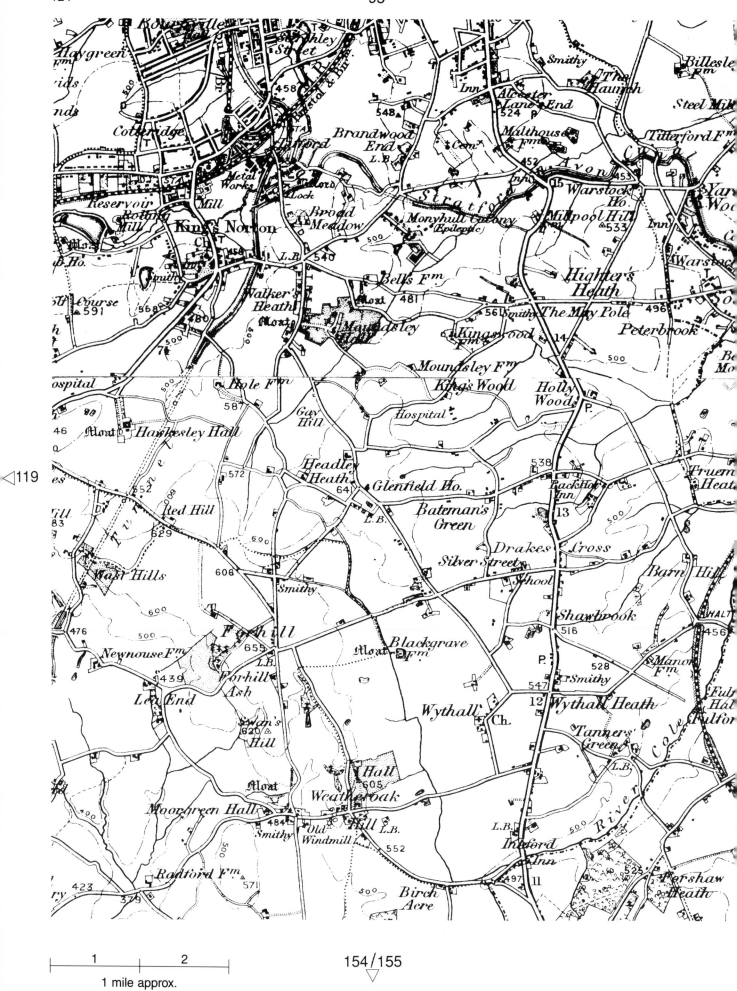

1      2

1 mile approx.

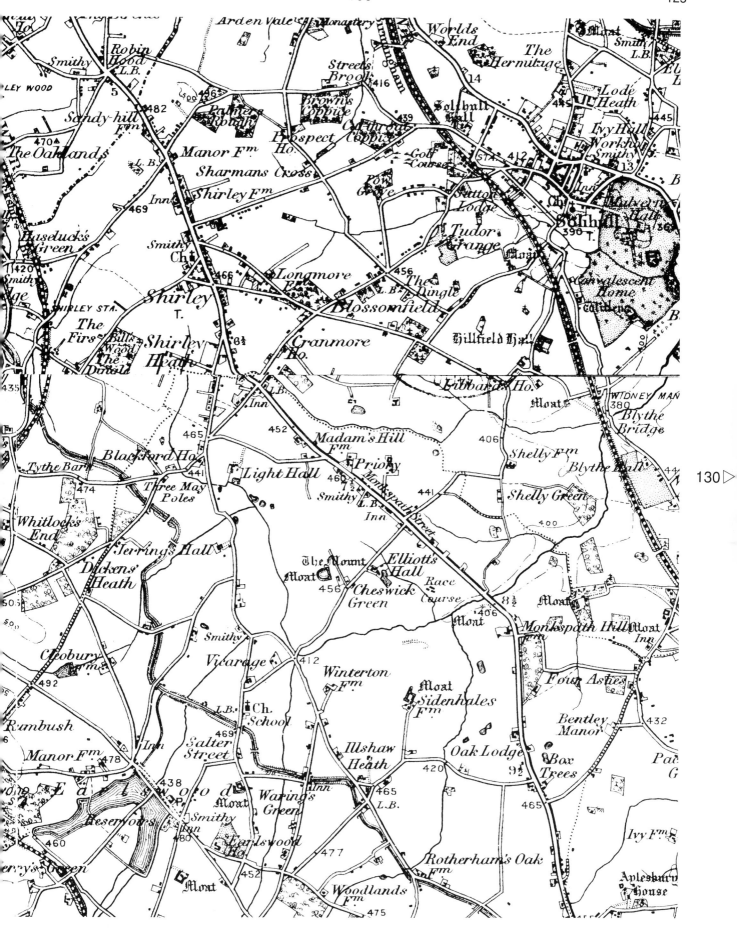

Surveyed 1881 - 88. Revised 1906 - 7. Published 1908 - 09.

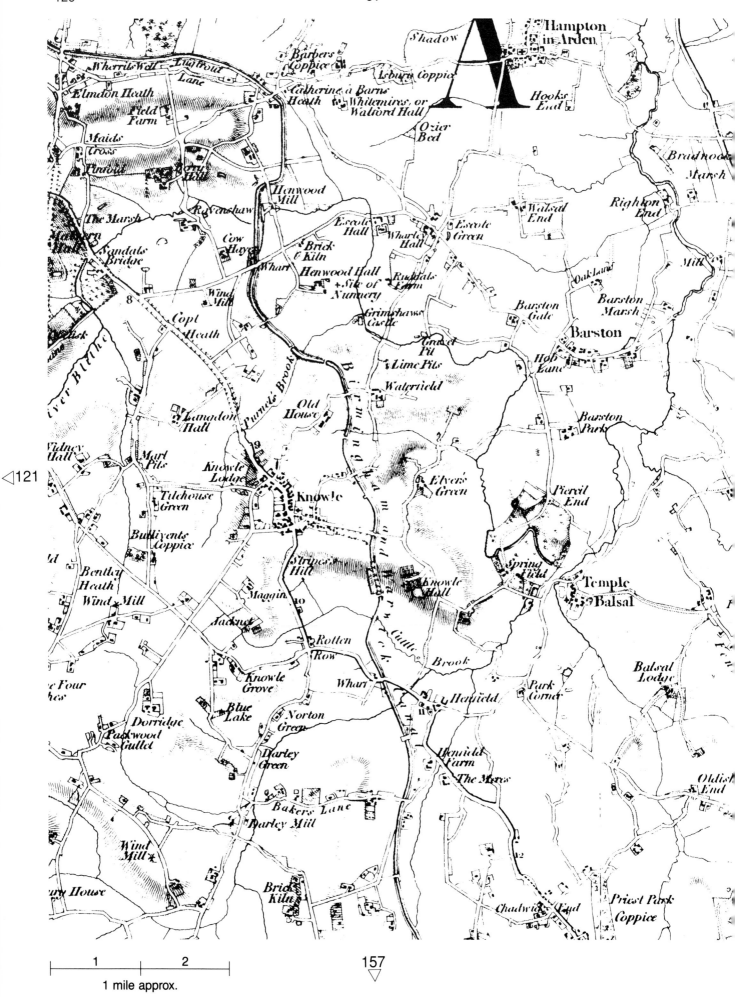

1          2

1 mile approx.

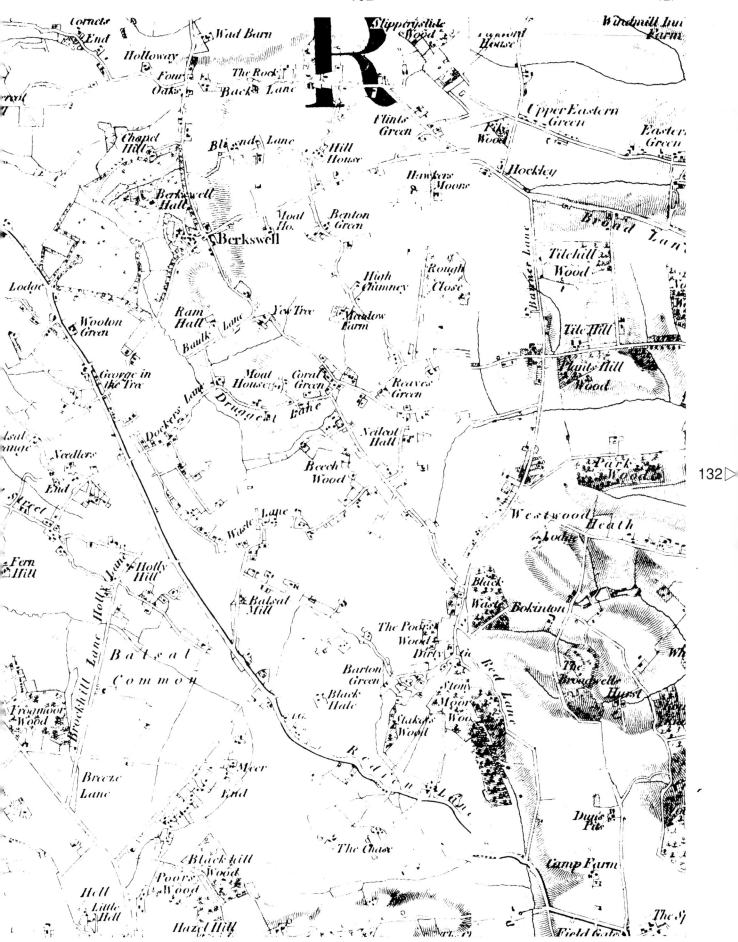

Published 1831 - 1834.

132▷

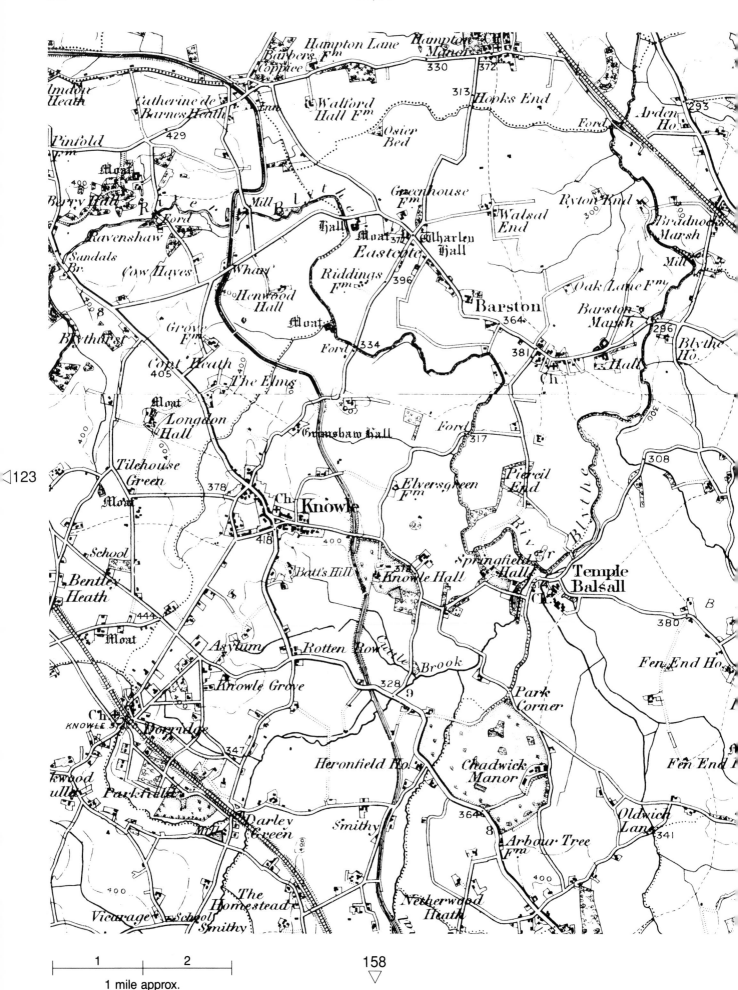

1 mile approx.

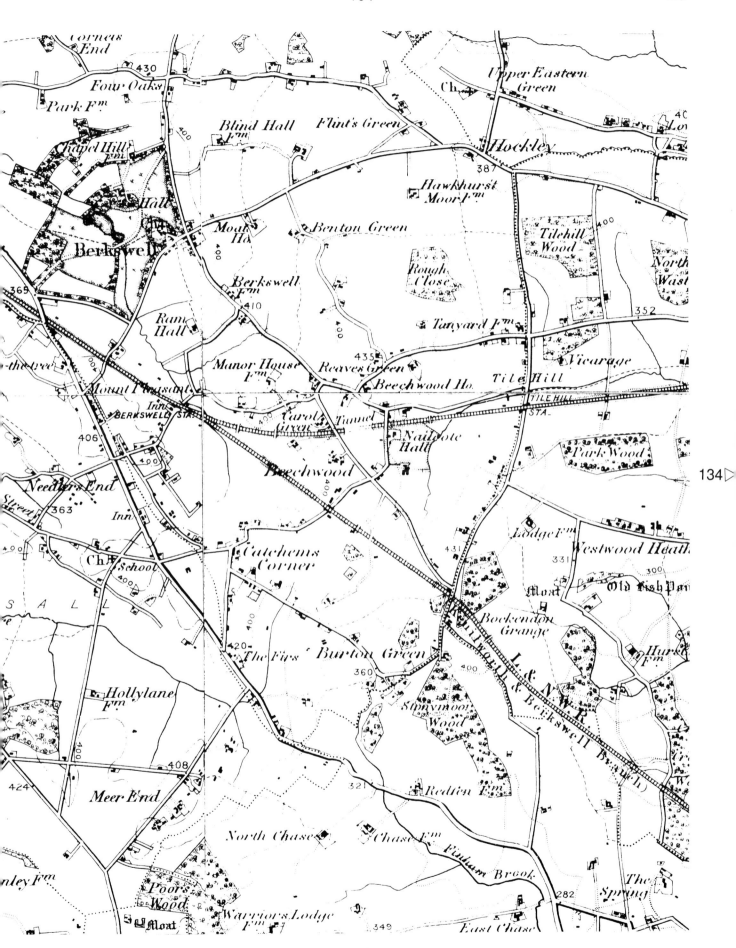

134 ▷

Surveyed 1881 - 88.  Published 1892 / 1895.

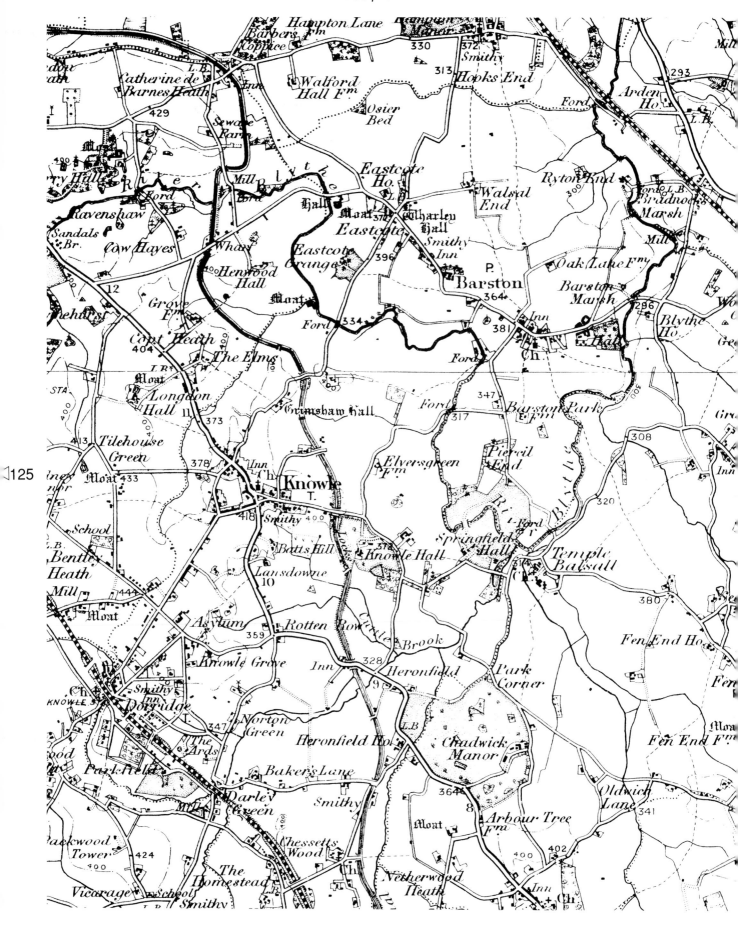

1        2

1 mile approx.

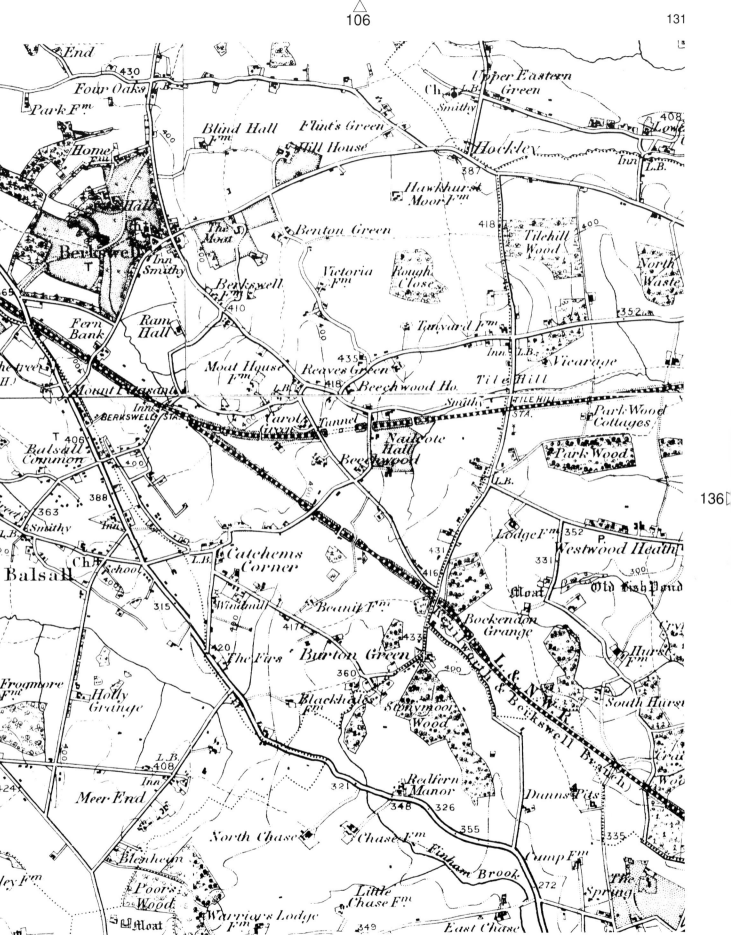

Surveyed 1881 - 88.  Revised 1906 - 7.  Published 1908 - 09.

Allesley

Allesley
Park

Site of
Castle

Radford

Inn

Guphill Ford

Mount Nod

Whoburley

COVENTRY

Chapel Fields

Mill  Spon Street

91

Gosford
Green

Heawood

Common

Fletchamstead
Hall

Fletchamstead

Pinley Lane

T.G.

The

Park

COVENTRY

Charter
House

Mill

Swift
Corner
Mill

Pensilling
Wood

Gibralter

Stivichall
Common

Quinton Pool

Mount
Tree

Stivichall

Whitley
Common

Mill

Canley

Burnt
Post

Hall

Whitley
Cottage

Kirby Corner

Grange

Howes Lane

Cheylesham

Mill

Fosil
House

Baginton

Mill

The Lunt
House

field
pice

Osfield

Wainbody
Wood

Green Lane

Hill

Hall

Baginton

Row

Marshall
Wood

Finham
Green

Finham
Grove

Millburn
Bridge

Pipes
Mill

Crackley

Millburn
Grange

Worsley Bridge

Finbury

Elliots Grove

Dale House

Chantry Heath

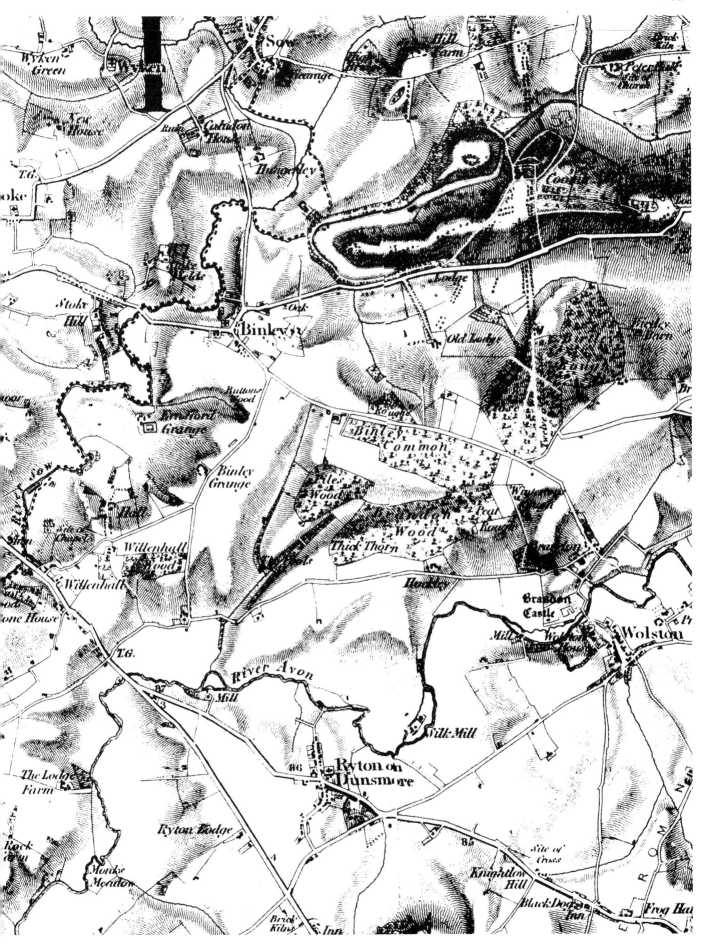

Published 1834.

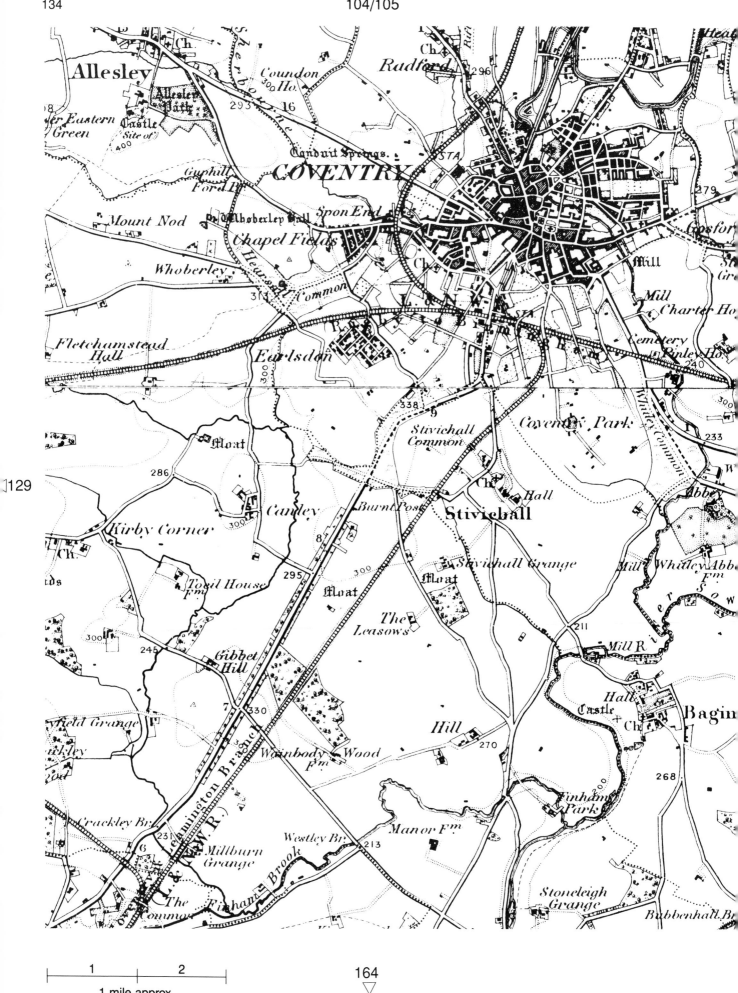

Allesley

Coundon 300 Ho. 16

293

Ch.

Radford 296

STA

Eastern Castle Green Site of? 400

Conduit Springs.

COVENTRY

279

Mount Nod

Guphill Ford Br.

Whoberley Hall Spon End

Chapel Fields

Cosfor

Mill

Whoberley

Heursall Common 310

Ch.

Mill Charter Ho

Fletchamstead Hall

Earlsdon 300

Cemetery Pinley Ho 240

129

Moat 286

338 9

Stivichall Common

Coventry Park 233

Whitley Common 300

Canley 300

Burnt Post

8

Ch. Hall

Stivichall

Kirby Corner 300

Abbe

Ch. ds

Toail House Fm 295

Moat 300

Stivichall Grange

Moat

Mill Whitley Abbey Fm Sow

300

245

Gibbet Hill

The Leasows

211

Mill R

7 330

Hill 270

Hall Castle Ch. + Bagin

268

field Grange

Wainbody Wood Fm

Finham Park

kley od

Crackley Br 231

W.R.) Leamington Branch

Millburn Grange

Westley Br 213

Manor Fm

Stoneleigh Grange

6

The Common Finham Brook

Bubbenhall Br

1        2

1 mile approx.

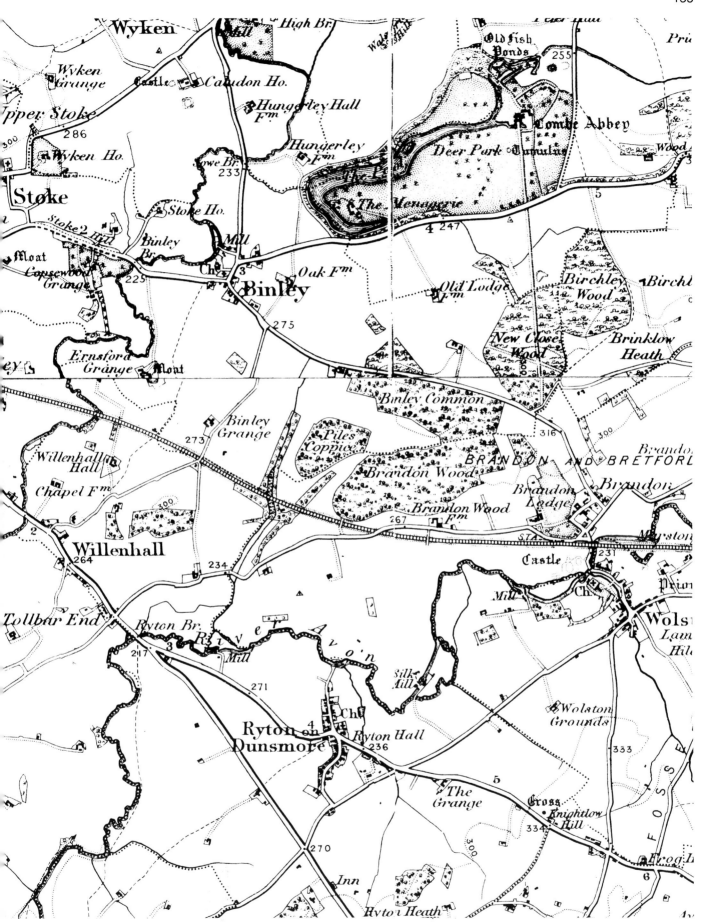

Surveyed 1883 - 86. Published 1892.

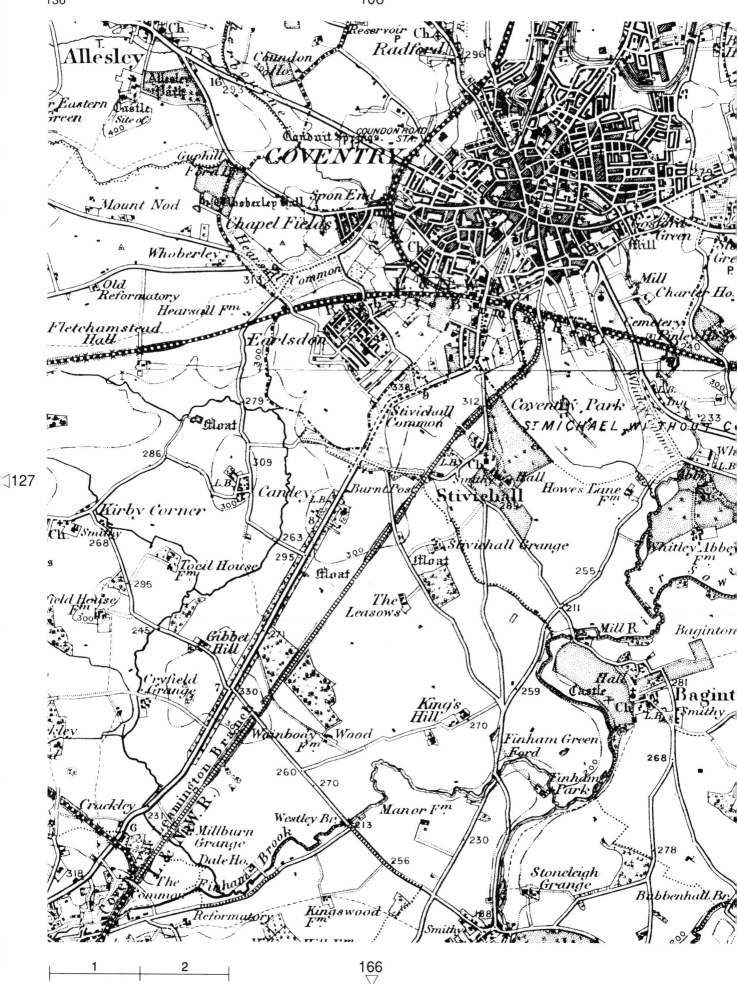

Allesley

Reservoir
Radford

COVENTRY

Mount Nod

Chapel Fields

Whoberley

Old Reformatory

Hearsall Fm

Fletchamstead Hall

Earlsdon

Moat

Canley

Stivichall Common

Coventry Park
ST MICHAEL WITHOUT

Stivichall

Howes Lane Fm

Whitley Abbey

Kirby Corner

Burnt Post

Stivichall Grange

Moat

Tocil House Fm

Moat

The Leasows

Gibbet Hill

King's Hill

Mill R

Baginton

Crofield Grange

Finham Green Ford

Hall Castle

Baginton

Wainbody Fm Wood

Finham Park

Cruckley

Millburn Grange

Dale Ho.

Westley Br

Manor Fm

Stoneleigh Grange

Bubbenhall Br

The Common

Finham Brook

Reformatory

Kingswood Fm

Smithy

1 — 2
1 mile approx.

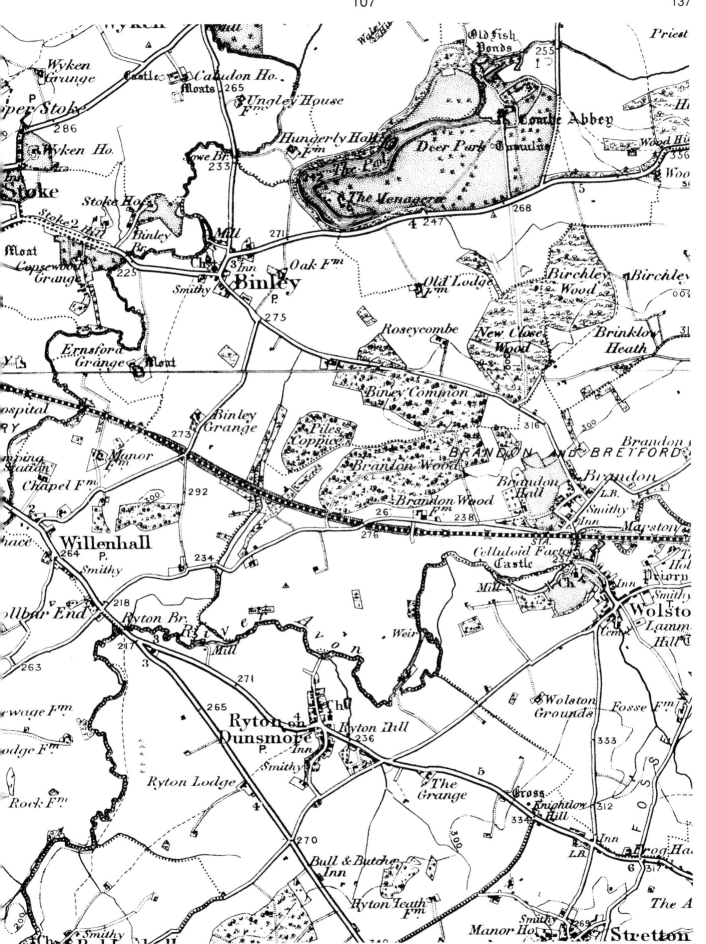

Surveyed 1882 - 86. Revised 1906 - 7. Published 1908.

1 mile approx.

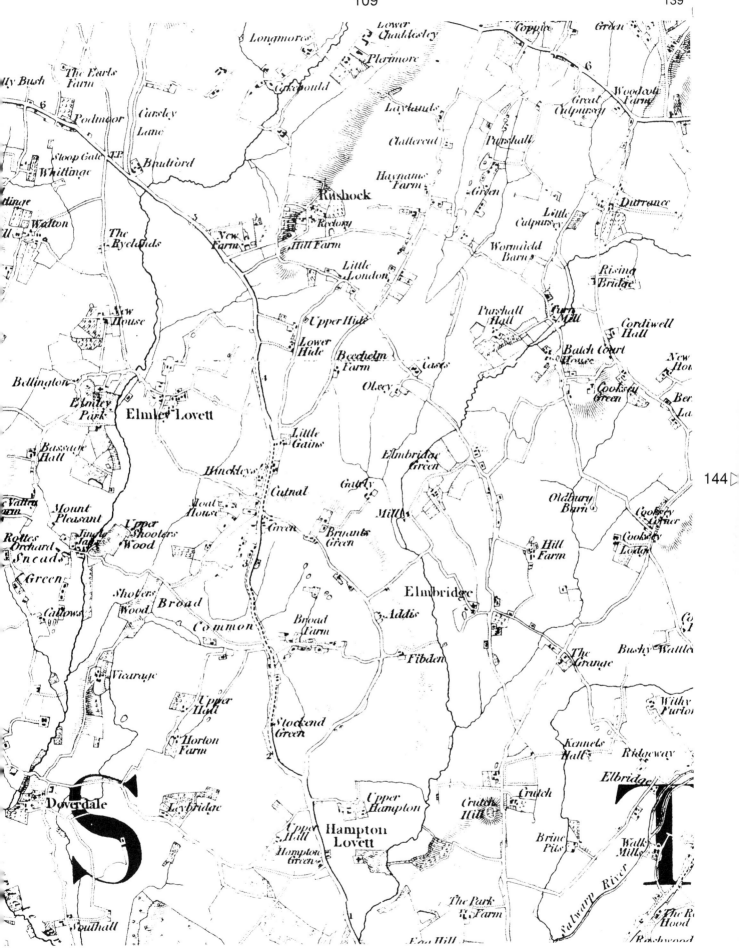

144 ▷

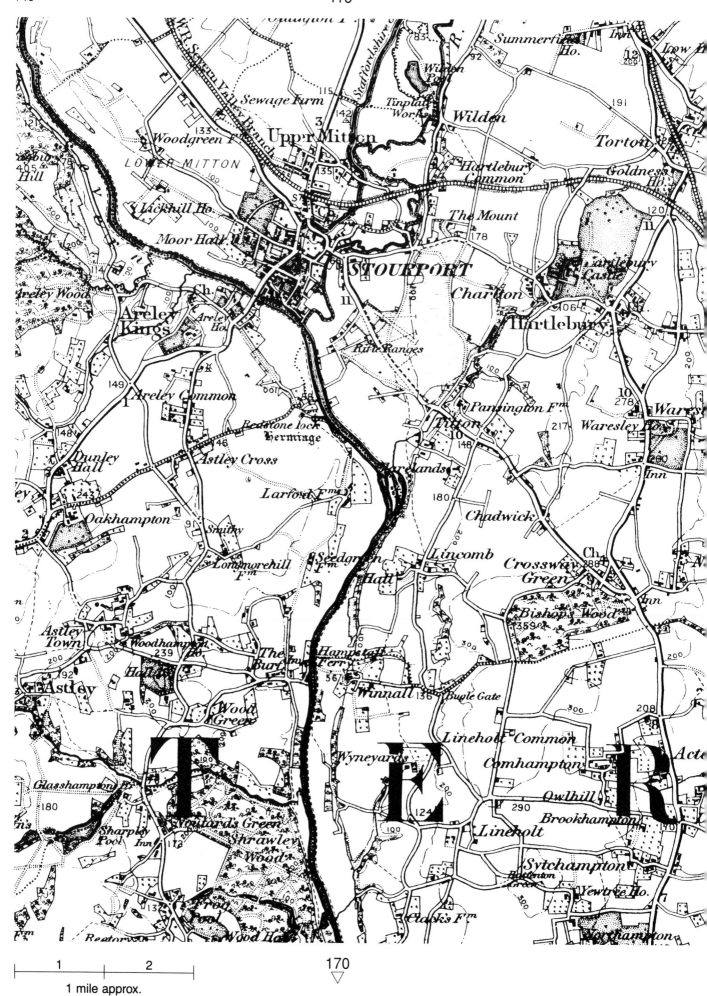

W. R. Severn Valley Branch

Sewage Farm

Staffordshire

Summerfield Ho.

Wilden Po.

Tinplate Works

Wilden

Torton

133

Woodgreen Fm.

Upp'r Mitton

115

142

3

Hartlebury Common

Goldness Ho.

191

LOWER MITTON

100

35

120

Lickhill Ho.

The Mount

II

405

278

Moor Hall

178

Ch.

STOURPORT

Charlton

Hartlebury Castle

114

Areley Wood

11

Hartlebury

206

Areley Kings

Areley Ho.

Rifle Ranges

200

149

Areley Common

100

Pansington Fm.

Ware

10

278

148

061

88

Titton

Waresley Ho.

10

148

200

Redstone lock Hermitage

46

Inn

148

Astley Cross

Irelands

Chadwick

Dunley Hall

Larford Fm.

180

243

Lincomb

Crossway Green

388

Ch.

Oakhampton

9

Smithy

Seedgreen Fm.

Bishops Wood

Inn

359

Longmorehill Fm.

Hall

200

Astley Town

Woodhampton

239

The Burf

Hampstall Ferr.

300

Winnall

136

Bugle Gate

208

Astley

Holt

56

Linehott Common

Acto

Wood Green

Wyneyards

Comhampton

200

Glasshampton

180

Owlhill

290

Sharpley Pool Inn

172

Noutard's Green

124

Lineholt

Brookhampton

190

Shrawley Wood

100

Sytchampton

132

Clacks Fm.

Yewtree Ho.

Wood Ho.

Reastow

Worhampton

| 1 | 2 |

1 mile approx.

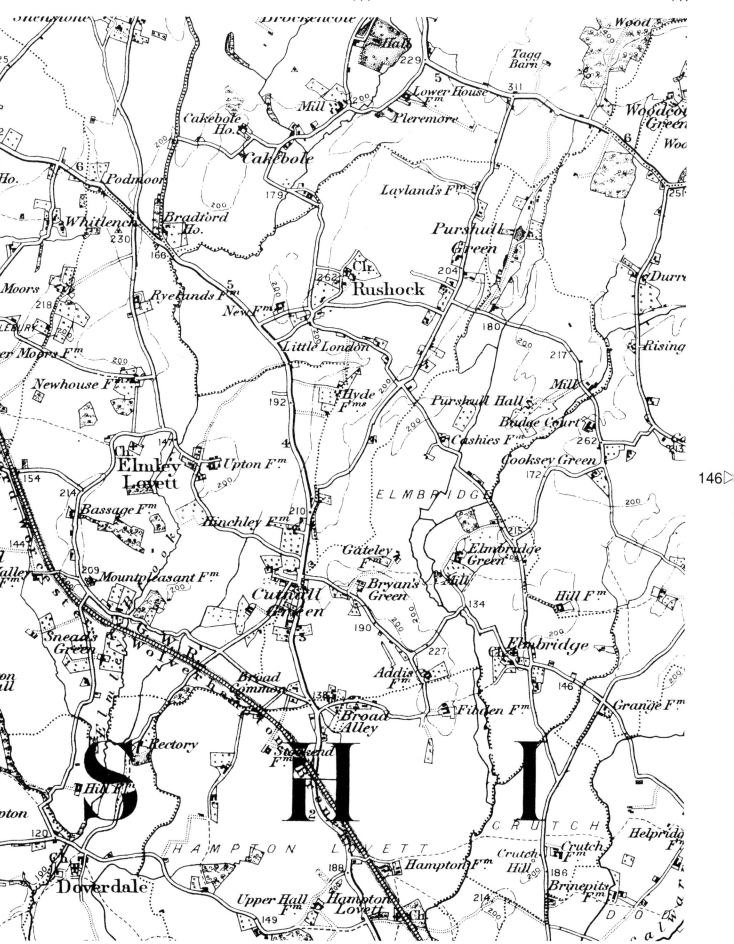

Shenstone

Brockencote

Hall

229

Tagg

Barn

5

Lower House

Fm

311

Wood

Woodcot

Green

Woo

Mill

200

Pleremore

Cakebole

Ho.

Cakebole

6

Podmoor

179

Layland's Fm

Purshull

Green

251

Whitlench

Bradford

Ho.

230

166

200

Cir.

262

204

Durr

Moors

218

Ryelands Fm

5

New Fm

Rushock

180

Rising

LEBURY

200

200

Little London

200

200

217

Mill

er Moors Fm

200

192

Hyde

Fm

Purshull Hall

Budge Court

262

Newhouse Fm

4

200

Cashies Fm

Cooksey Green

172

Ch

Elmley

Lovett

147

Upton Fm

200

ELMBRIDGE

200

154

214

210

215

Bassage Fm

Hinchley Fm

Elmbridge

Green

200

144

209

Mountpleasant Fm

Gateley

Fm

Mill

Hill Fm

alley

Fm

Bryan's

Green

134

Snead's

Green

G.W.R.

Cutnall

Green

190

200

Elmbridge

3

227

Ch

146

Broad

Common

Addis

Fm

Fihden Fm

Grange Fm

200

Broad

Alley

13

Rectory

Stockend

Fm

CRUTCH

Helprido

Hill Fm

2

Crutch

Hill

Crutch

Fm

186

120

HAMPTON

LOVETT

Hampton Fm

200

Brinepits

Fm

Ch

Hampton Fm

188

Hampton

Lovett

214

200

D

Doverdale

Upper Hall

Fm

149

Ch

Surveyed 1882 - 84. Published 1895.

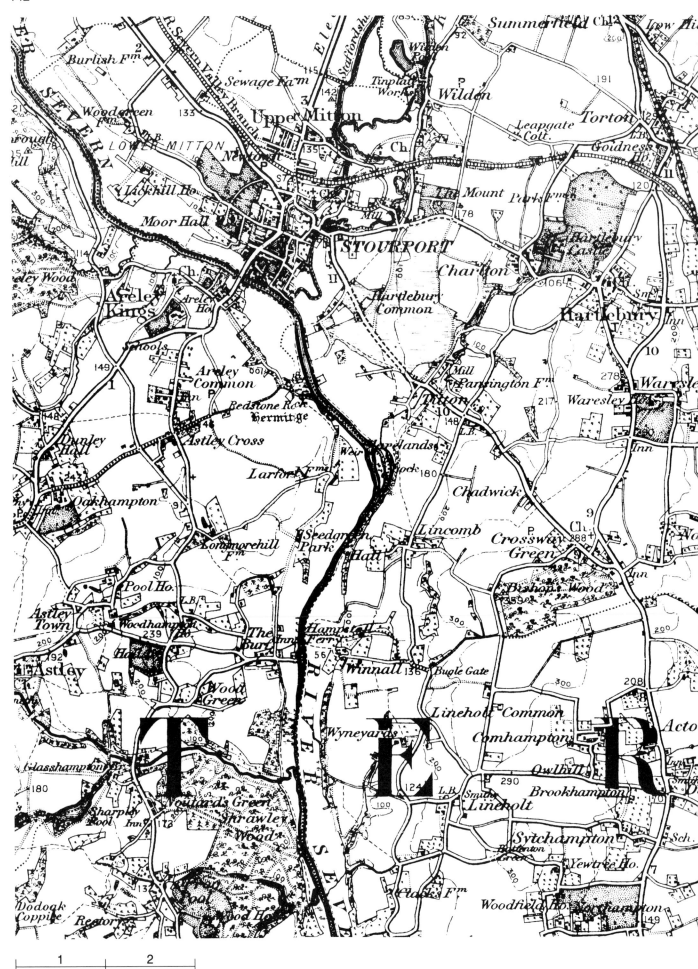

1 mile approx.

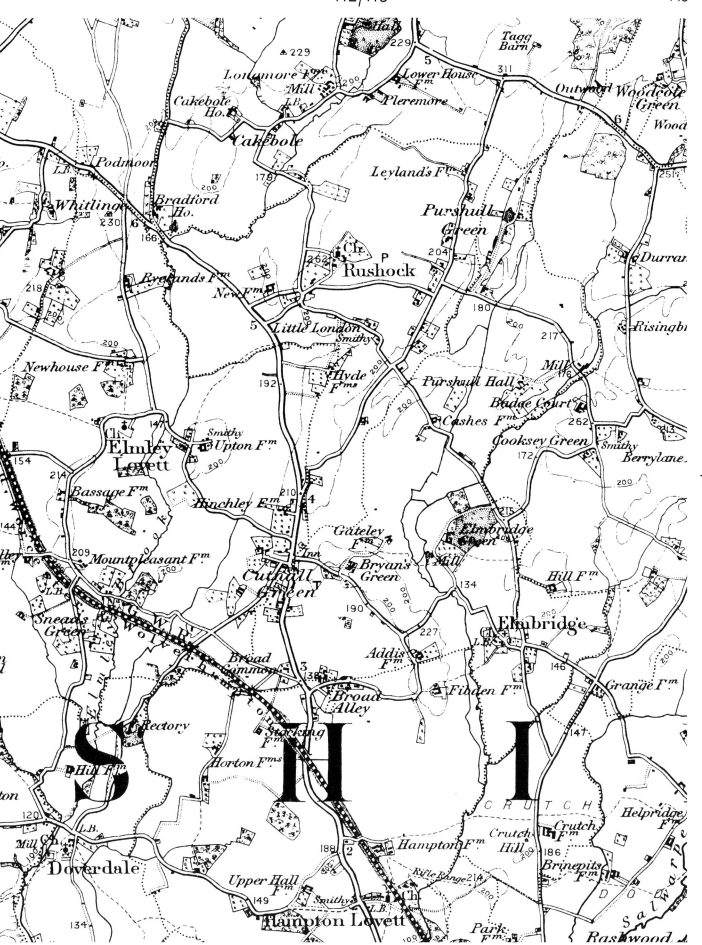

148 ▷

Surveyed 1882 - 84. Revised 1907. Published 1909.

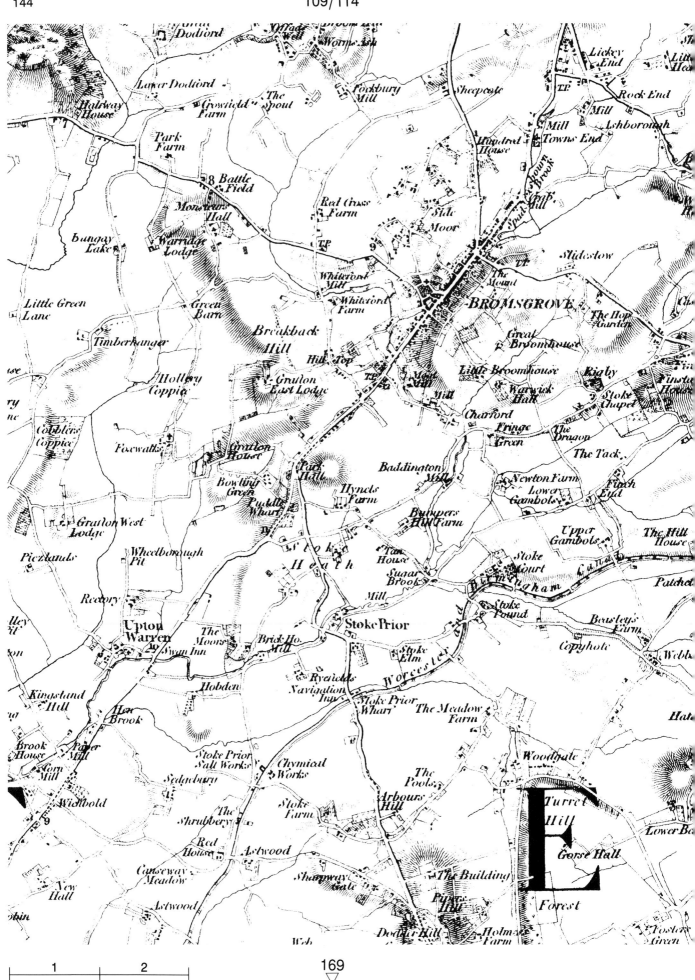

◁139

Dodford
Offad
Worm Ash
Lower Dodford
The Spout
Foxbury Mill
Sheepcote
Lickey End
Rock End
Mill
Halfway House
Growfield Farm
Mill
Ashborough
Park Farm
Hundred House
Towns End
8 Battle Field
Red Cross Farm
Side Moor
Monsrott Hall
Slideslow
Bungay Lake
Warridge Lodge
TP
9
The Mound
Whiteford Mill
BROMSGROVE
Little Green Lane
Green Barn
Whiteford Farm
The Hop Garden
Timberhanger
Breakback Hill
Great Broomhouse
Hollery Coppice
Hill Top
Little Broomhouse
Rigby
Grafton East Lodge
TP
Mill
Warwick Hall
Stoke Chapel
Cobblers Coppice
Foxwalls
Grafton House
Mill
Charford
Fringe Green
The Dragon
The Tack
Bowling Green
Pack Hill
Baddington Mill
Newton Farm
Finch End
Puddle Wharf
Hynets Farm
Lower Gambols
Grafton West Lodge
Bumpers Hill Farm
Upper Gambols
The Hill House
Pieztands
Wheelborough Pit
Stoke Heath
Tan House
Stoke Mount
Canal
Patchet
Rectory
Sugar Brook
Stoke Pound
Beasley's Farm
Upton Warren
The Moons
Brick Ho. Mill
Mill
Stoke Prior
Stoke Elm
Copyhote
Webb
Swan Inn
Kingsland Hill
Hobden
Ryefields
Navigation Inn
Stoke Prior Wharf
The Meadow Farm
Hen Brook
Stoke Prior Wharf
Brook House
Paper Mill
Stoke Prior Salt Works
Chymical Works
Woodgate
Corn Mill
Sedgebury
The Pools
Turret Hill
Wichbold
Stoke Farm
Arbours Hill
Gorse Hall
The Shrubbery
Lower Ba
Red House
Astwood
The Building
Forest
New Hall
Causeway Meadow
Shanway Gate
Piper Hill
Astwood
Web
Dodar Hill
Holms Farm
Foster Green

Published 1832.

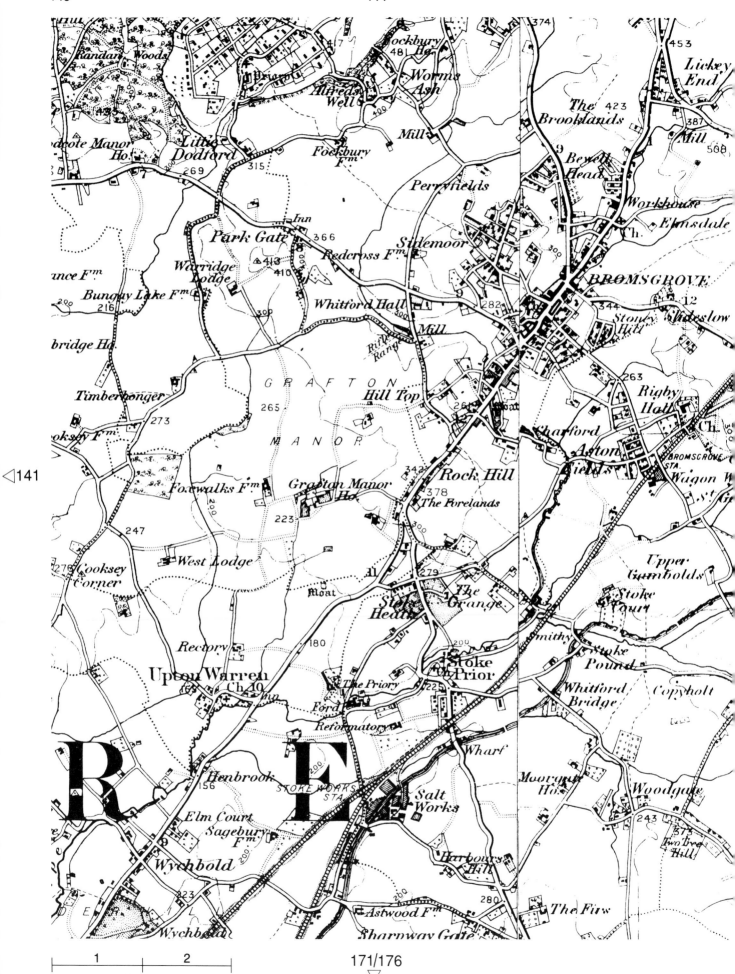

Randan Woods

Priory G

Alfred's Well

Dodcote Manor Ho.

Little Dodford

Fockbury Fm.

269

315

Park Gate

Inn

366

413

410

Warridge Lodge

ance Fm.

Bungay Lake Fm.

216

200

bridge Ho.

300

Timberhonger

273

oksey Fm

265

GRAFTON

MANOR

Foxwalks Fm.

200

223

247

Cooksey Corner

West Lodge

200

Moat

Rectory

180

Upton Warren

Ch

The Priory

Ford

Reformatory

Henbrook

156

STOKE WORKS
STA

Salt
Works

Elm Court

Sagebury
Fm.

200

Wychbold

223

Wychbold

Astwood Fm.

Sharpway Gate

481

Fockbury
Ho.

Worms
Ash

400

Mill

Fockbury
Fm.

Perryfields

Sidemoor

Redcross Fm.

Whitford Hall

Rifle
Range

Mill

300

Hill Top

282

265

Grafton Manor
Ho.

342

Rock Hill

378

The Forelands

300

Stoke
Heath

The
Grange

279

300

Stoke
Prior

422

Wharf

Harbours
Hill

280

374

453

Lickey
End

The
Brooklands

423

387

Mill

508

Bewell
Head

Workhouse

Elmsdale

Th.

BROMSGROVE

300

344

12

Stoney Alderslow
Hill

263

Rigby
Hall

Charford

Aston
Fields

BROMSGROVE
STA.

Wagon W

243

St Gr

Upper
Gambolds

Stoke
Court

Smithy

Stoke
Pound

Whitford
Bridge

Copyholt

Moorgate
Ho.

Woodgate

243

375

Two Tree
Hill

The Firs

R F

1          2

1 mile approx.

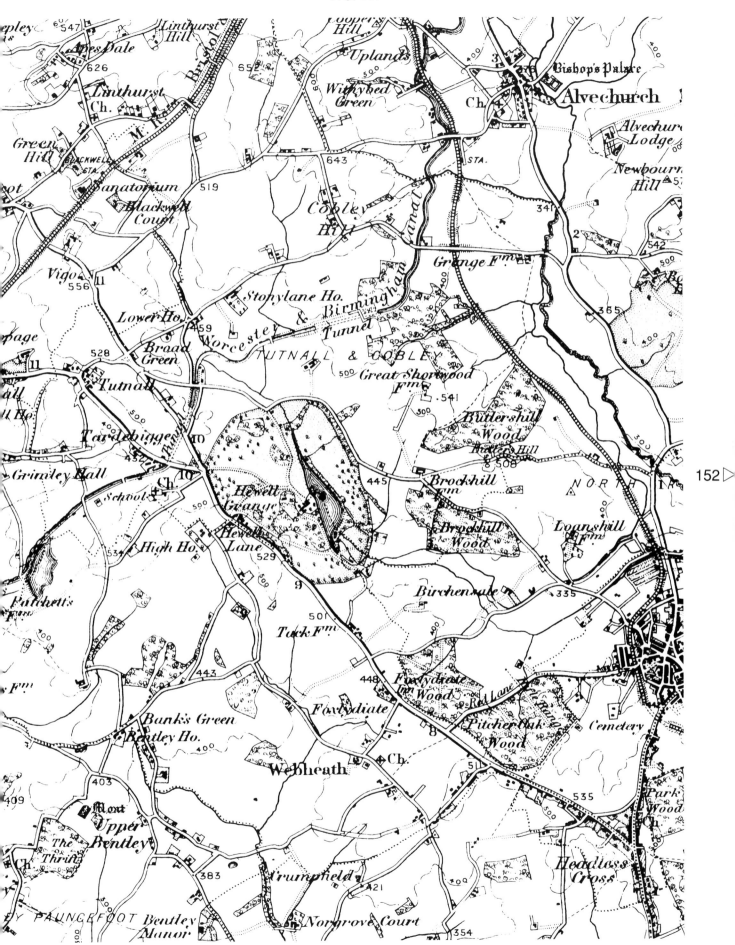

Randan
Wood
435

ote Manor
Ho.
L.B.

Little
Dodford
269

315

Ch.
Priory
L.B.

Alfred's
Well

Rockbury Ho.
481

Worms
Ash
400

Pumping Station

Inn

Lickey
End
P.

423

387

Mill
508

Lunatic
Asylum

Bewell
Head

Mill

Park Gate
L.B.
366

Smithy

418
410

Inn

300

Perryfields

Sidemoor
Smithy

Inn
P.

Workhouse
Ch.
Elmsdale

321

BROMSGROVE

Warridge
Lodge

Whitford Hall

Mill

400

Venn

Stone
Hill
Slideslow

344
297

ce Fm

Bungay Lake Fm
216

333

Rifle
Range

GRAFTON

Hill Top

263

ridge Ho.

300

MANOR

Cours Hosp!
L.B.

Rock Hill
NORTH

Rigby
Hall
Ch.

Timberhonger
273

265

Charford
Ch.

Aston
Fields
P.

Inn
BROMSGROVE
STA.

143

Cobbler's
Coppice

Foxwalks Fm

Grafton Manor
Ho.
223

342

The Forelands
BROMSGROVE
(DET.)

Wagon W
St.

247

West Lodge

11

279

The
Grange

Upper
Gambolds

Cooksey
Corner

Moat

Stoke
Heath
Inn

Mill

Stoke
Court

Rectory

180

200

Smithy
L.B.

Stoke
Pound
296

Upton Warren
Ch. 10
L.B.

Inn

The Priory

Mills
Reformatory

Stoke
Prior
P.

Mill

Whitford
Bridge

Copyholt

R

F

Stoke
Wharf

Henbrook
156

STA

Salt
Works

Moorgate
Ho.

Woodgate

Mill

Elm Court
Sagebury
Fm

Smithy

Inn

Stoke
Works

Harbours
Hill

243

Inn

Two Tree
Hall

285

303

Wychbold
Inn
T
323
Ch.

200

Astwood Fm

280

Vicarage Fm

Wychbold
Hall
200

Locks
Sharpway Gate

The Firs

1        2

1 mile approx.

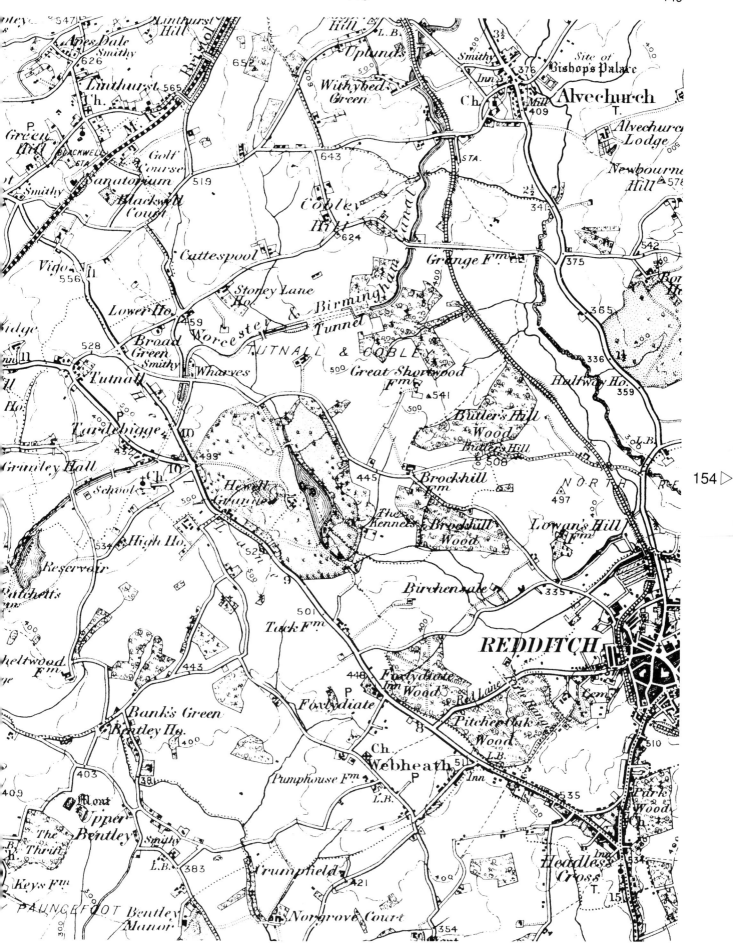

154 ▷

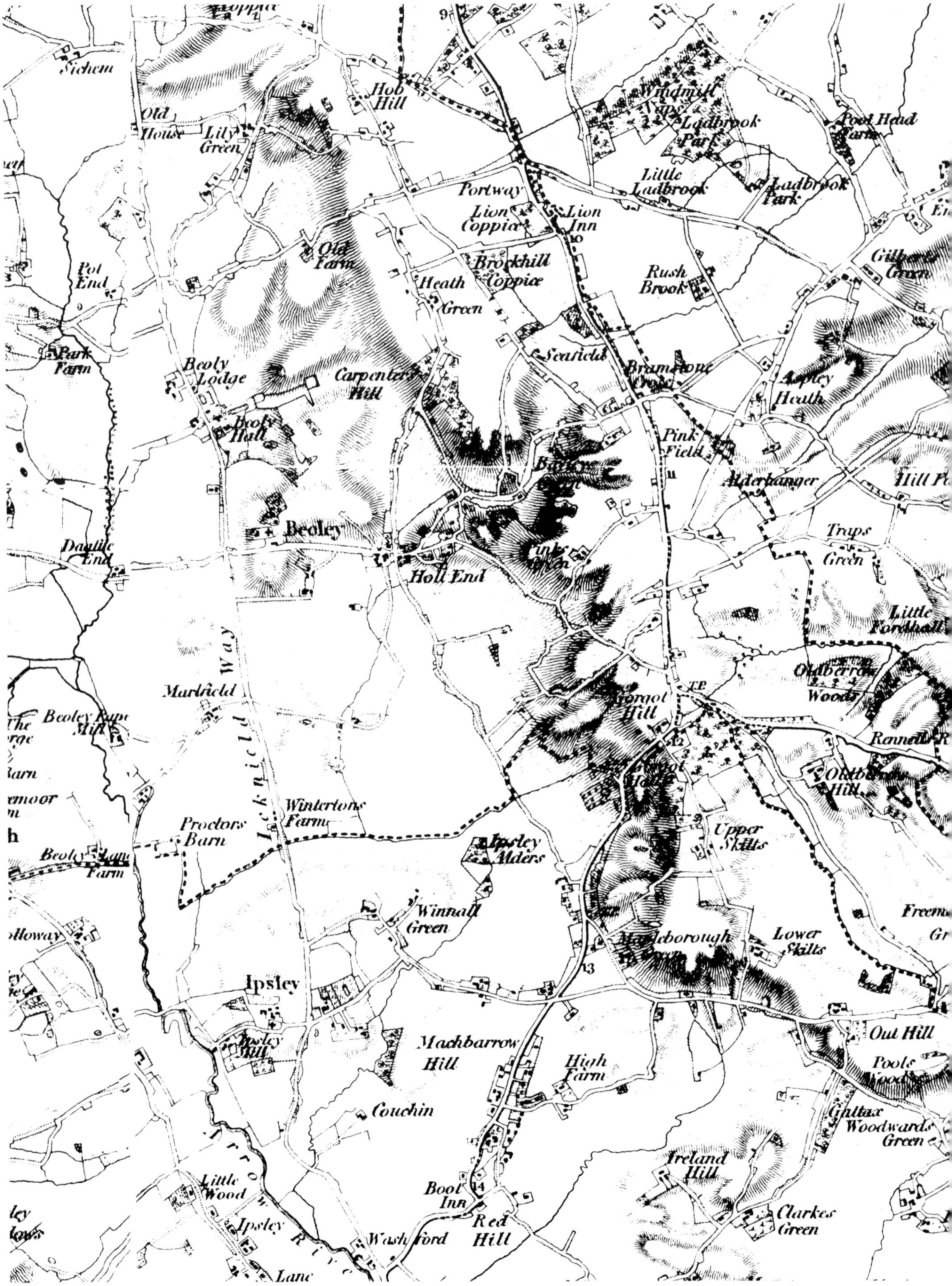

Sichem
Old House
Lily Green
Coppice
Hob Hill
Portway
Lion Coppice
Lion Inn
Windmill
Ladbrook Park
Little Ladbrook
Ladbrook Park
Pool Head Farm
Pot End
Old Farm
Heath Green
Brockhill Coppice
Rush Brook
Bramstone
Gilbert's Green
Park Farm
Beoly Lodge
Carpenters Hill
Seafield
Pink Field
Apsley Heath
Beoly Hall
Barrow
Alderhanger
Hill Pool
Beoley
Links Green
Traps Green
Daisic End
Hall End
Little Forshall
Icknield Way
Marlfield
Gorcot Hill
Oldberrow Woods
145
Beoley Rape Mill
The Gorge
Barn
moor
h
Proctors Barn
Wintertons Farm
Gorcot Hall
Rennall R.
Oldberrow Hill
Ipsley Alders
Upper Skilts
Beoley Lane Farm
Winnall Green
Holloway
Moreborough Green
Lower Skilts
Freeman Gr.
Ipsley
Out Hill
Ipsley Hill
Machbarrow Hill
High Farm
Pools Wood
Couchin
Galtax Woodwards Green
Little Wood
Boot Inn
Red Hill
Ireland Hill
Clarkes Green
Ipsley River
Washford
Lane

1   2

1 mile approx.

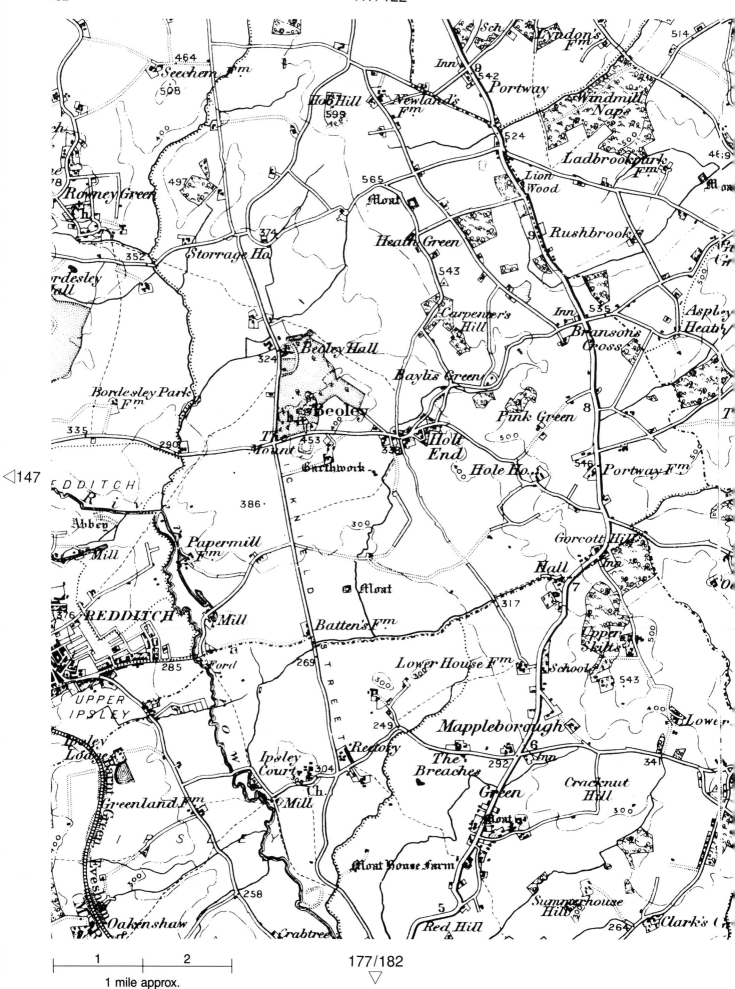

◁147

1                    2

1 mile approx.

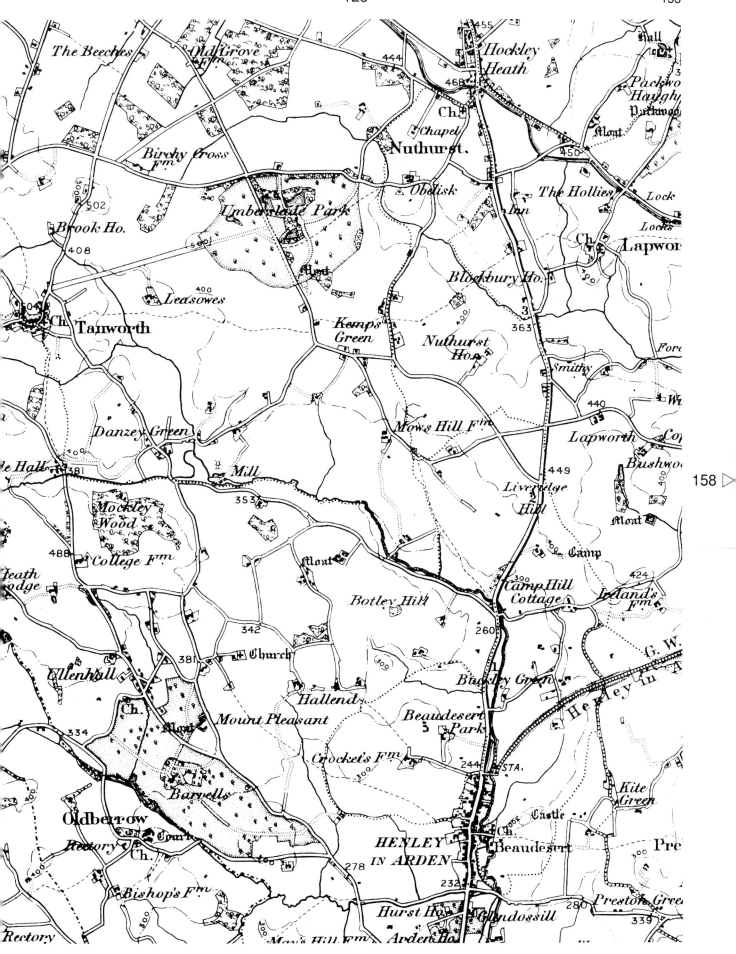

The Beeches

Old Grove F<sup>m</sup>

Hockley Heath

Hall

Packwo Haugh

Parkwo

Mont

Ch.

Birchy Cross F<sup>m</sup>

Nuthurst.

Chapel

Obelisk

The Hollies

Lock

Umberslade Park

Inn

Brook Ho.

408

500

502

Mont

Blackbury Ho.

Ch.

Lapwor

Locks

Leasowes

400

Kemps Green

Nuthurst Ho.

363

Ch.

Tanworth

Smithy

Mows Hill F<sup>m</sup>

440

Danzey Green

Lapworth

449

Bushwo

Co

Mill

Liveridge Hill

Moat

Mockley Wood

353

488

College F<sup>m</sup>

Camp

Heath Lodge

342

Botley Hill

Camp Hill Cottage

260

Ireland's F<sup>m</sup>

424

381

Church

300

Buckley Green

G. W.

Ellenhall

Hallend

Beaudesert Park

Henley in A

334

Mont

Mount Pleasant

Crocket's F<sup>m</sup>

300

244

STA.

Kite Green

Barrells

Castle

Oldberrow

Con

Ch.

HENLEY IN ARDEN

Beaudesert

Pre

Rectory

Ch.

278

232

Preston Gree

Bishop's F<sup>m</sup>

Hurst Ho.

Glendossill

280

339

Rectory

Mows Hill F<sup>m</sup>

Arden Ho.

Surveyed 1882 - 86.  Published 1895.

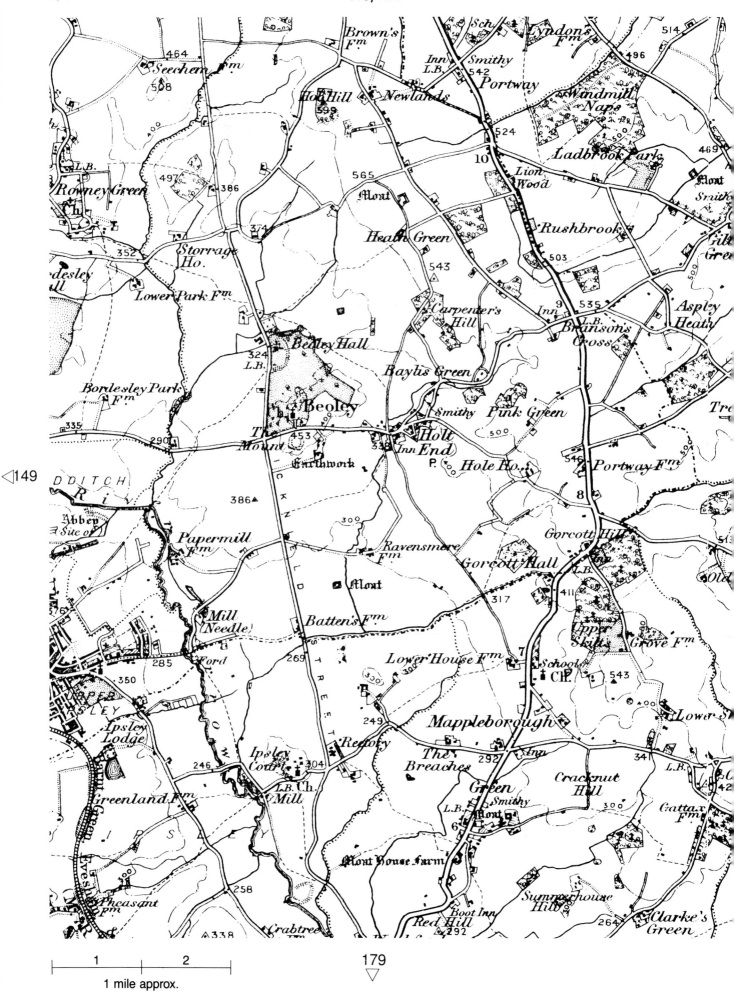

◁149

1                    2

1 mile approx.

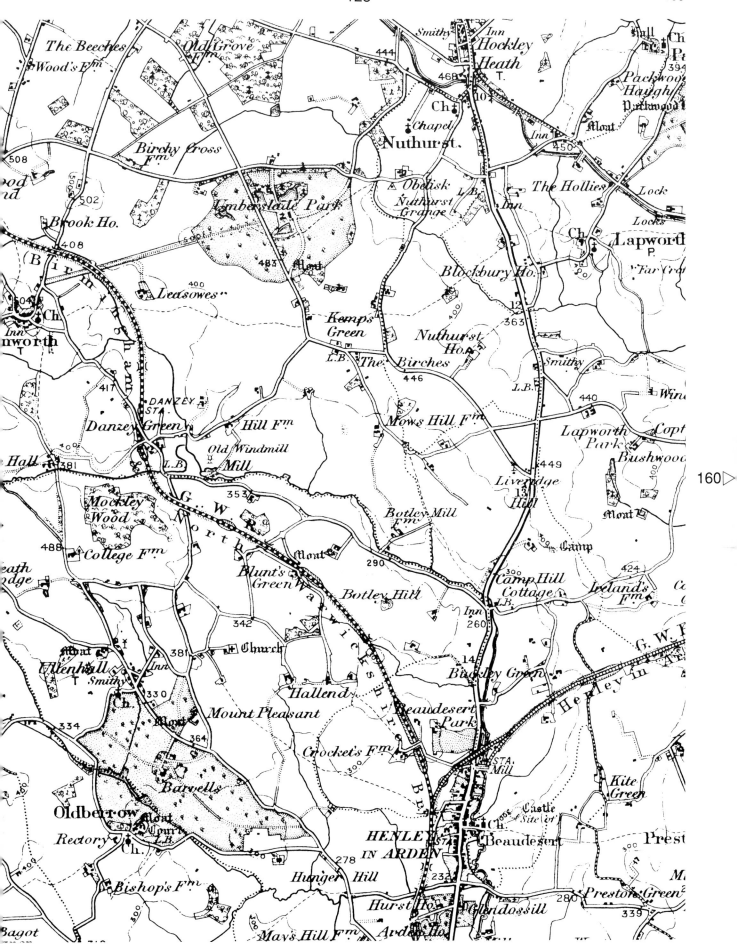

**184/185** Surveyed 1882 - 86. Revised 1906 - 7. Published 1909.

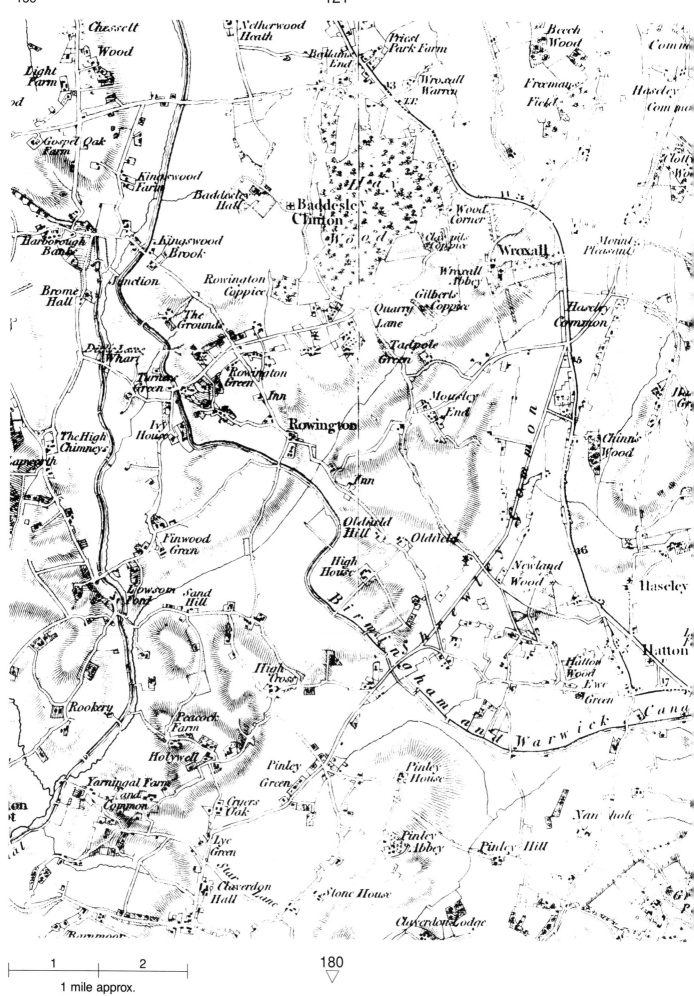

1     2

1 mile approx.

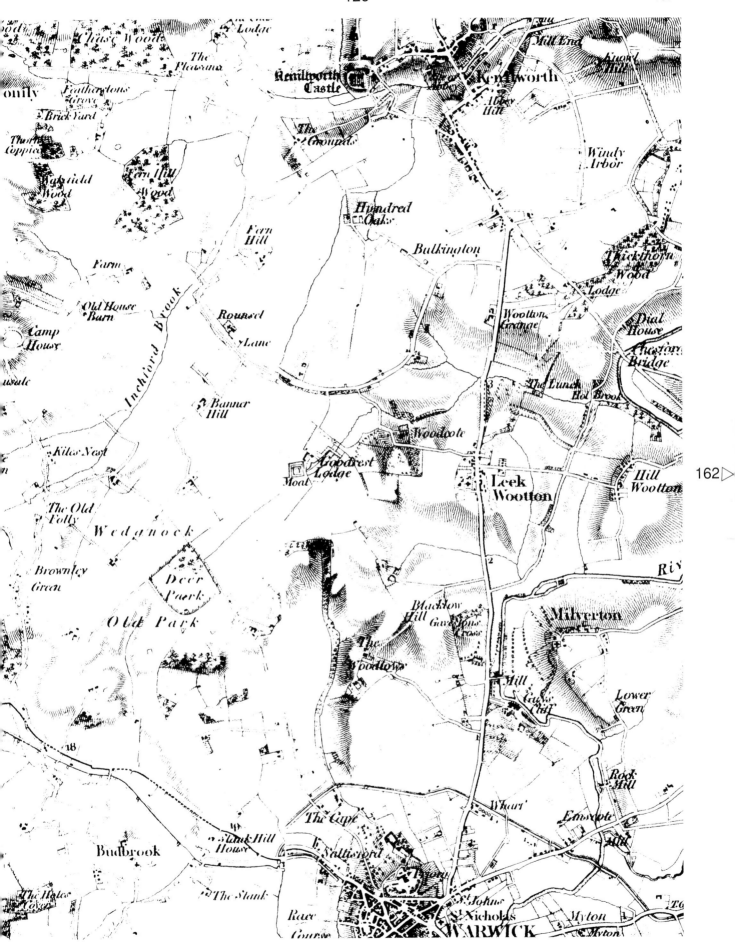

Published 1831 - 1834.

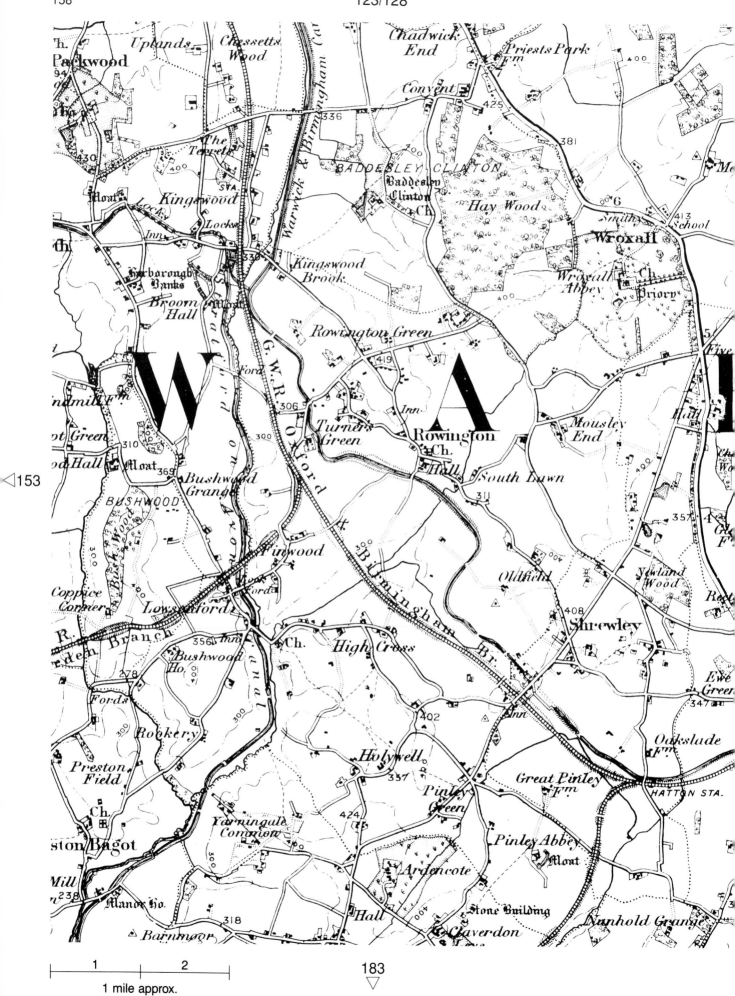

153

1        2

1 mile approx.

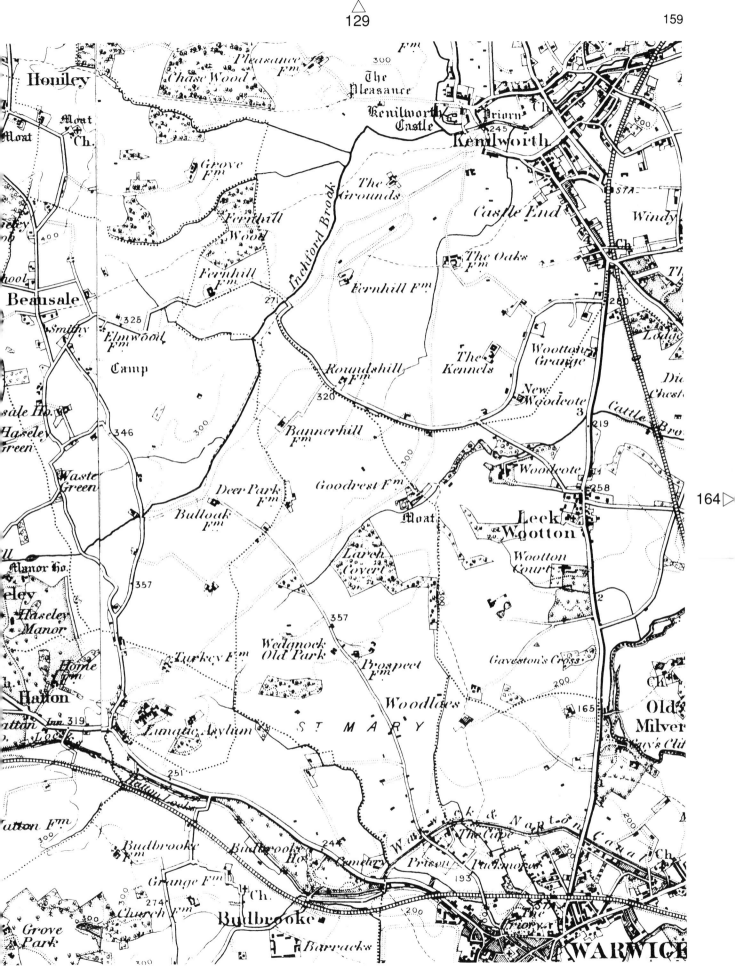

Honiley

Chase Wood

Pleasance Fm

The Pleasance

300

Moat Ch.

Moat

Grove Fm

Fernhill Wood

Kenilworth Castle

Priory

Kenilworth

245

STA

Windy

The Grounds

Castle End

Ch

Fernhill Fm

271

Inchford Brook

The Oaks Fm

Fernhill Fm

280

Beausale

325

Smithy

Elmwood Fm

Camp

Roundshill Fm

320

The Kennels

The Fm

Wootton Grange

New Woodcote

3

Die Chest

Cattle Bro

sale Ho.

Haseley Green

346

300

Bannerhill Fm

300

Woodcote

219

258

164 ▷

Waste Green

Deer Park Fm

Goodrest Fm

Moat

Leek Wootton

Bulloak Fm

Larch Covert

Wootton Court

ll Manor Ho.

eley

357

Haseley Manor

Wedgnock Old Park

357

2

Gaveston's Cross

200

Old Milver

Home Fm

Turkey Fm

Prospect Fm

165

Hatton

Inn 319

Lunatic Asylum

Woodloes

S T   M A R Y

attan Lock

251

Warwick & Narton Canal

Hatton Locks

Grove Park

natton Fm

300

Budbrooke Fm

Budbrooke Ho.

24

Cemetery

The Cape

Warwick

Priory Packmores

193

Grange Fm

Ch.

274

Church Fm

Budbrooke

200

The Priory

Grove Park

300

Barracks

WARWICK

Surveyed 1882 - 86.  Published 1892.

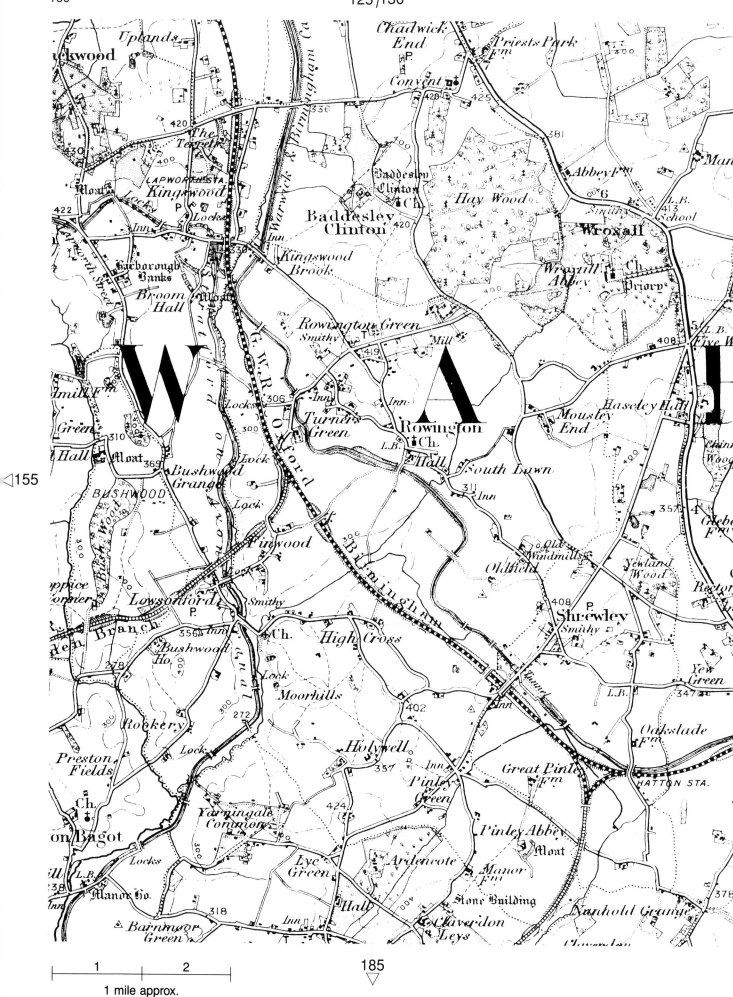

◁155

1      2

1 mile approx.

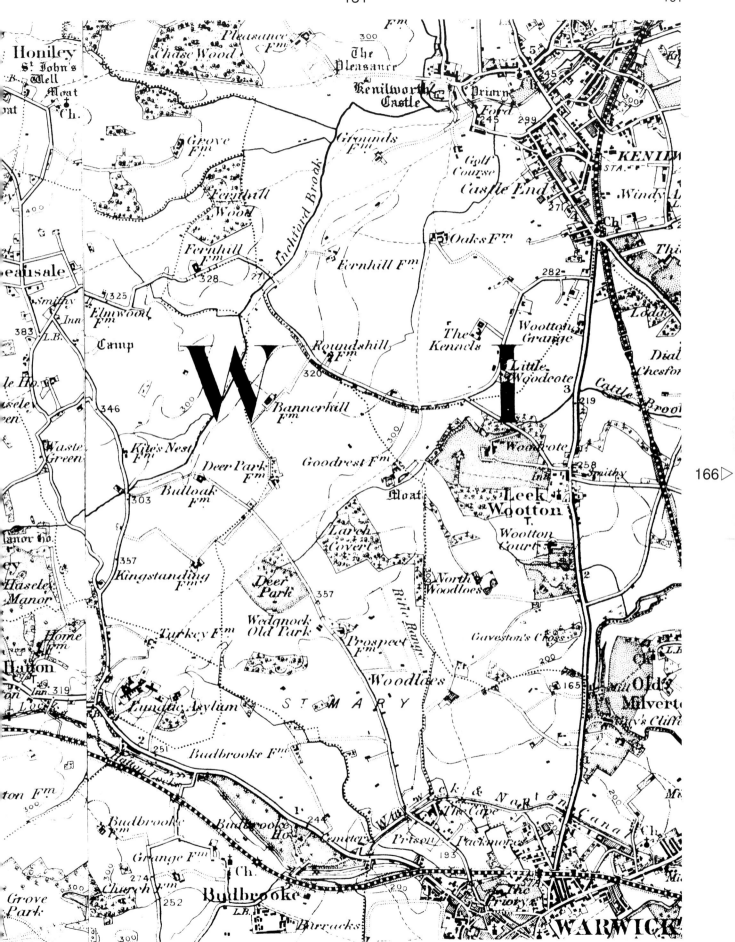

166 ▷

Honiley
St John's
Well
Moat
Ch.

Chase Wood

Pleasance
Fm

The
Pleasance

300

Kenilworth
Castle

Priory
Ford

245

299

KENIL

STA.

Windy

Grove
Fm

Grounds
Fm

Golf
Course

Castle End

Ch.

Fernhill
Wood

Oaks Fm

282

The
Kennels

Wootton
Grange

Lodge

eausale

Fernhill
Fm

328

27

Fernhill Fm

Dial
Chesfor

Smithy
Inn
Elmwood
Fm

325

Roundshill
Fm

The
Kennels

Little
Woodcote
3

Cattle
Broo

383

L.B.

Camp

320

219

Waste
Green

346

300

Bannerhill
Fm

Woodcote

258

Smithy

Kite's Nest
Fm

Deer Park
Fm

Goodrest Fm

300

Leek
Wootton
T.

166 ▷

Bulloak
Fm

303

Moat

Wootton
Court

Larch
Covert

Manor Ho.

357

Deer
Park

357

North
Woodloes

Haseley
Manor

Kingstanding
Fm

Wedgnock
Old Park

Rifle Range

Gaveston's Cross

200

Home
Farm

Turkey Fm

Prospect
Fm

165

Old
Milverton

Hatton

319

Lunatic Asylum

ST. MARY

Woodloes

Cliffe

251

Budbrooke Fm

Warwick & Napton Canal

The Cape

Budbrooke

Budbrooke
Ho.

Cemetery

244

Prison

Packmores

193

Grove
Park

274

Grange Fm

Church Fm

Ch.

252

The
Priory

Budbrooke

L.B.

Barracks

WARWICK

Surveyed 1883 - 86. Revised 1906 - 7. Published 1908.

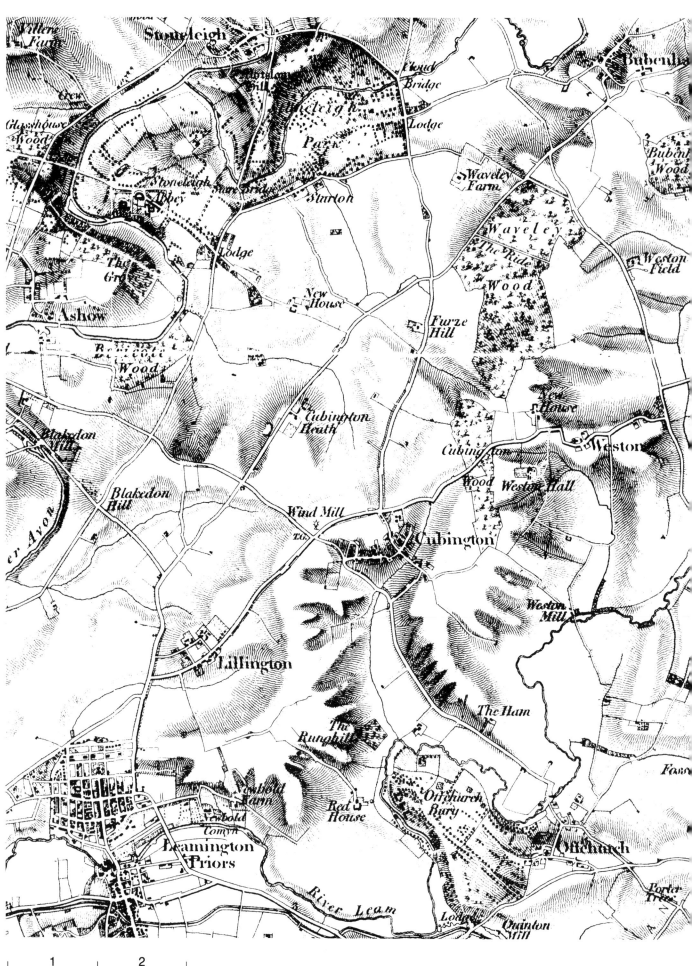

1      2

1 mile approx.

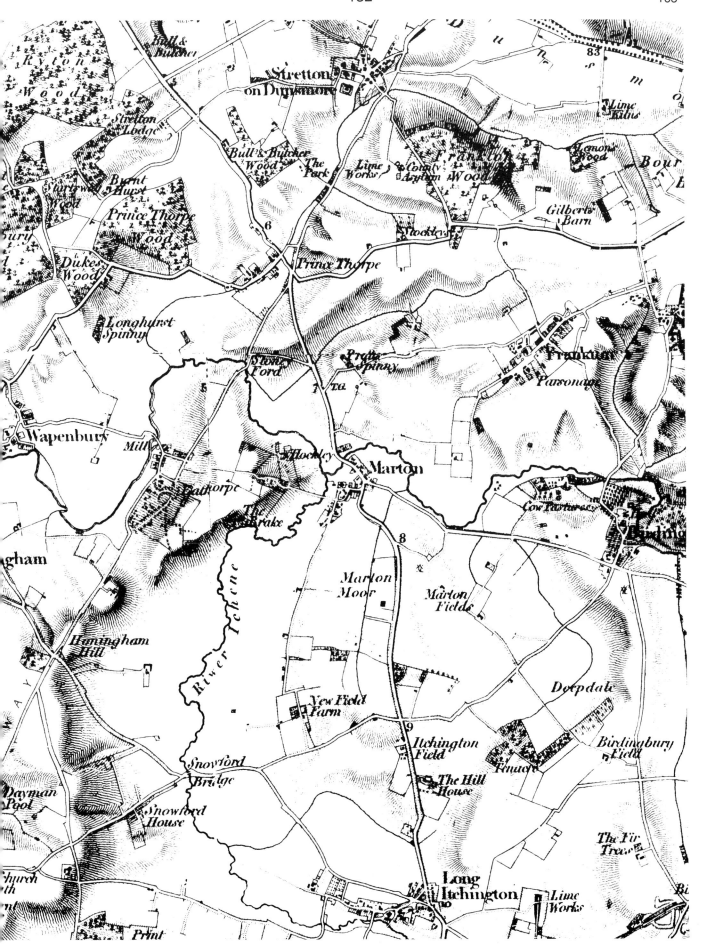

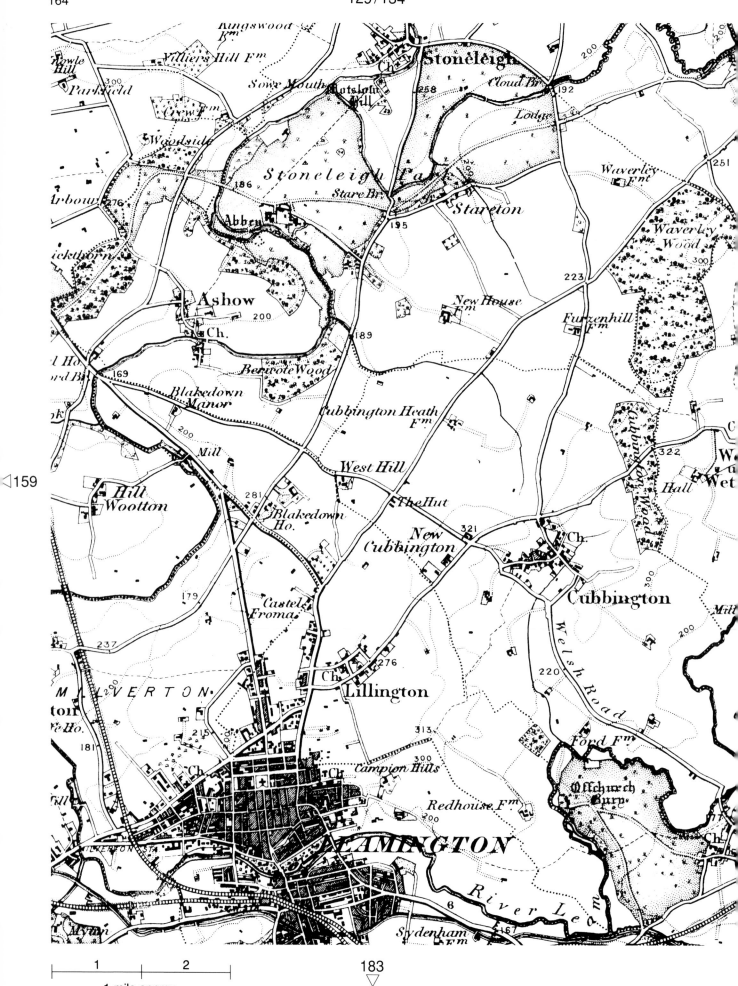

1 mile approx.

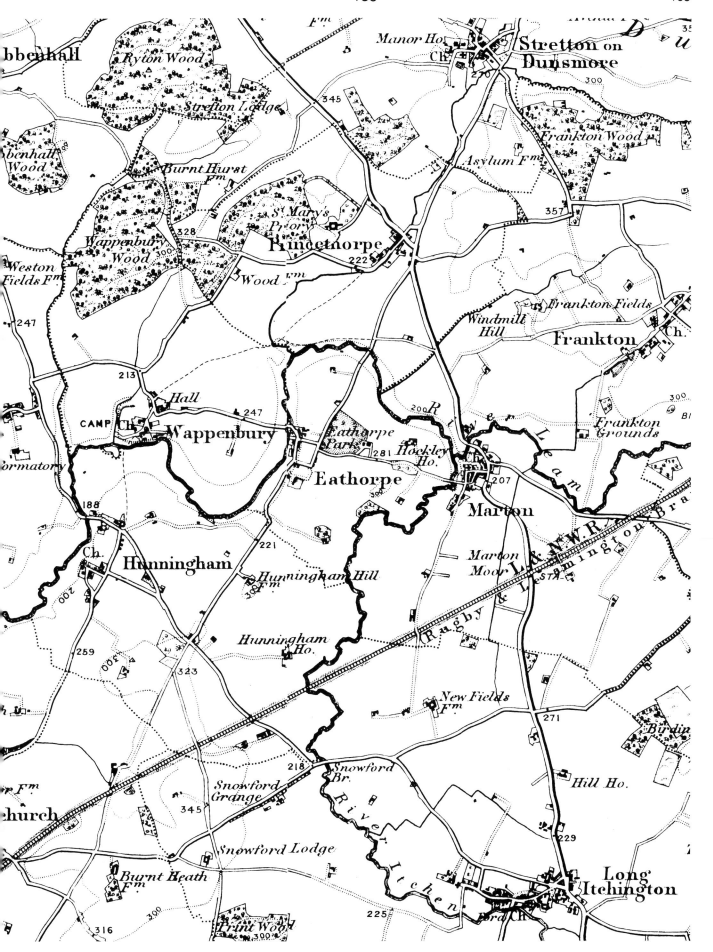

Surveyed 1883 - 86. Published 1892.

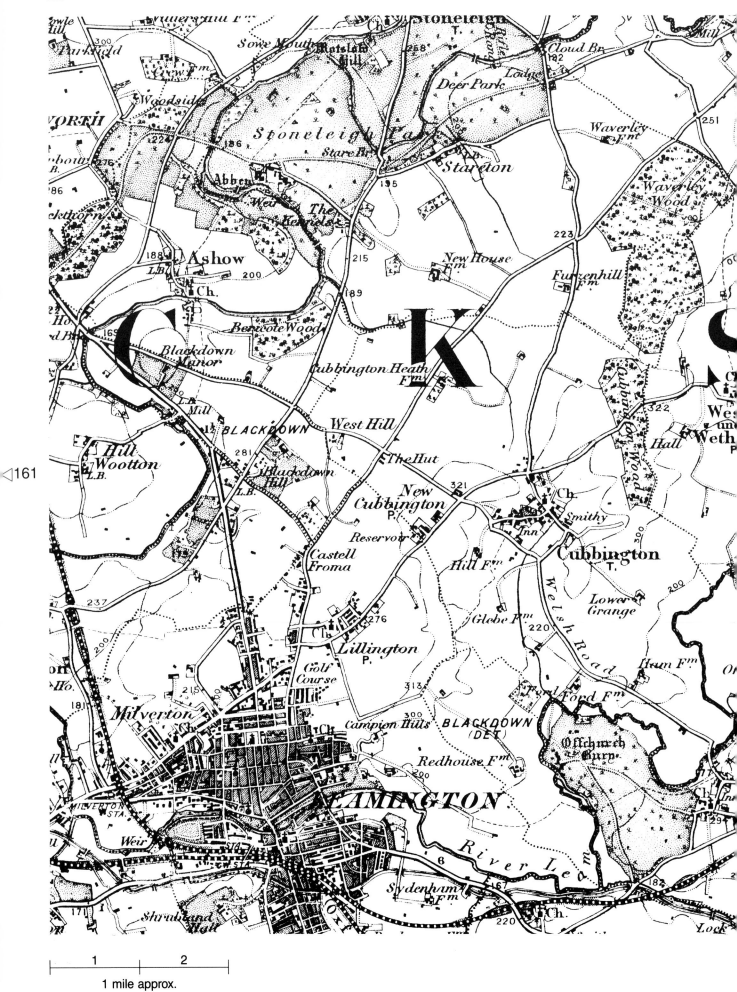

1 mile approx.

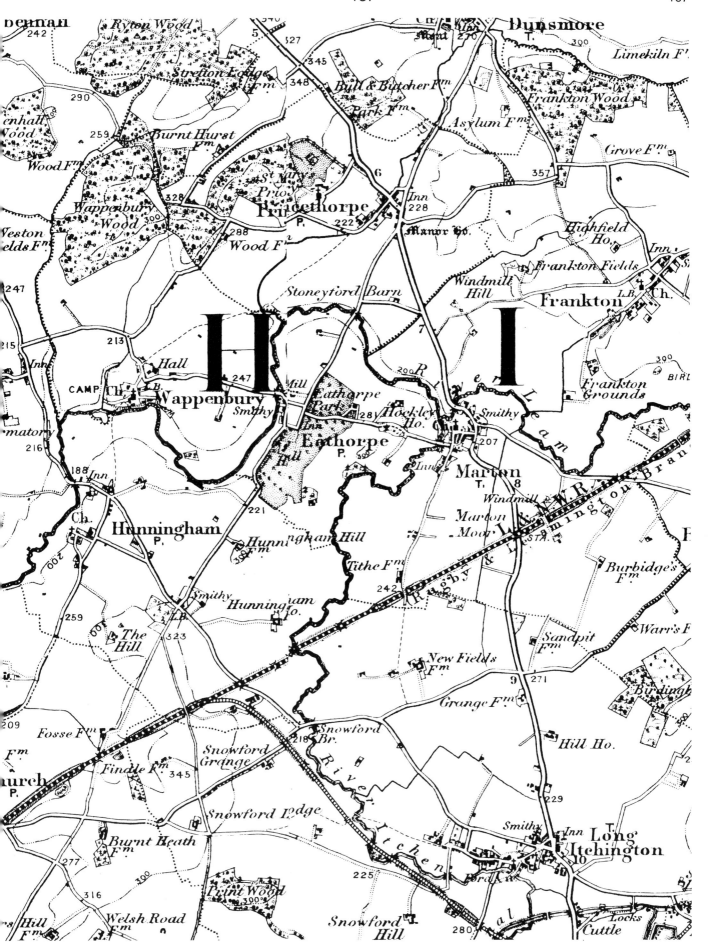

Surveyed 1883 - 86. Revised 1906 - 7. Published 1908.

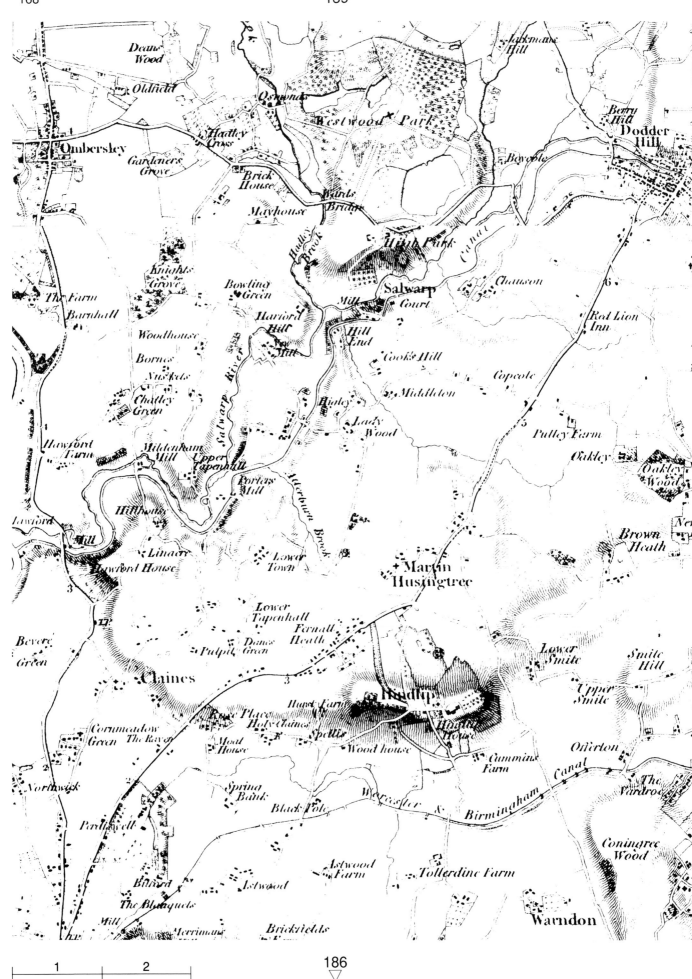

Deans Wood

Oldfield

Oswonds

Westwood Park

Jackmans Hill

Berry Hill

Dodder Hill

Ombersley

Hadley Cross

Gardeners Grove

Brick House

Mayhouse

Wards Bridge

Bevere

High Park

Canal

Knights Grove

Bowling Green

Hadley Brook

Salwarp

Chauson

6

The Farm

Barnhall

Woodhouse

Harford Hill

Mill

Hill End

Cook's Hill

Red Lion Inn

Bornes

Nuskets

Chatley Green

Salwarp River

Higley

Lady Wood

Middleton

Copcote

5

Pulley Farm

Oakley

Oakley Wood

Hawford Farm

Mildenham Mill

Upper Tapenhill

Porters Mill

Adderburn Brook

Brown Heath

New F

Hawford

Hillhouse

Linacr

Hawford House

3

Lower Town

Martin Hasingtree

Lower Tapenhall

17

Fernall Heath

Lower Smite

Smite Hill

Bevere Green

Pulpit

Danes Green

Upper Smite

Claines

3

Hadlip

Coremeadow Green

The Ray

Hunt Farm

Rose Place

Holy Claines

Spettis

Hadlip House

Offerton

Moat House

Wood house

Cumming Farm

Northwick

2

Spring Bank

Worcester &

Birmingham

Canal

The Vardroc

Parliwell

Black Pole

Coningree Wood

Billford

Astwood Farm

Astwood

Tollerdine Farm

The Blanquets

Mill

Merriman

Brickfields

Warndon

1          2

1 mile approx.

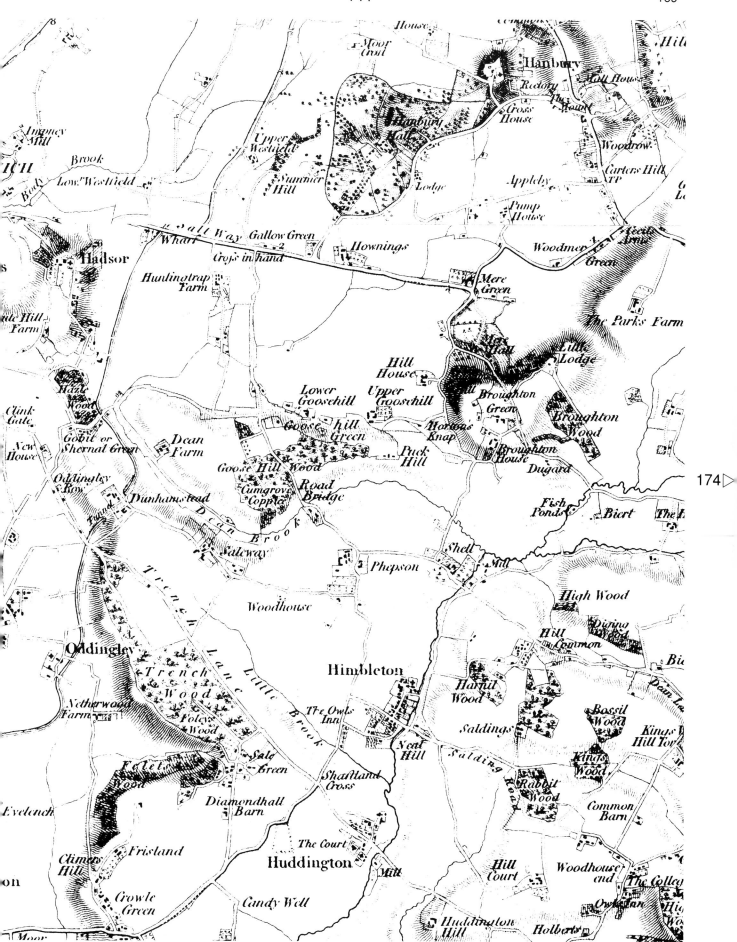

174 ▷

Published 1831.

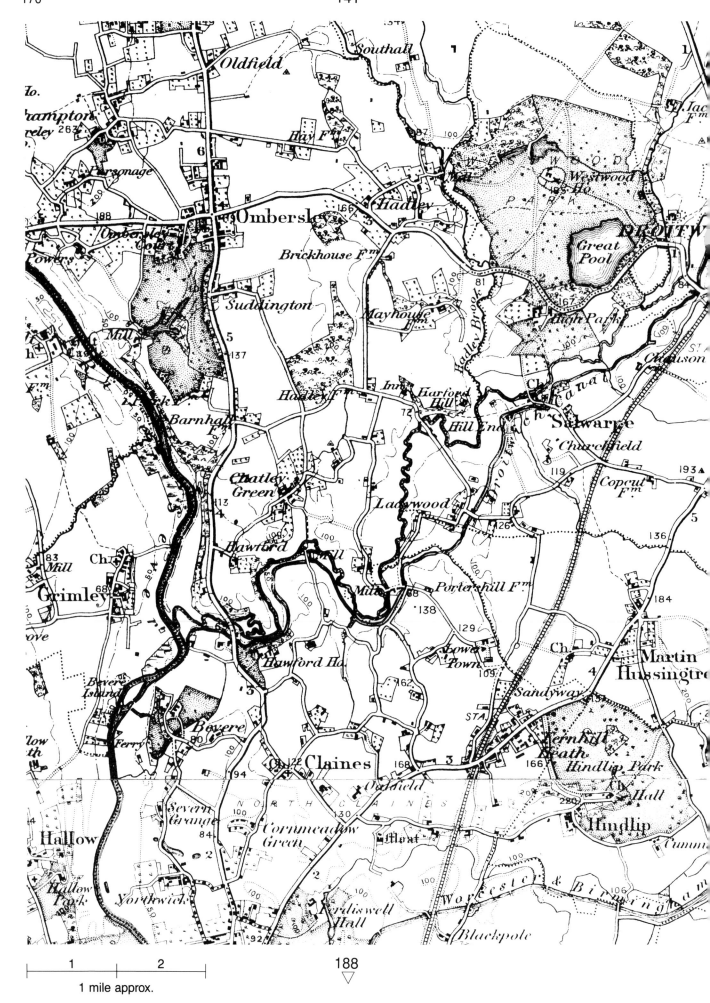

1       2

1 mile approx.

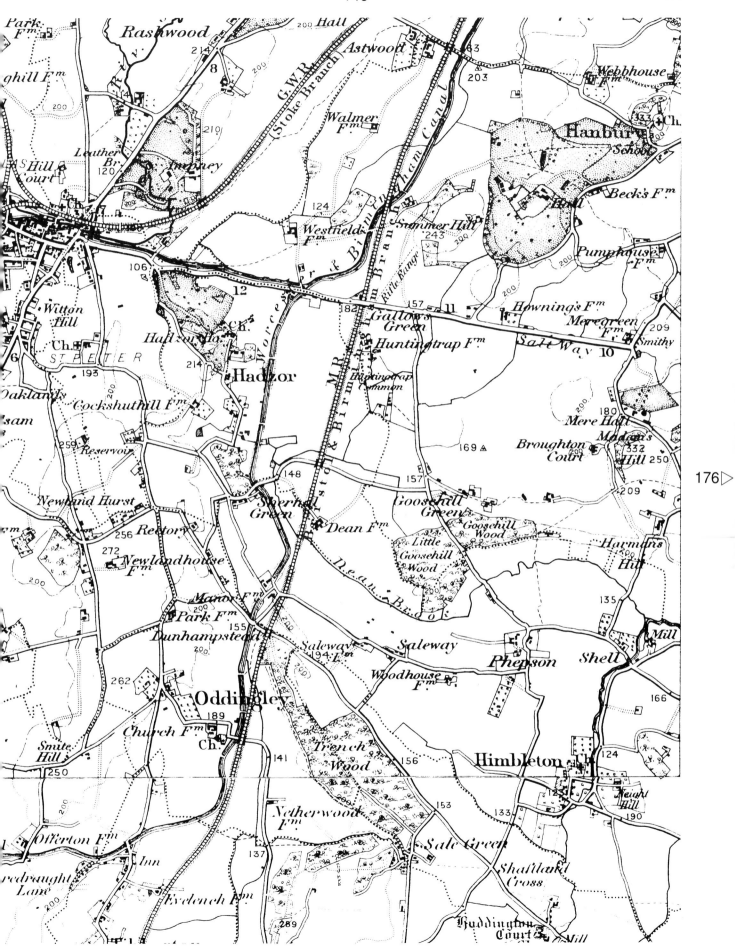

Surveyed 1882 - 86. Published 1893 / 1895.

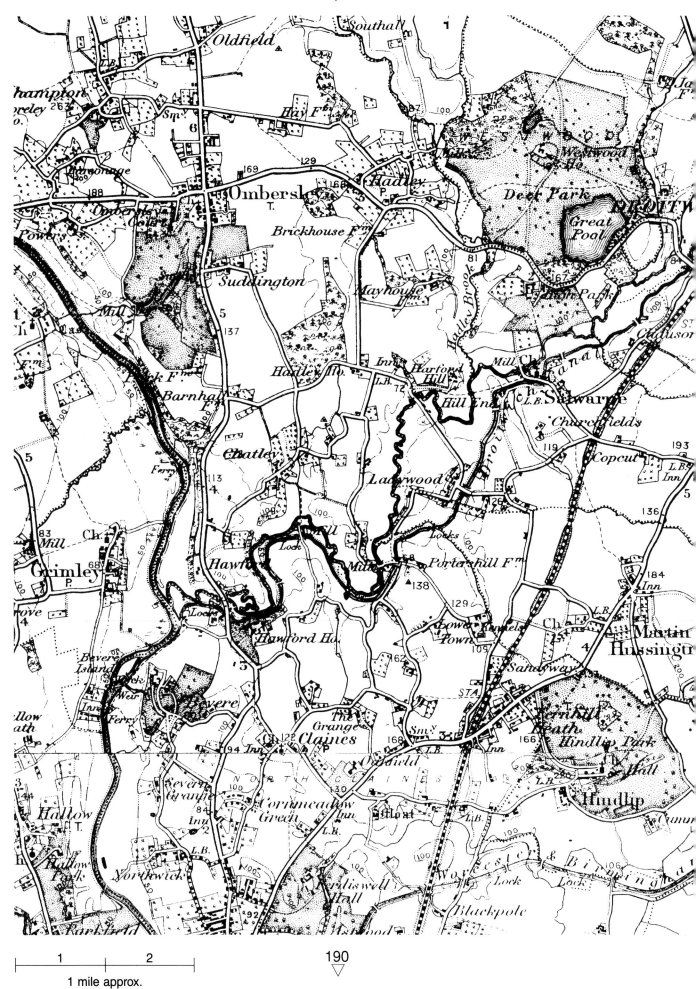

1     2

1 mile approx.

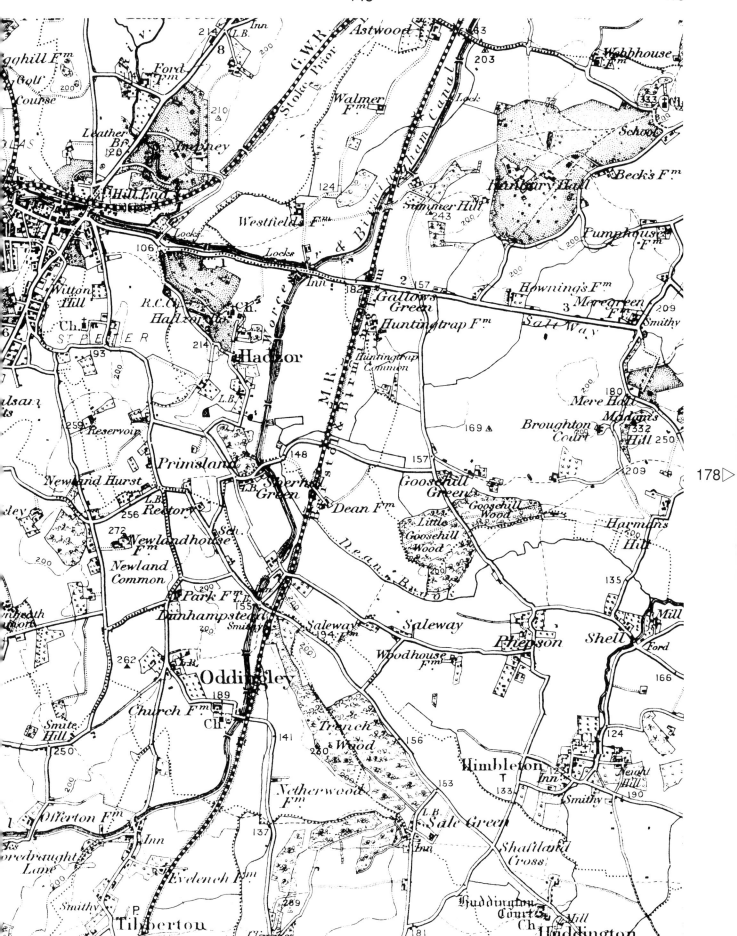

178▷

Surveyed 1882 - 86. Revised 1907. Published 1909.

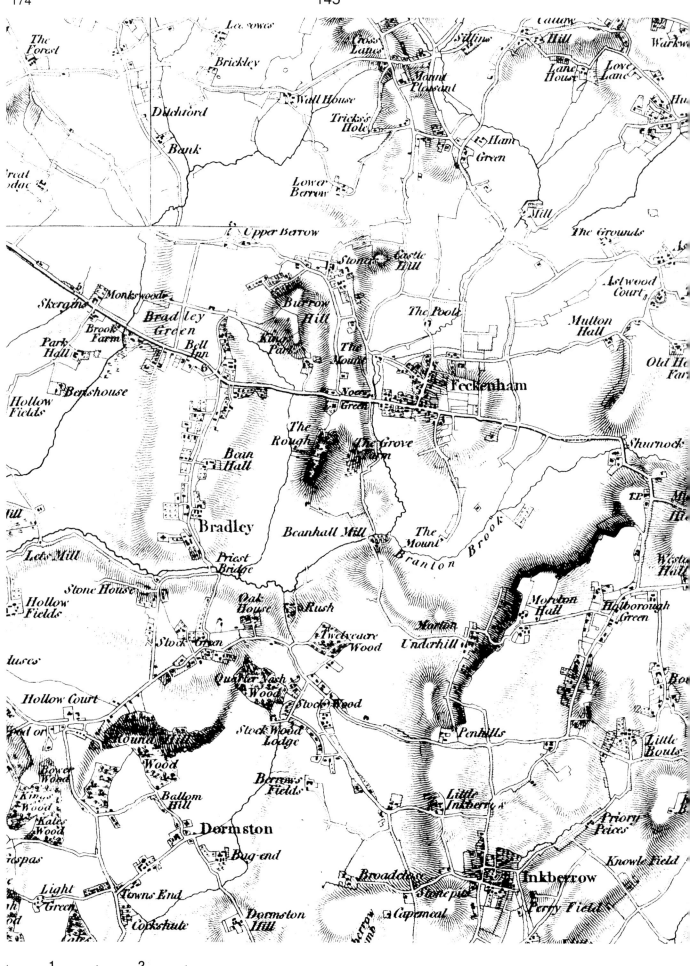

169

The Forest

Brickley

Ditchford

Bank

Great Lodge

Leasowes

Wall House

Trick's Hole

Cross Lanes

Mount Pleasant

Siftins

Hill

Lane House

Lower Lane

Warkwe

Catswe

Lower Berrow

Ham Green

Mill

The Grounds

Upper Berrow

Stone

Castle Hill

The Pool

Astwood Court

Monkswood

Skergins

Bradley Green

Burrow Hill

Kings Park

The Mount

Feckenham

Multon Hall

Old He Far

Brook Farm

Bell Inn

Noor Green

Shurnock

Park Hall

Benshouse

Hollow Fields

The Rough

Bean Hall

The Grove Farm

T.P.

Mi Hi

Hill

Bradley

Beanhall Mill

The Mount

Branton Brook

Westa Hall

Lets Mill

Priest Bridge

Morton Hall

Holborough Green

Stone House

Hollow Fields

Oak House

Rush

Twelveacre Wood

Morton

Underhill

Stock Green

Quarter Nash Wood

Stock Wood

Penhills

Little Bouts

Hollow Court

uses

od or

Mount Wood

Stock Wood Lodge

Bower Wood

Kings Wood

Kates Wood

Ballom Hill

Berrow's Fields

Little Inkberro

Priory Peices

Dormston

Bug end

Broadclose

Stonepits

Inkberrow

Knowle Field

Grispas

Light Green

Towns End

Cookshute

Dormston Hill

Capmeal

Perry Field

herro

1      2

1 mile approx.

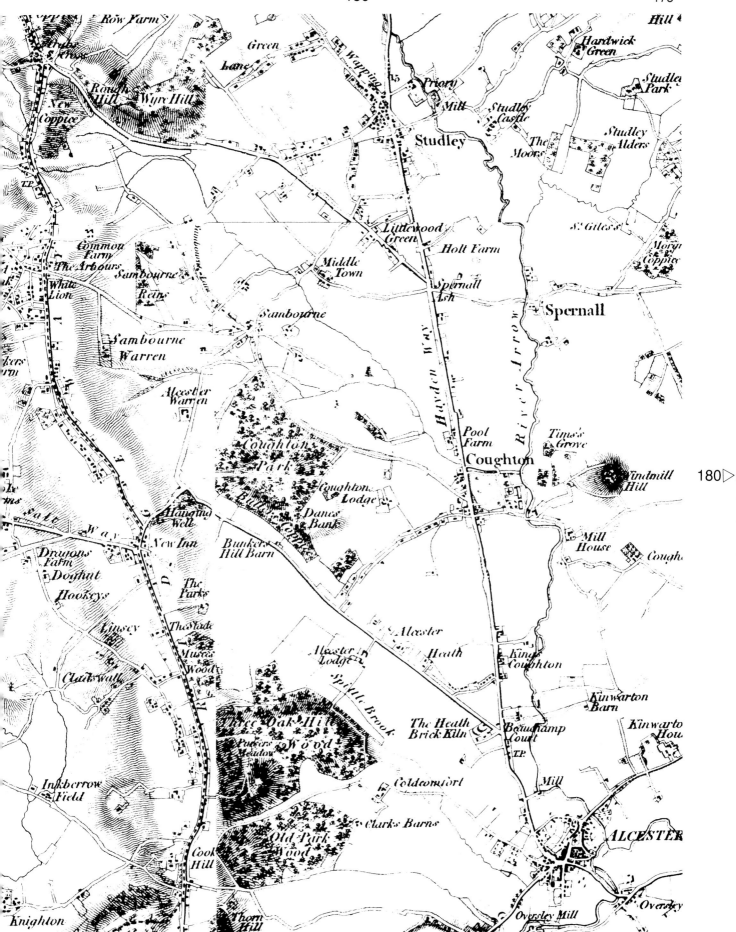

△

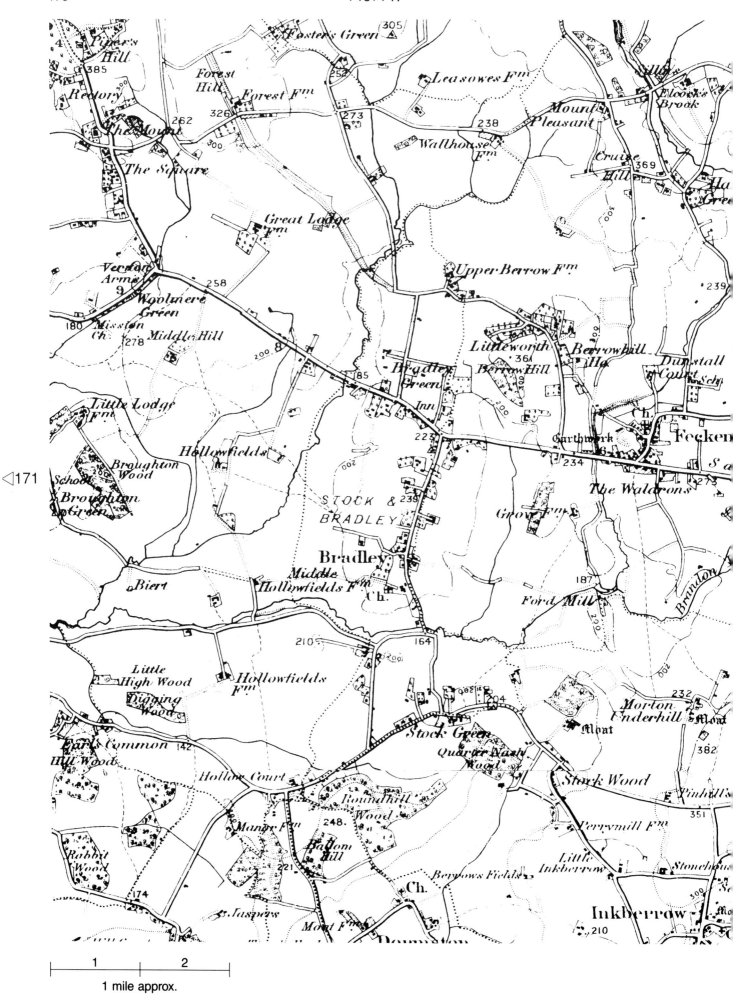

4 *Piper's*
*Hill*
385

*Forest*
*Hill*

*Foster's Green*
305 △

252

*Leasowes Fm*

*Elcock's*
*Brook*

*Rectory*
262
326 *Forest Fm*
273
238
*Mount*
*Pleasant*

300

*The Mount*
300

*Walthouse*
*Fm*

*Cruise*
*Hill* 369
300

*The Square*

*Great Lodge*
*Fm*

*Upper Berrow Fm*

239

*Vectar*
*Arms*
9 258

*Woolmere*
*Green*

180 *Mission*
*Ch.* 278 *Middle Hill*
200 8

*Littleworth*
*Berrow Hill*
361
300
*Berrowhill*
*Ha*

*Dunstall*
*Court* *Sch*

85 *Bradley*
*Green*

*Inn*
200

*Ch.*

*Feck*

*Little Lodge*
*Fm*

*Hollowfields*
200
223

*Earthwork*
6

234
273

*School*
*Broughton*
*Wood*
200

STOCK &
BRADLEY
239

*Grove Fm*

*The Waldrons*

*Broughton*
*Green*

*Bradley*

*Biert*
*Middle*
*Hollowfields Fm*
*Ch.*

187
*Ford Mill*
290

*Brandon*

210
164
200

*Little*
*High Wood*
*Hollowfields*
*Fm*

204

232
*Morton*
*Underhill* *Moat*

*Digging*
*Wood*

380
300

*Moat*
382

*Earls Common*
*Hill Wood* 142

*Hollow Court*

*Stock Green*

*Quarter Nash*
*Wood*
*Stock Wood*

*Pinhill's*
351

*Roundhill*
*Wood*
*Perrymill Fm*

*Rabbit*
*Wood*
*Manor Fm*
248

*Little*
*Inkberrow*
*Stonehou*

*Batton*
*Hill*
221

174
*Ch.*
*Berrows Fields*

*St Jaspers*
*Mort Fm*
*Ch.*
*Inkberrow*
210
300

◁171

◁171

1          2

1 mile approx.

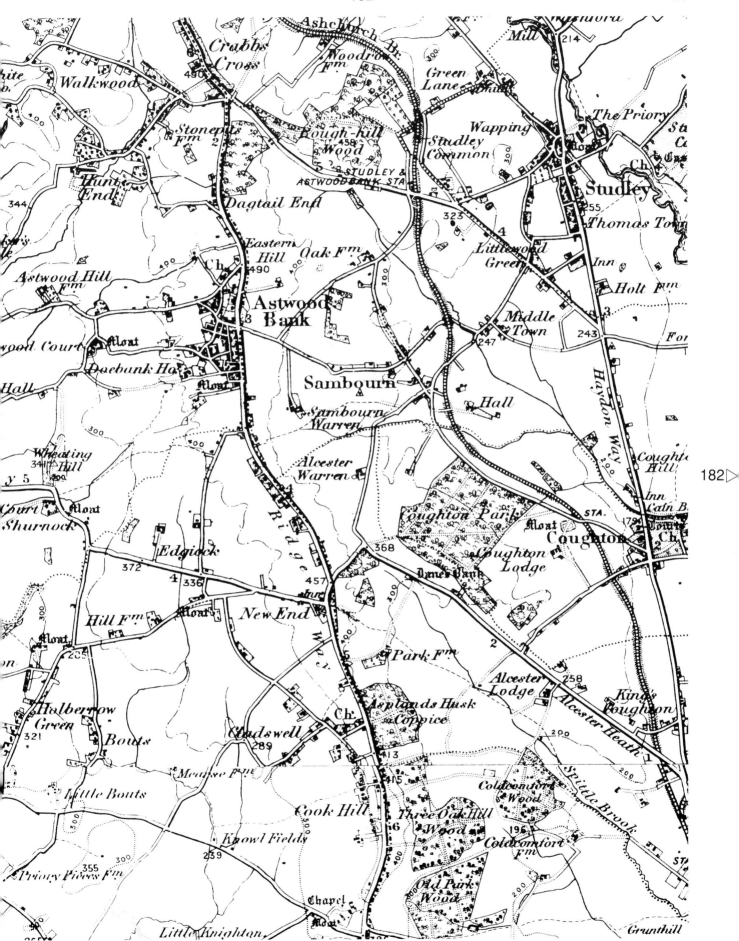

Surveyed 1882 - 85.  Published 1892.

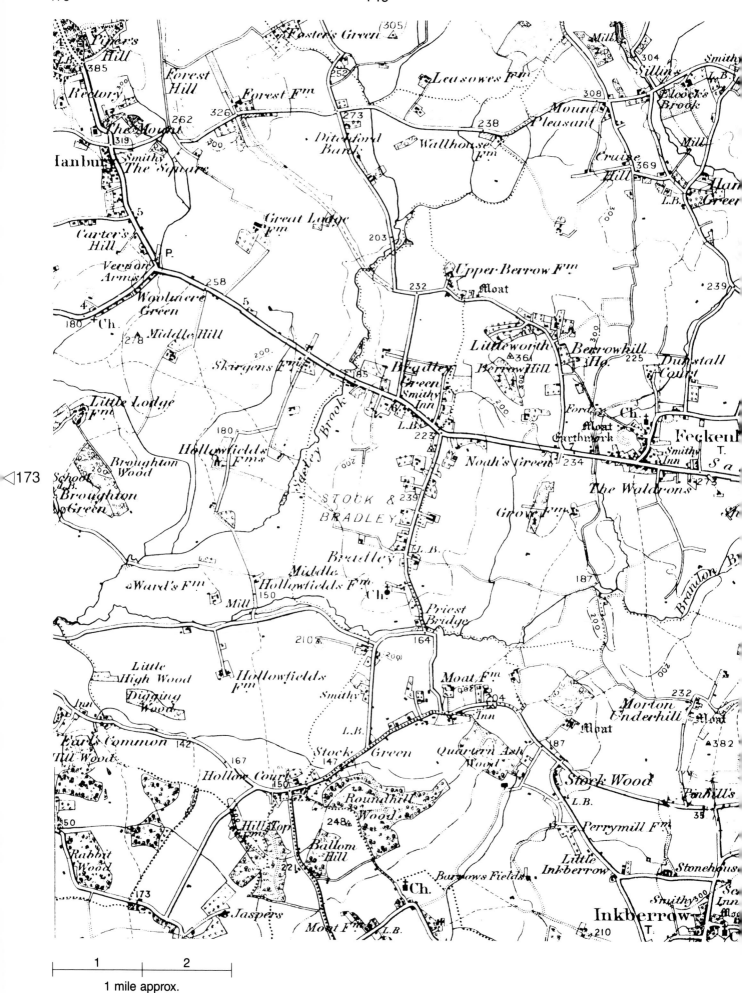

149

173

Piper's Hill
385

Forest Hill

Foster's Green
(305)

Leasowes Fm

Mill
304
Smith
Gilling

Ilcock's Brook

Rectory

Forest Fm

262
326

273

252

238

Mount Pleasant

308

The Mount
319

Ditenford Bank

Wallhouse Fm

Mill

Hanbury

Smith's
The Square

300

Cruise Hill
369

L.B.

Han Green

5

Great Lodge Fm

203

Upper Berrow Fm

Moat

300

239

Carter's Hill

P.

Vernon Arms

258

232

Woolmere Green

5

Littleworth
361

Berrowhill

Dunstall Court

180
Ch.

Middle Hill
278

200

Skargens Fm

185

Bradley Green

Smithy Inn

Berrow Hill

225

300

200

Forde

Ch.

Little Lodge Fm

180

Sapley Brook

L.B.
223

Garthwork

Moat

Feckenh

T.

Hollowfields Fms

007

Noah's Green

234

Smith Inn

Sa

School

Broughton Wood

L.B.

239

STOCK &

Grove Fm

The Waldrons

Broughton Green

BRADLEY

200

Ward's Fm

Middle Hollowfields Fm

Bradley

L.B.

Mill
150

Ch.

187

Brandon B.

Priest Bridge

Little High Wood

210

164

Moat Fm

Morton Underhill

232

Digging Wood

Hollowfields Fm

200

204

Smithy

Moat

382

Inn

L.B.

Inn

187

Earl's Common
142

Stock Green
147

Quarurn Ash Wood

Stock Wood

Till Wood

167

Hollow Court
150

Roundhill Wood

L.B.

Perrymill Fm

Pinhill's
35

50

Hill Top Fm

248

221

Little Inkberrow

Stonehous

Rabbit Wood

Ballom Hill

Barrows Fields

Smithy
Sa Inn

173

Jaspers

Moat Fm

L.B.

Ch.

Inkberrow
210
T.

1          2

1 mile approx.

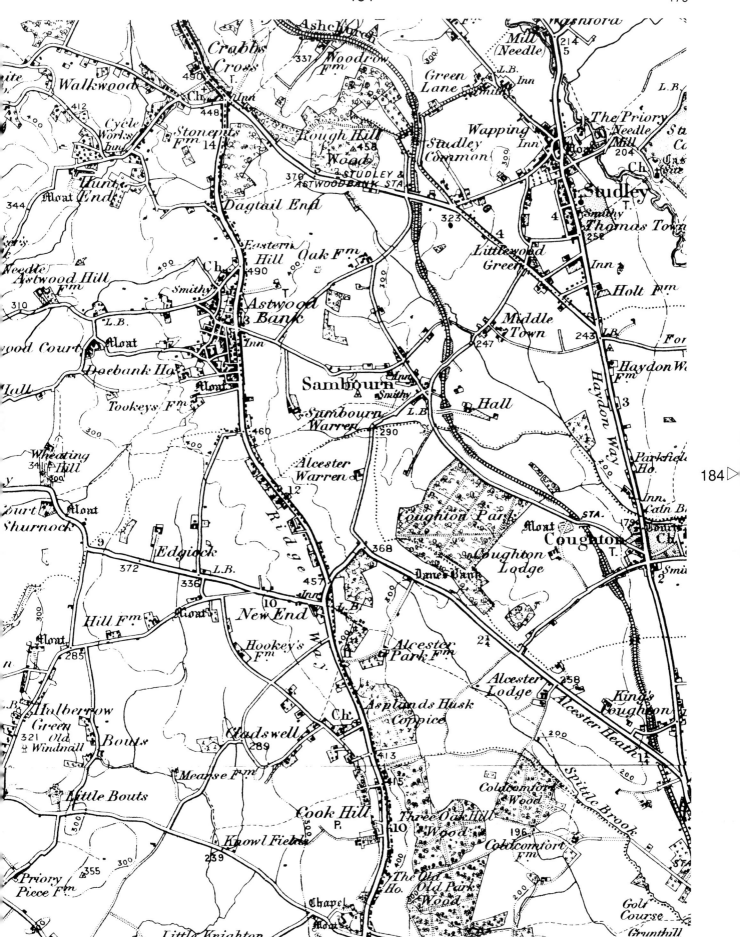

Surveyed 1882 - 85. Revised 1906 - 7. Published 1908.

Morton
Mill

Morton Bagot

Forest Nap
Bannams
Wood

Browns
Wood

Five
Acres

Merryfield
Green

Farm

Mill
Wood

Gibb
Bag

Greenhill
Green

Morton
Common

Wawens Moor

Torewood
Farm

Wootton
Wawen

Wootton Ha

Par

Stoopers
Wood

Badbury
Hill

Spernall
Park

Shelfield

Shelfield
Lodge

Shelfield

Burford Lane

Clayhill
Farm

Wootton
Park

Mill

The H

Upper
Spernall

Pennyford

Collister
Wood

Shelfield
Green

Gray
Mill

Alne
Wood

Browns
Wood

Wood
House

Little
Alne

Hills

The Folly
Farm

Silo

New End

Field
Barn

on fields

Aston
Cantlow

Newnh

Great Alne

Alne
End

Gt Alne
Work
House

Aston
Barn

Gipsey
Hall

Alne River

Mill

Hasler
Grounds

Holdings
Farm

Wood
Barn

Kinwarton

Walcote

Grove

Home Mill

Hazeler

Wibmoo

Trench Lane
T.P

Barn

6

Upton

Green

The Hill

Withcome
Wood

Billesley

Published 1831.

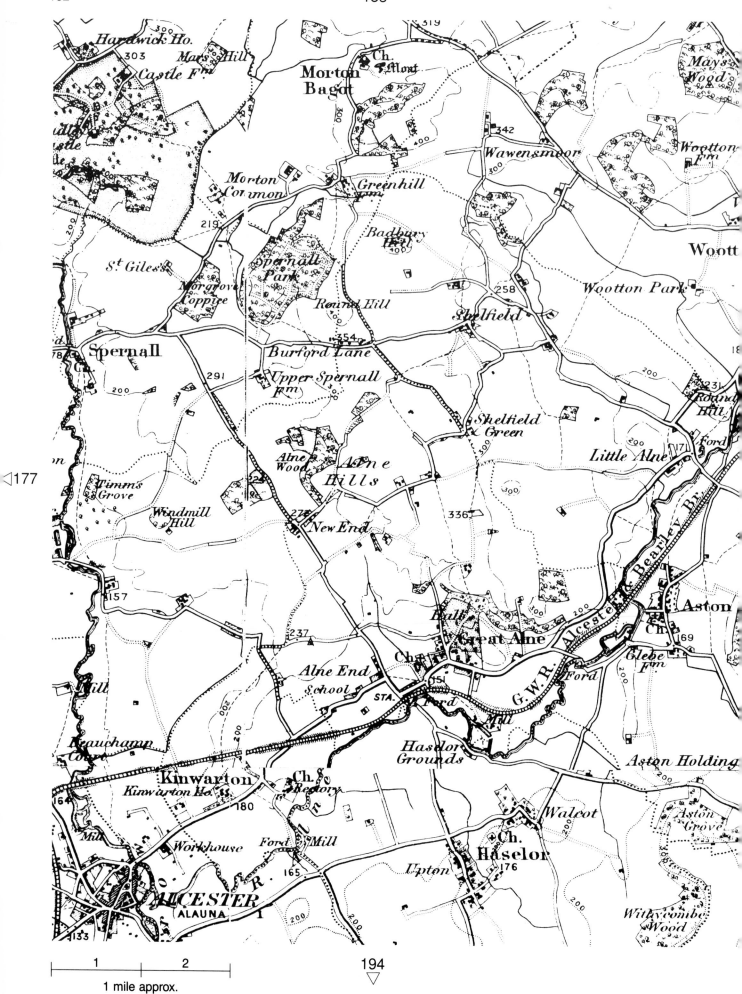

Hardwick Ho.

303

Mars Hill

Castle Fm

Morton
Bagot

Ch.

Moat

319

Mays
Wood

342

Wawensmoor

Wootton
Fm

300

Morton
Common

Greenhill
Fm

300

Woott

200

219

St Giles's

Spernall
Park

Badbury
Hill

400

258

Wootton Park

Morgrove
Coppice

Round Hill

Shelfield

18

354

Burford Lane

200

Spernall

291

Upper Spernall
Fm

231

Round
Hill

200

Ford

177

200

Timm's
Grove

Alne
Wood

Alne
Hills

Shelfield
Green

300

200

Little Alne

171

336

Windmill
Hill

275

New End

300

157

Aston

237

Hall

Great Alne

Ch.

69

Alne End
School

Ch.

Glebe
Fm

Ford

200

STA.

Ford

Mill

G.W.R.

Alcester & Bearley Br.

Beauchamp
Court

Haselor
Grounds

Aston Holding

200

Kinwarton

Ch.

Rectory

Walcot

200

Aston
Grove

164

Kinwarton Ho.

180

Mill

Workhouse

Ford

Mill

Ch.

Haselor

176

165

Upton

200

ALCESTER

ALAUNA

200

200

Withycombe
Wood

133

1          2

1 mile approx.

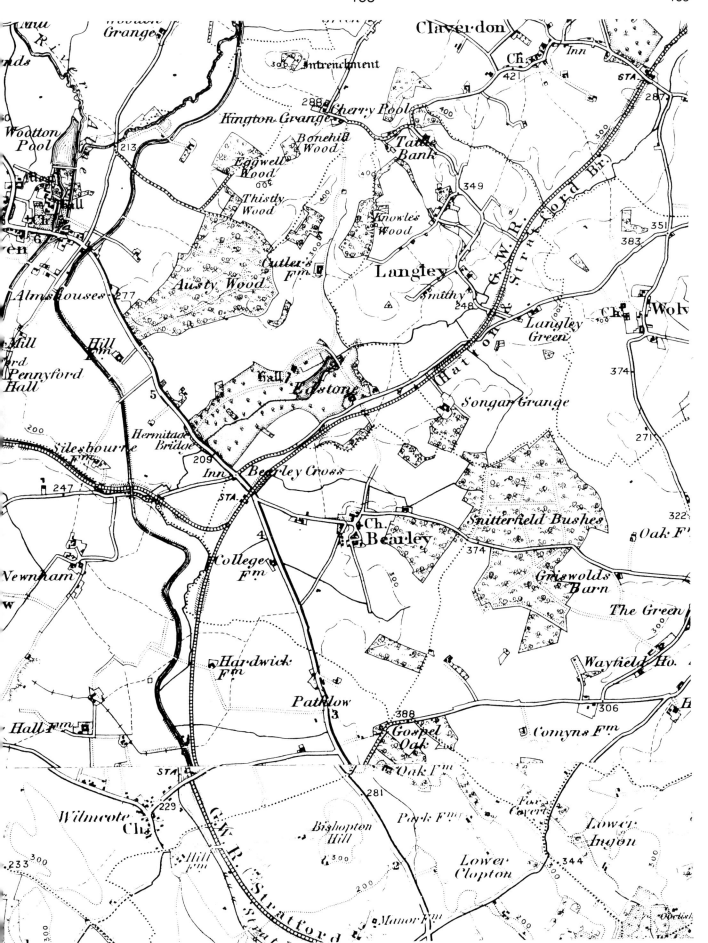

Surveyed 1882 - 85.  Published 1892.

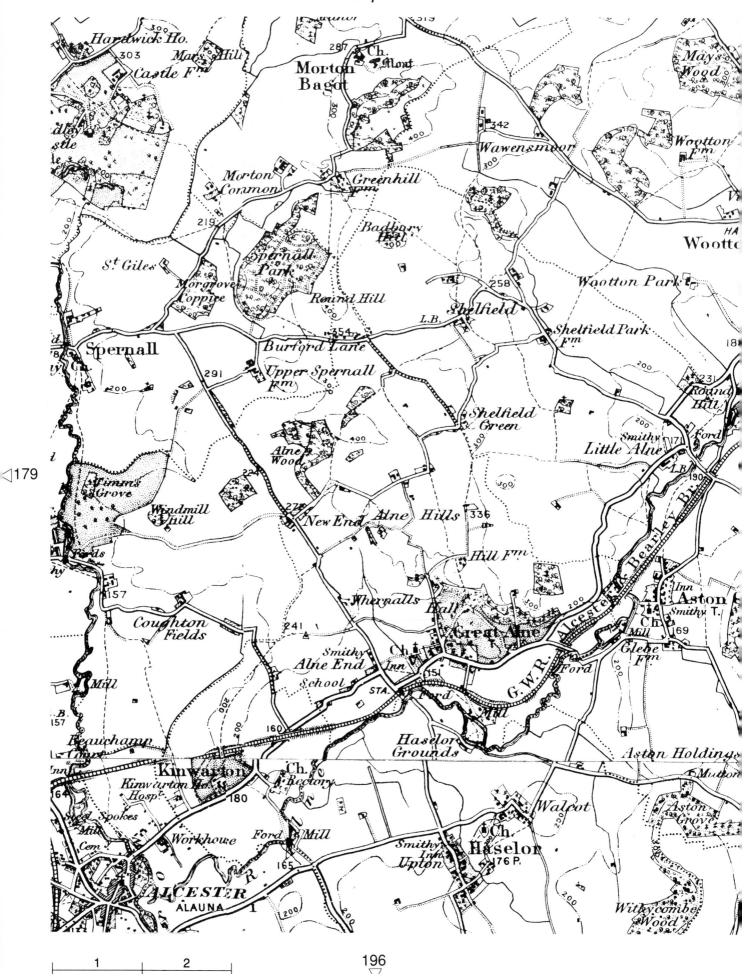

1          2

1 mile approx.

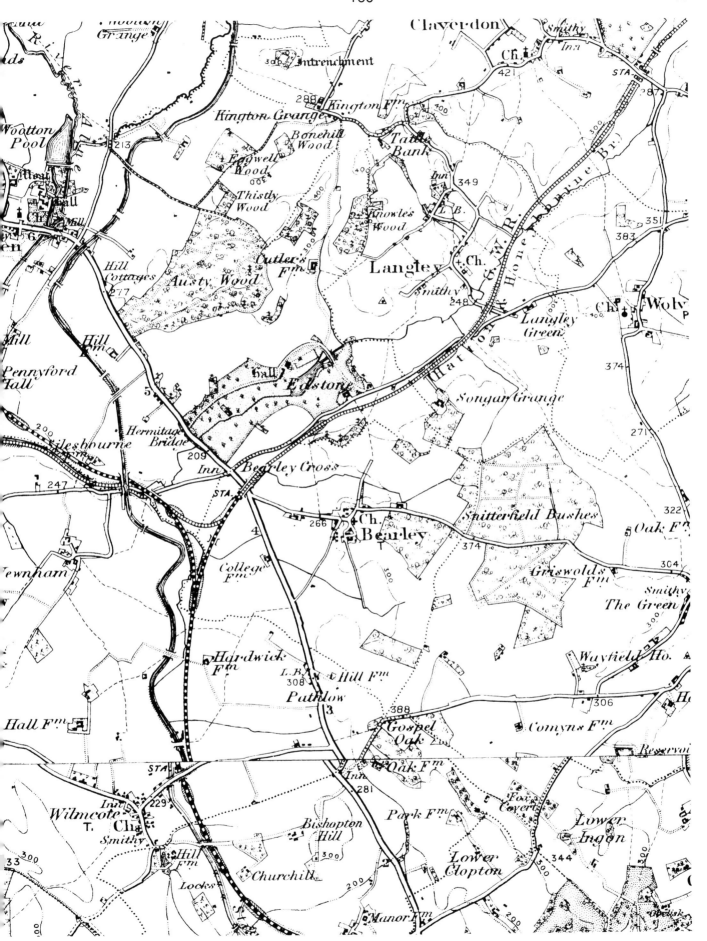

Surveyed 1882 - 85. Revised 1906 - 7. Published 1908.

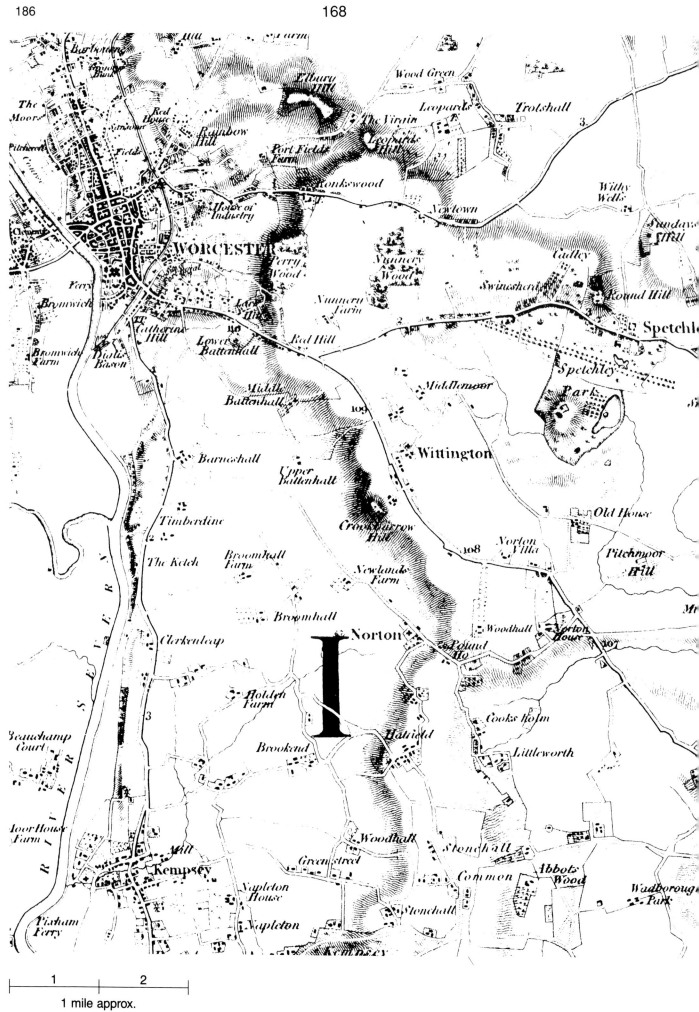

1 mile approx.

Published 1831.

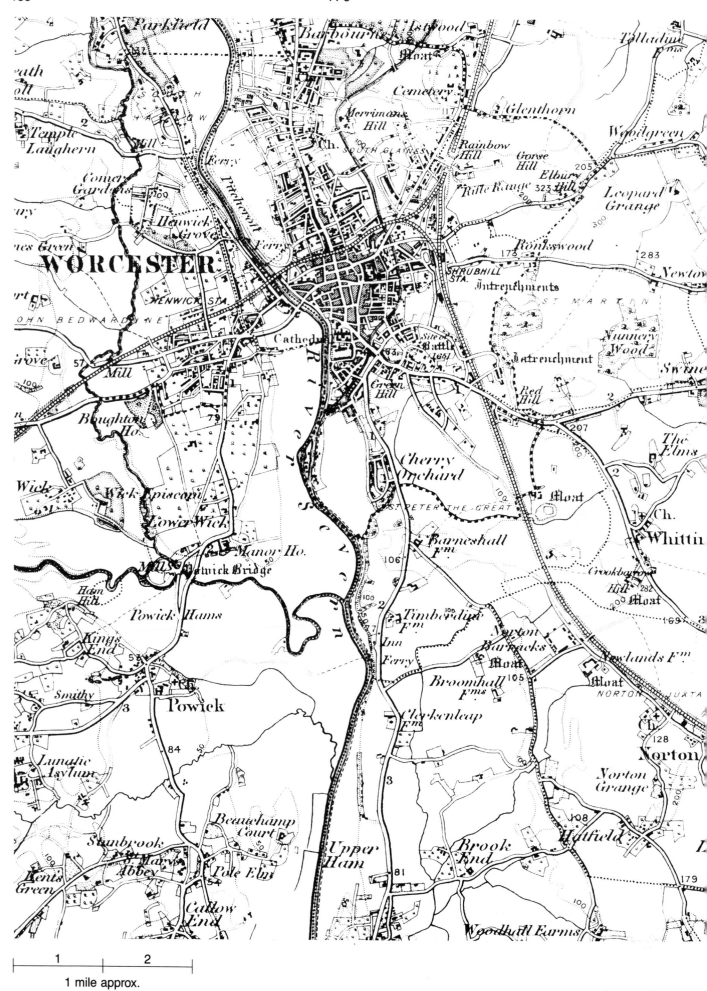

1 mile approx.

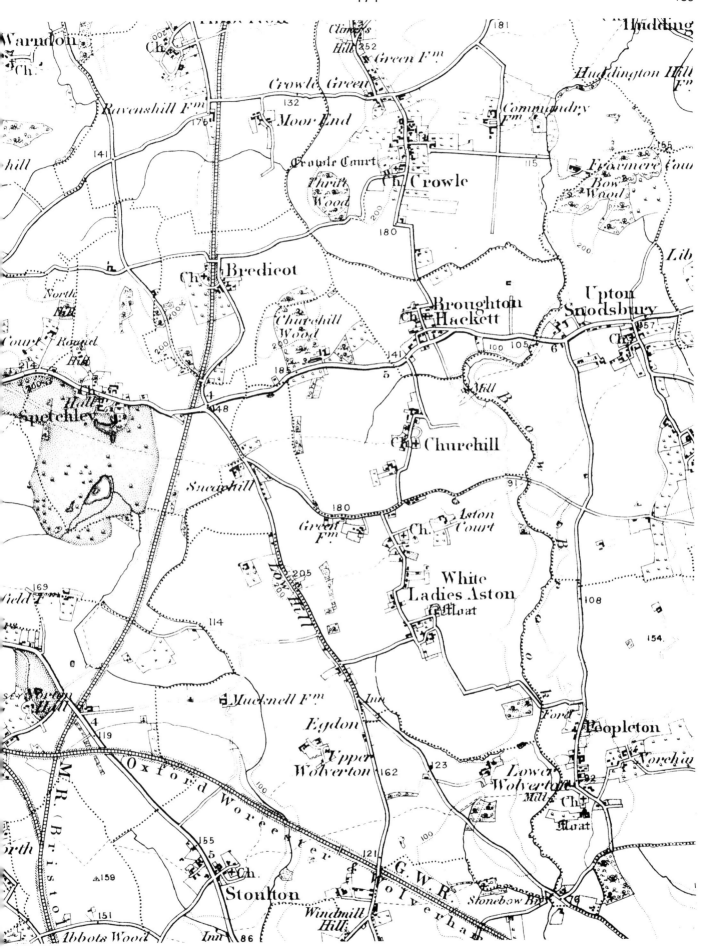

Surveyed 1882 - 86. Published 1893.

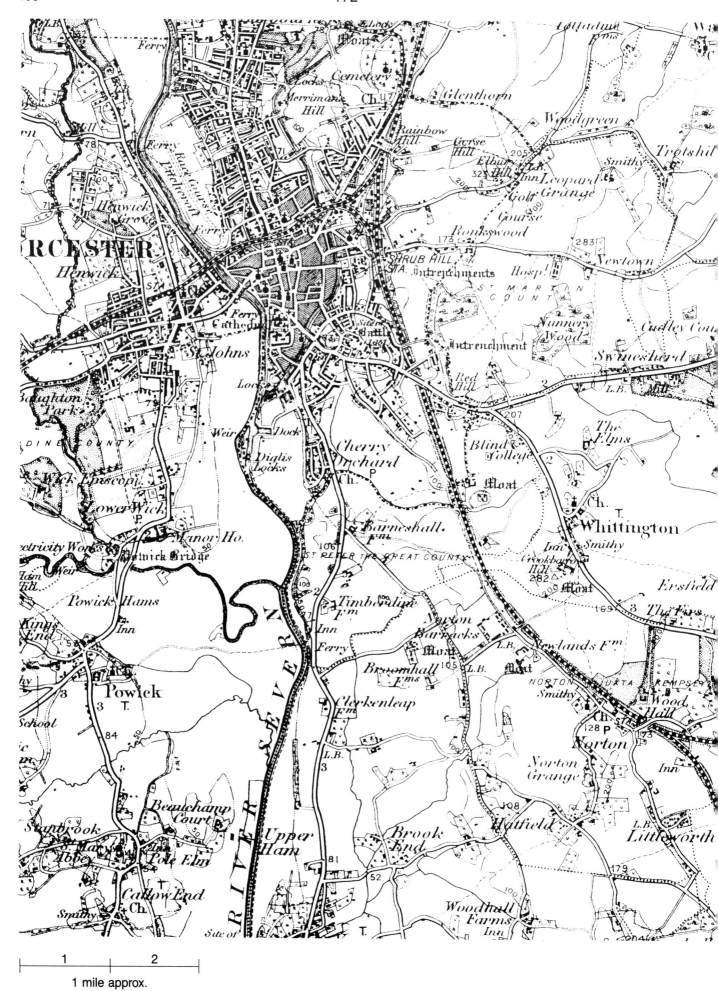

1

2

1 mile approx.

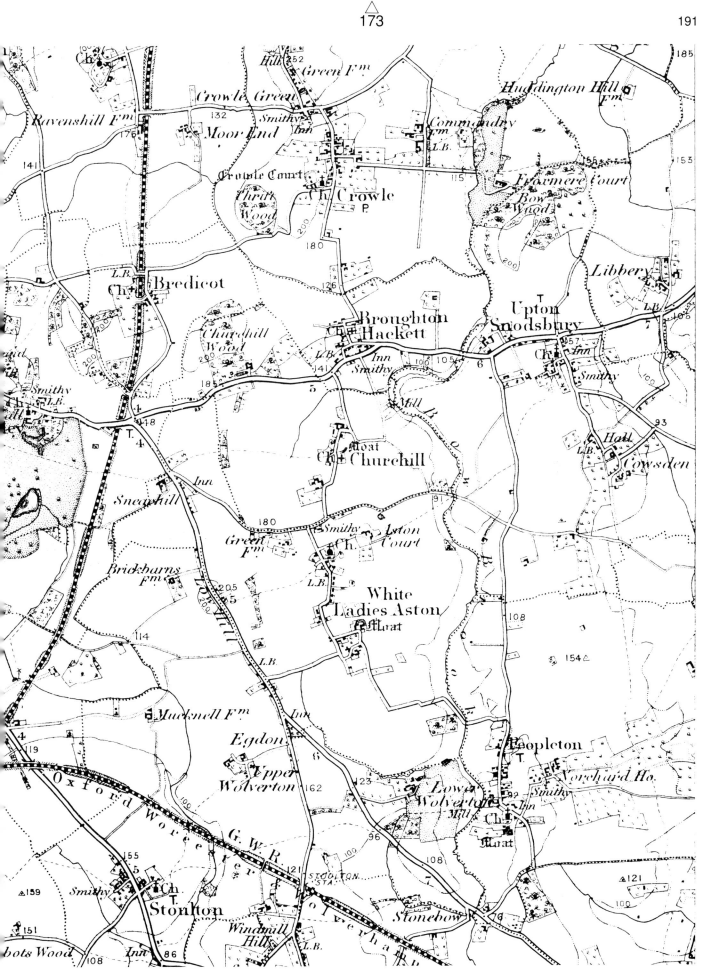

Surveyed 1882 - 86.  Revised 1907.  Published 1909.

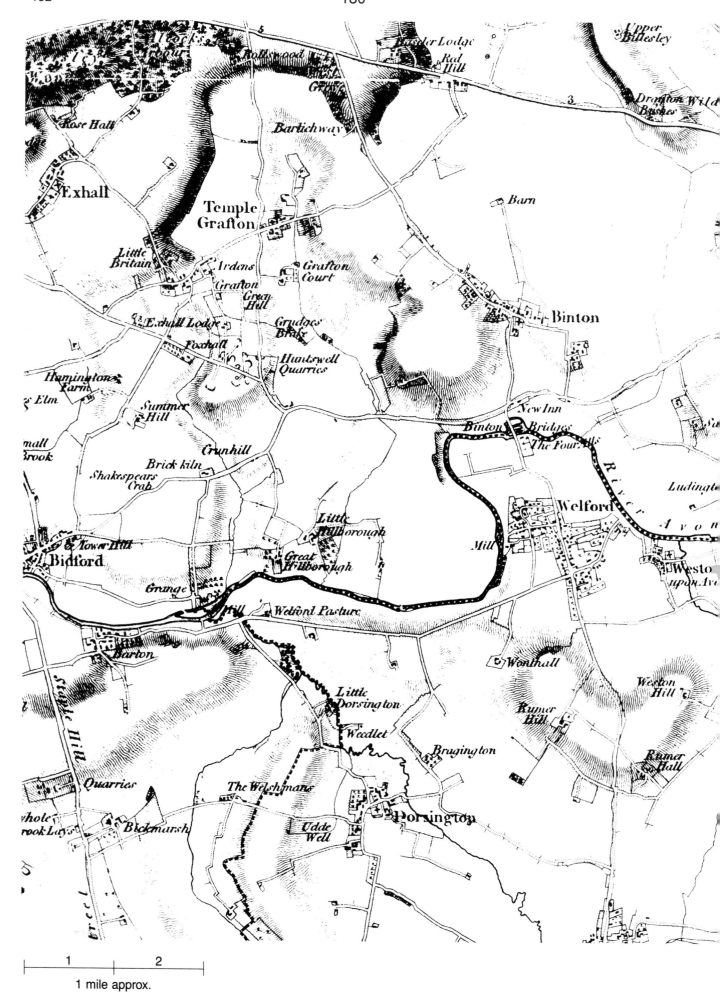

Upper
Bittesley

aster Lodge

Drayton Wild
Bushes

Red
Hill

3

Rose Hall

Bartichway

Barn

Exhall

Temple
Grafton

Little
Britain

Ardens

Grafton
Court

Binton

Grafton
Green
Hill

Exhall Lodge

Foxhall

Grudges
Bank

Hamingtons
Farm

Huntswell
Quarries

New Inn

's Elm

Summer
Hill

Binton
Bridges
The Four Alls

Welford

River

Ludingt

mall
Brook

Grinhill

Avon

Brick kiln

Mill

Shakespears
Crab

Little
Hillborough

Weston

& Tower Hill

Bidford

Great
Hillborough

upon Avon

Grange

Hill

Welford Pasture

Wonhall

Weston
Hill

Barton

Little
Dorsington

Rumer
Hill

Weedlet

Rumer
Hall

Braginton

Staple Hill

The Welschmans

Quarries

whole
rook Lays

Bickmarsh

Udde
Well

Dorsington

1              2

1 mile approx.

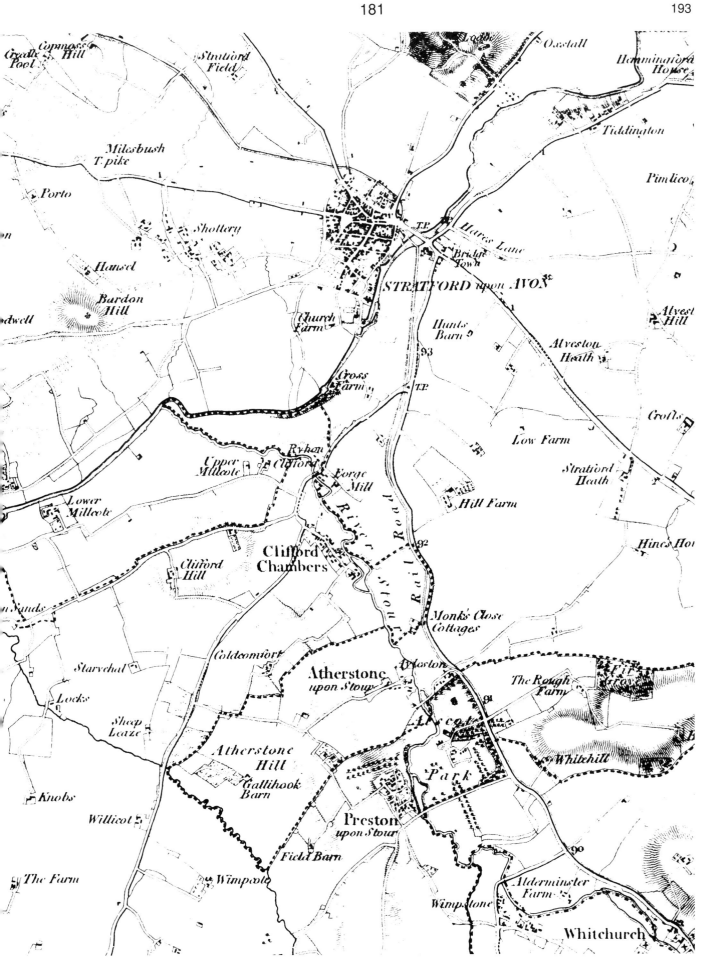

Published 1831.

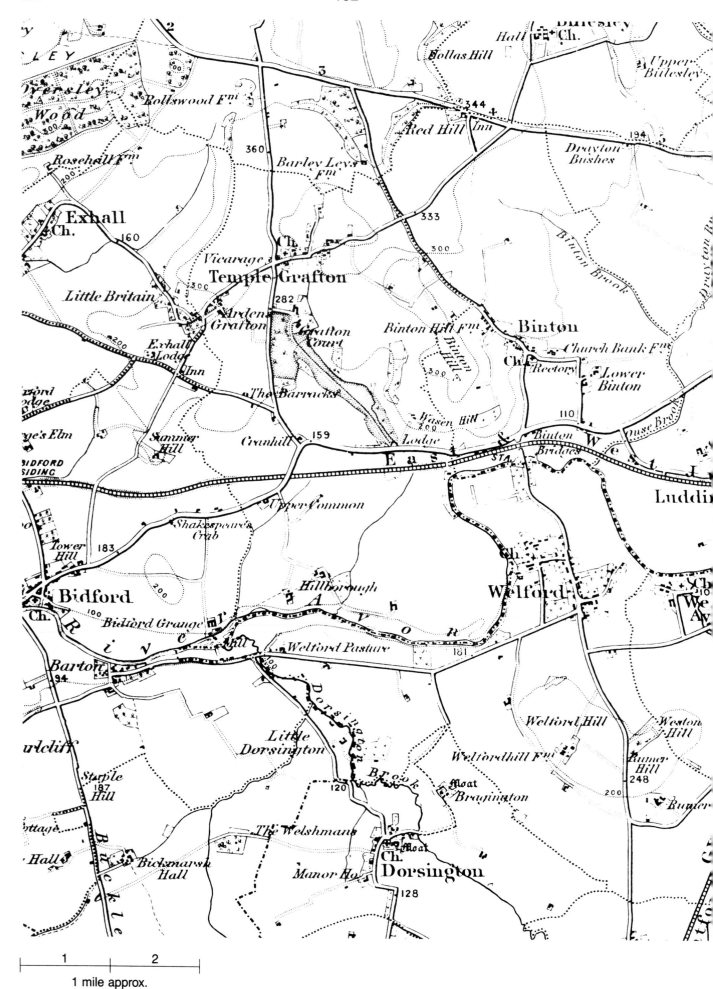

Wixford
Wood
300
Rosehill Fm
200
Rollswood Fm
360
Barley Leys Fm
Hollas Hill
Hall Ch.
Upper Bidesley
Red Hill Inn
344
4
194
Drayton Bushes
333
300
Binton Brook
Exhall Ch.
160
Ch.
Vicarage
Temple Grafton
Little Britain
300
282
Arden Grafton
Grafton Court
Binton Hill Fm
Binton
Ch.
Binton Hill
Church Bank Fm
Rectory
Lower Binton
110
Exhall Lodge
Inn
300
The Barracks
Wasen Hill
200
Lodge
Binton Bridges
W
ouse Brook
STA.
East
West
J
's Elm
BIDFORD SIDING
Summer Hill
Cranhill
159
Luddin
Upper Common
Shakespeare's Crab
200
Tower Hill
183
Hillborough
A
V
O
R
Welford
Ch.
We
A
Bidford
Ch.
100
Bidford Grange
R
i
v
e
Hill
Welford Pasture
181
Barton
94
Welford Hill
Weston Hill
Little Dorsington
Dorsington
Brook
Moat Braginton
Welfordhill Fm
200
Rumer Hill
248
Staple Hill
187
120
The Welshmans
Moat
Rumer
Hall
Bickmarsh Hall
Manor Ho
Ch.
Dorsington
128
Buckle

1          2

1 mile approx.

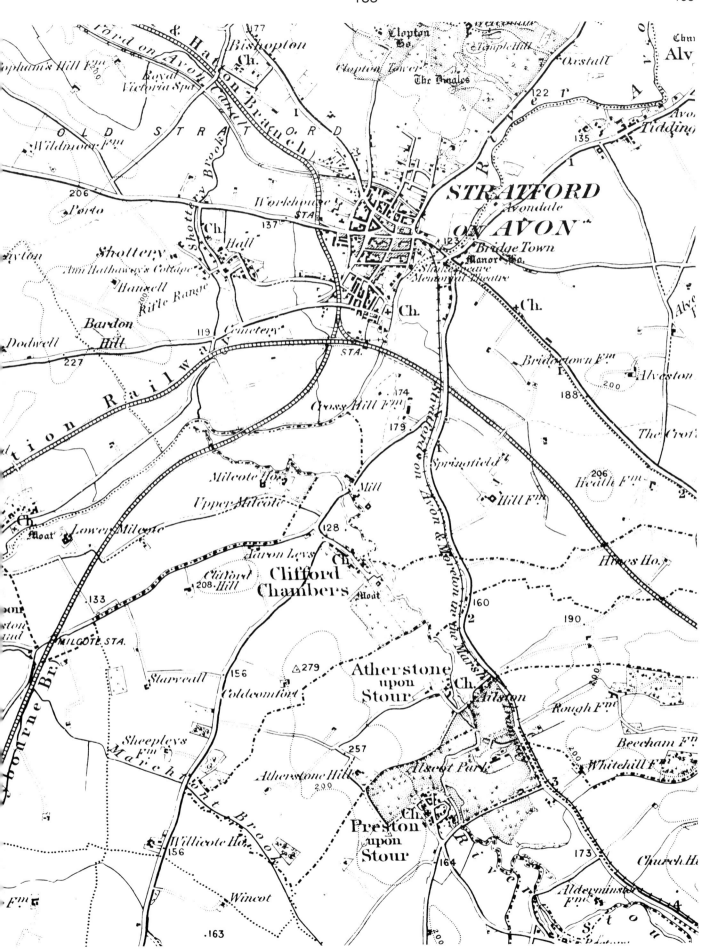

Surveyed 1882 - 85. Published 1892.

△
184

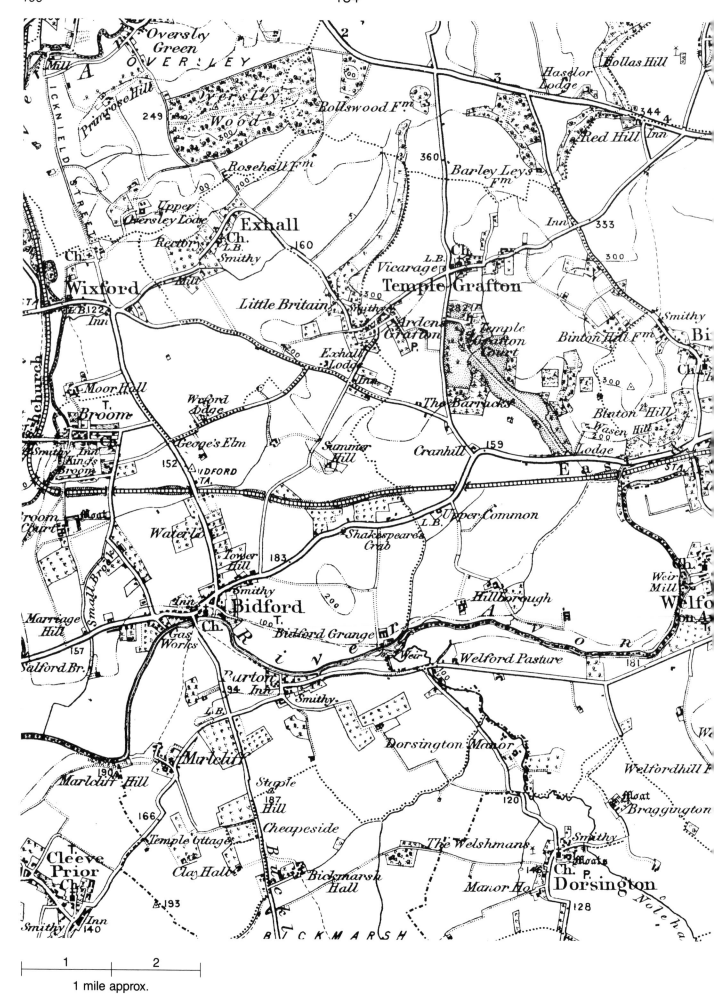

1 mile approx.

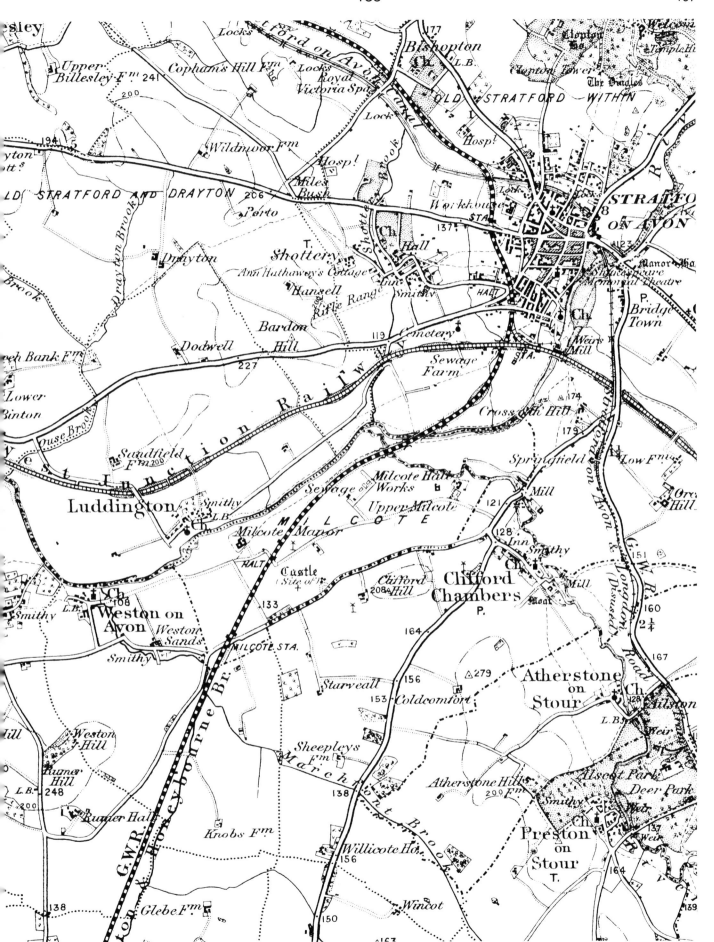

Surveyed 1882 - 85.  Revised 1906 - 7.  Published 1908.

# BIBLIOGRAPHY

The making of Victorian Birmingham by Victor Skipp. Publisher: Victor Skipp.

Cornish's Strangers Guide Through Birmingham 1858.

How Birmingham Became a Great City by John Whybrow and Rachel Waterhouse. Publishers: John Whybrow Limited.

The Black Country by Edward Chitham. Publishers: Longman.

The Victoria History of the Counties of England. Editor: Christopher Elrington. Publishers: Oxford University Press.

# *Gazetteer*

The following list of place names is not definitive; rather it is designed to stimulate the reader's interest and, used in conjunction with a modern day atlas, assists on a journey of re-discovering one's heritage.